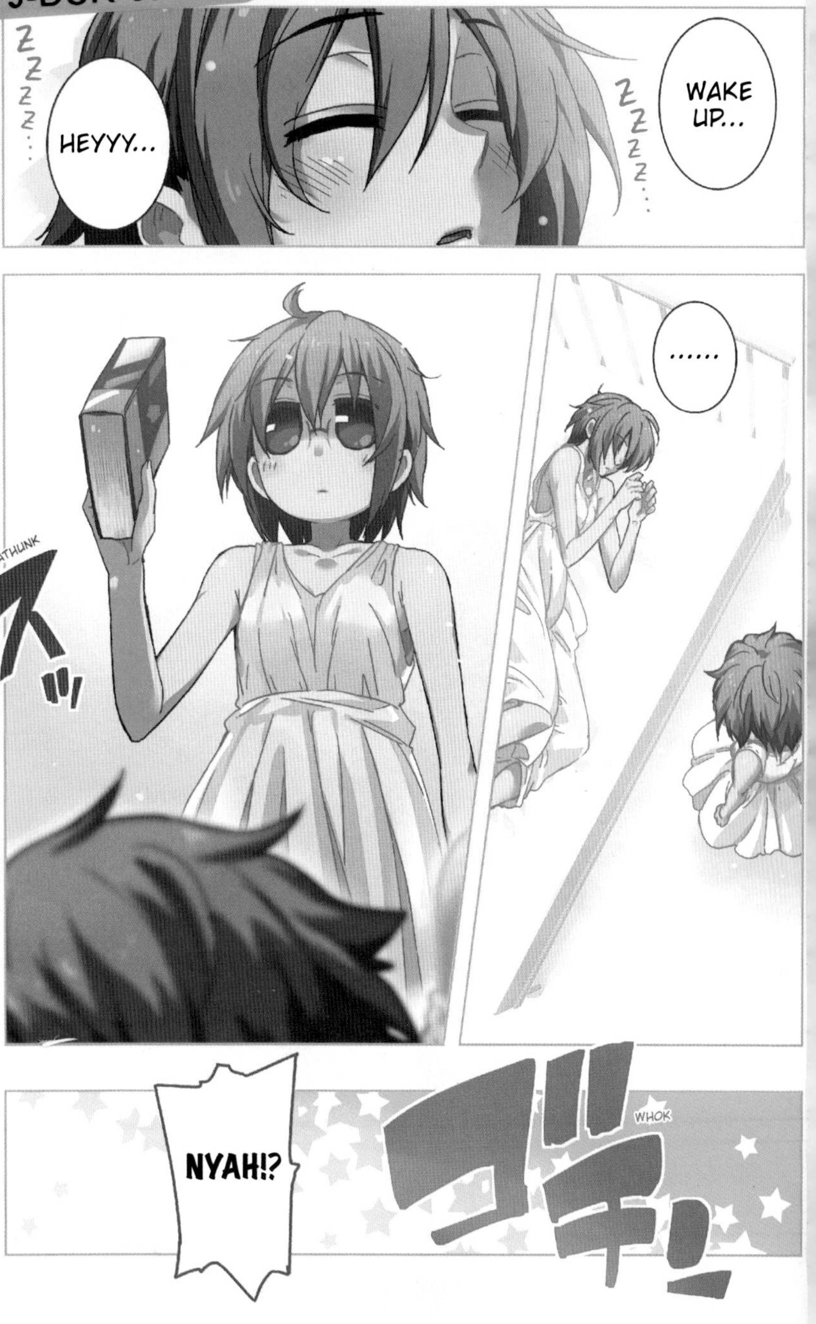
ZZZZ...
WAKE UP...
HEYYY...
ZZZZ...
......
KATHUNK
WHOK
NYAH!?

Epilogue 34>> Dream

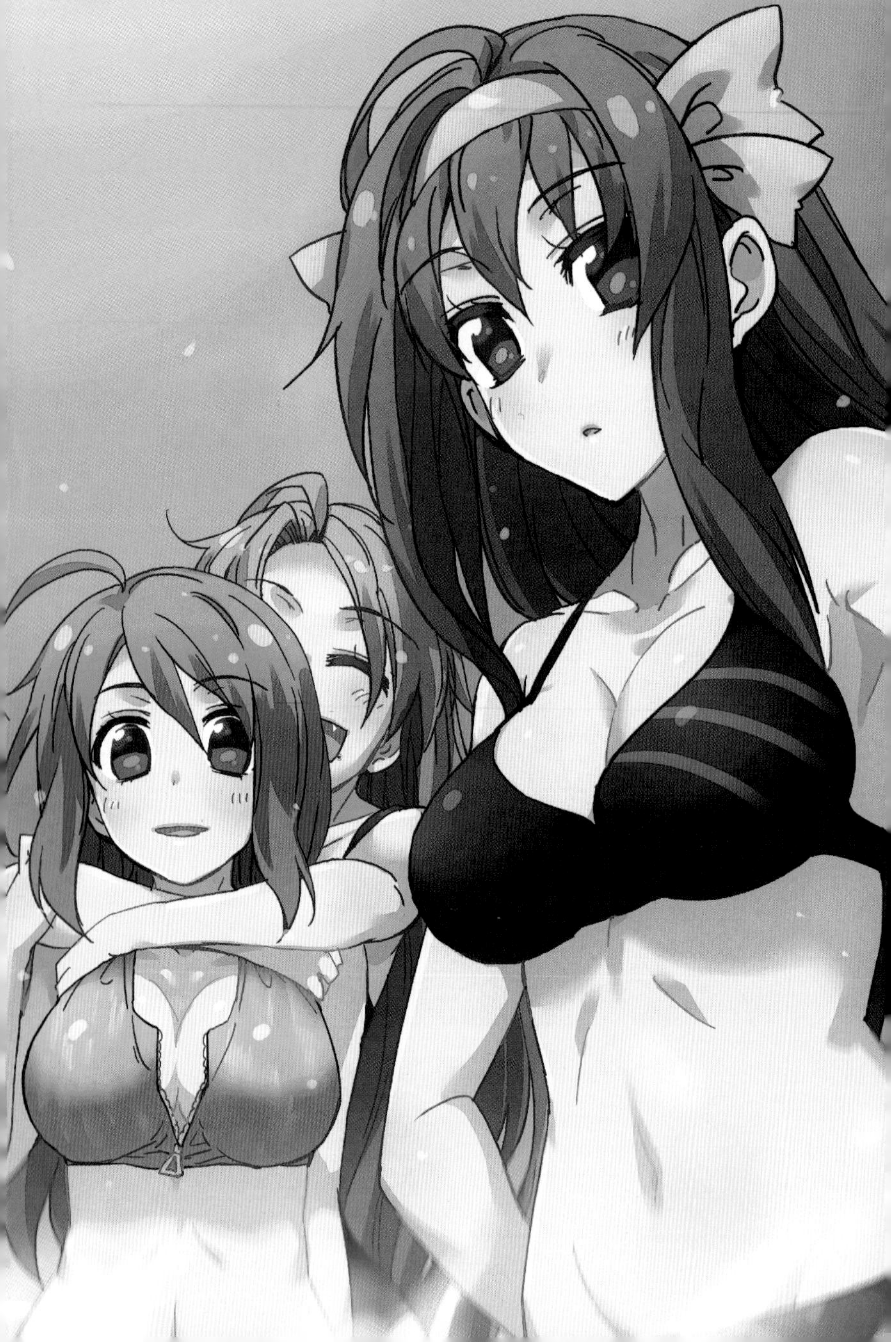

THE DISAPPEARANCE of NAGATO YUKI-CHAN

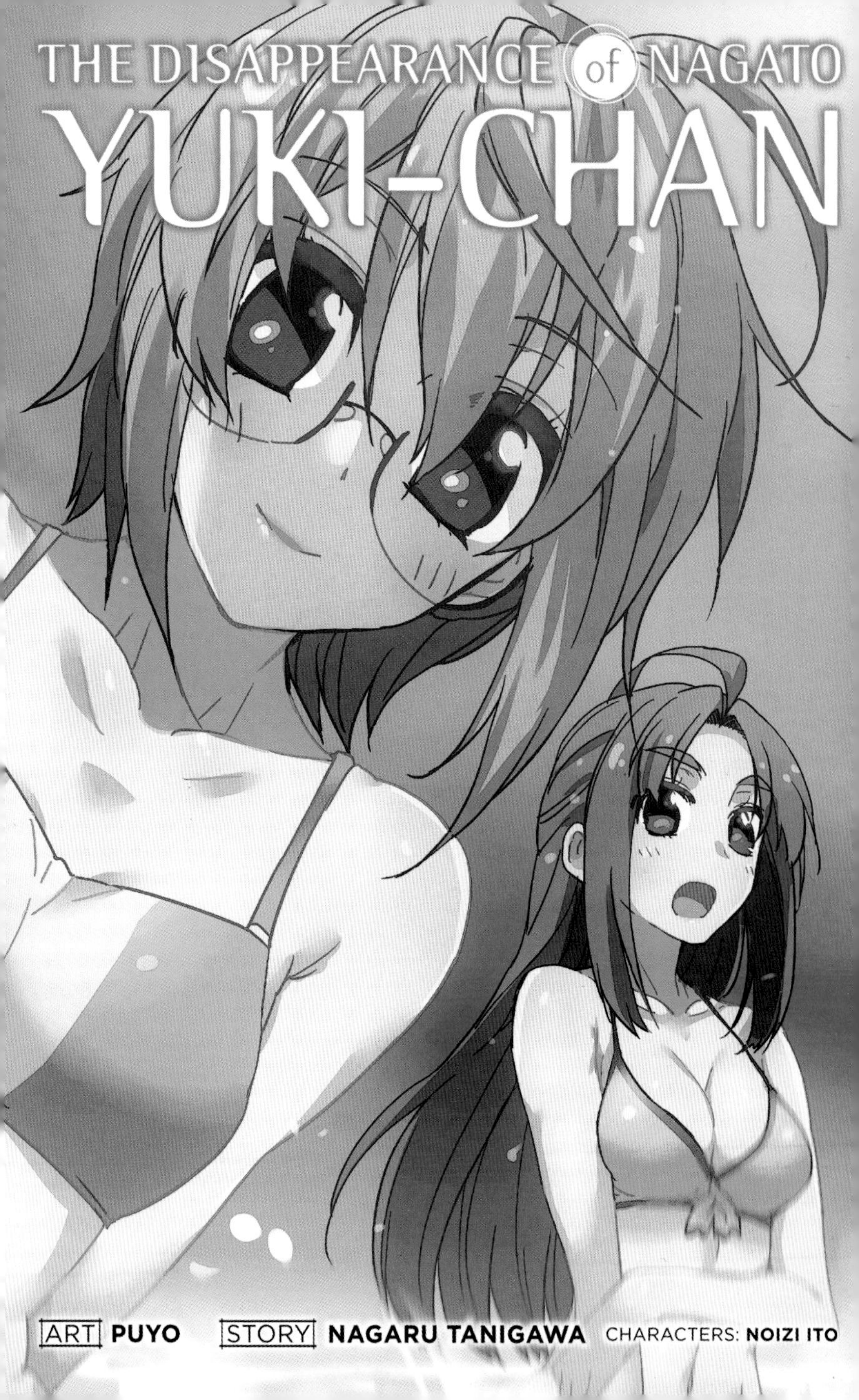

ART PUYO STORY NAGARU TANIGAWA CHARACTERS: NOIZI ITO

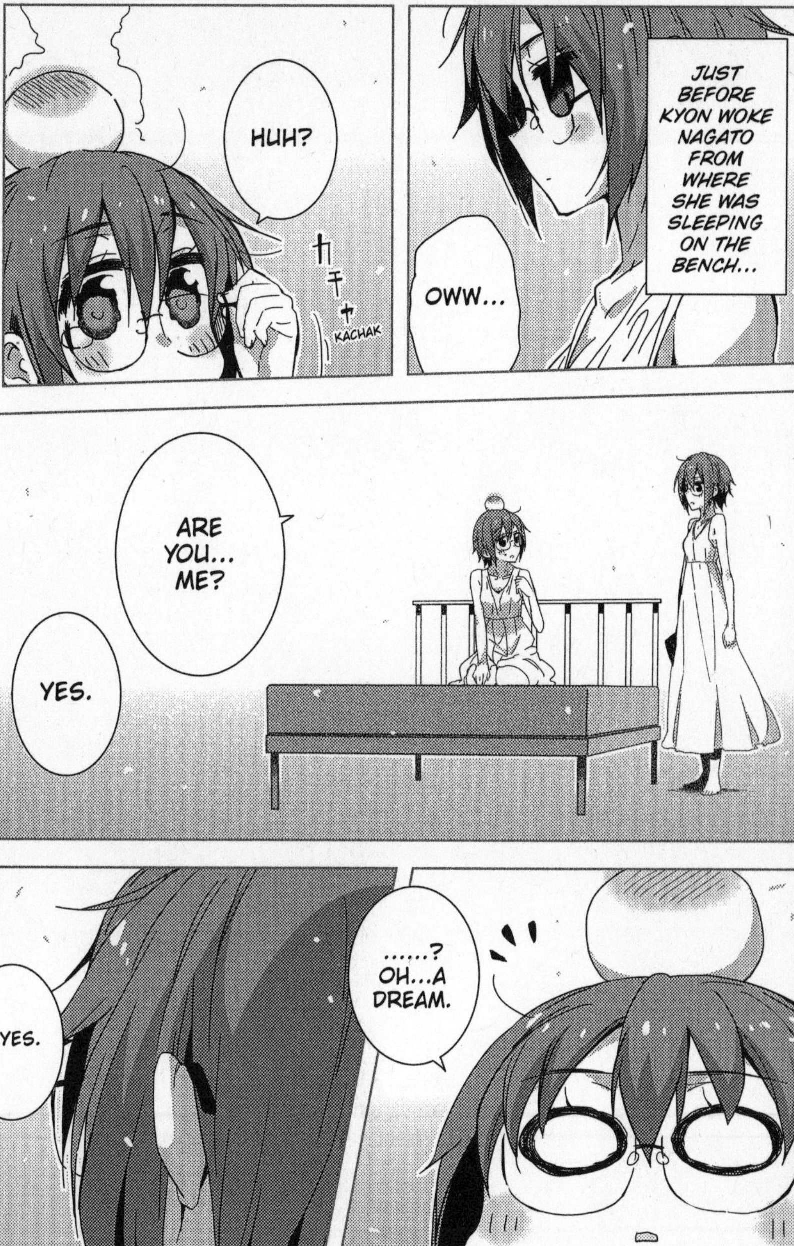
JUST BEFORE KYON WOKE NAGATO FROM WHERE SHE WAS SLEEPING ON THE BENCH...
OWW...
HUH?
カチャ
KACHAK
ARE YOU... ME?
YES.
......? OH...A DREAM.
...YES.

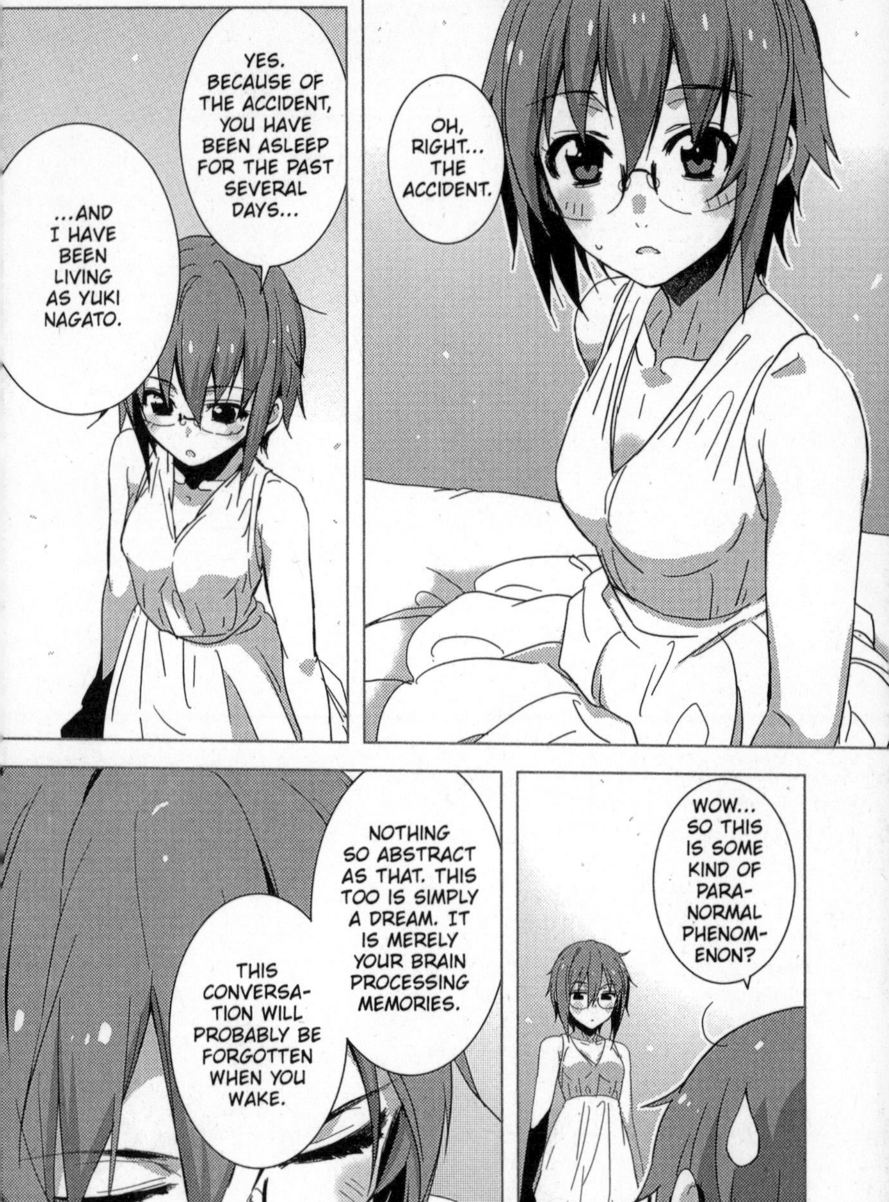
OH, RIGHT... THE ACCIDENT.
YES. BECAUSE OF THE ACCIDENT, YOU HAVE BEEN ASLEEP FOR THE PAST SEVERAL DAYS...
...AND I HAVE BEEN LIVING AS YUKI NAGATO.
WOW... SO THIS IS SOME KIND OF PARA-NORMAL PHENOM-ENON?
NOTHING SO ABSTRACT AS THAT. THIS TOO IS SIMPLY A DREAM. IT IS MERELY YOUR BRAIN PROCESSING MEMORIES.
THIS CONVERSA-TION WILL PROBABLY BE FORGOTTEN WHEN YOU WAKE.

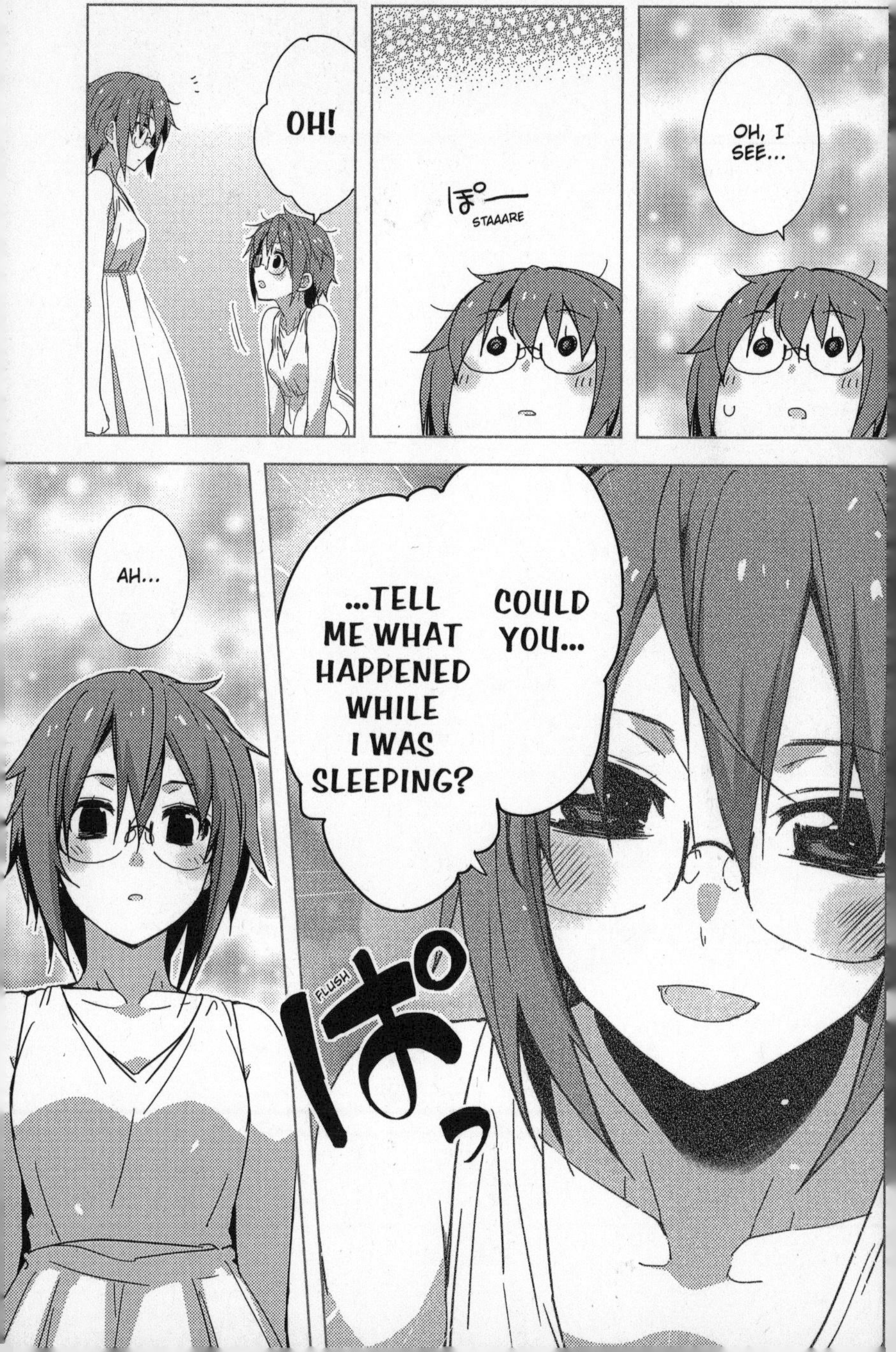
OH, I SEE...
ぽー
STAAARE
OH!
COULD YOU... ...TELL ME WHAT HAPPENED WHILE I WAS SLEEPING?
ぽっ
FLUSH
AH...

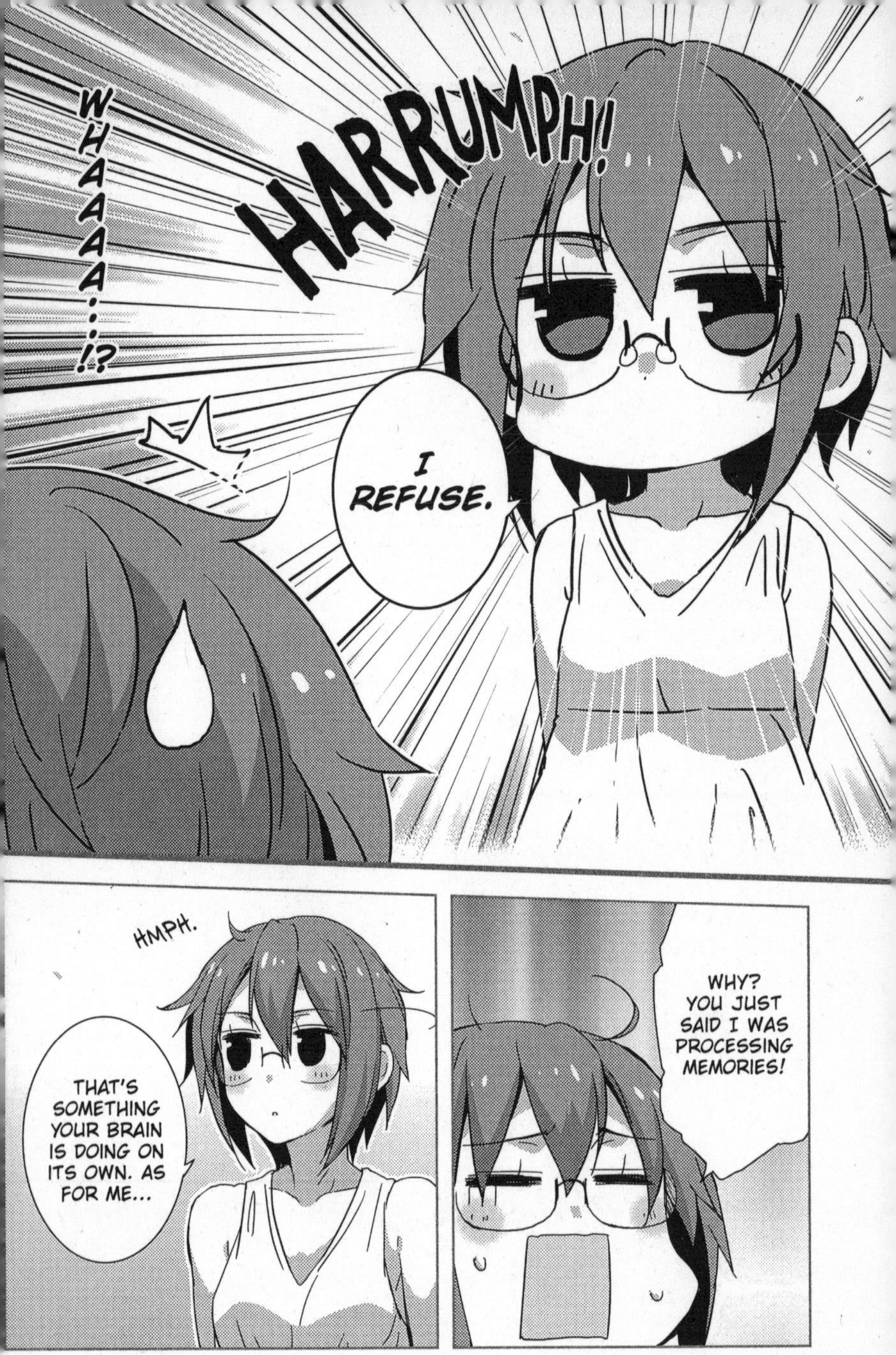
HARRUMPH!
I REFUSE.
WHAAAA...!?
WHY? YOU JUST SAID I WAS PROCESSING MEMORIES!
HMPH.
THAT'S SOMETHING YOUR BRAIN IS DOING ON ITS OWN. AS FOR ME...

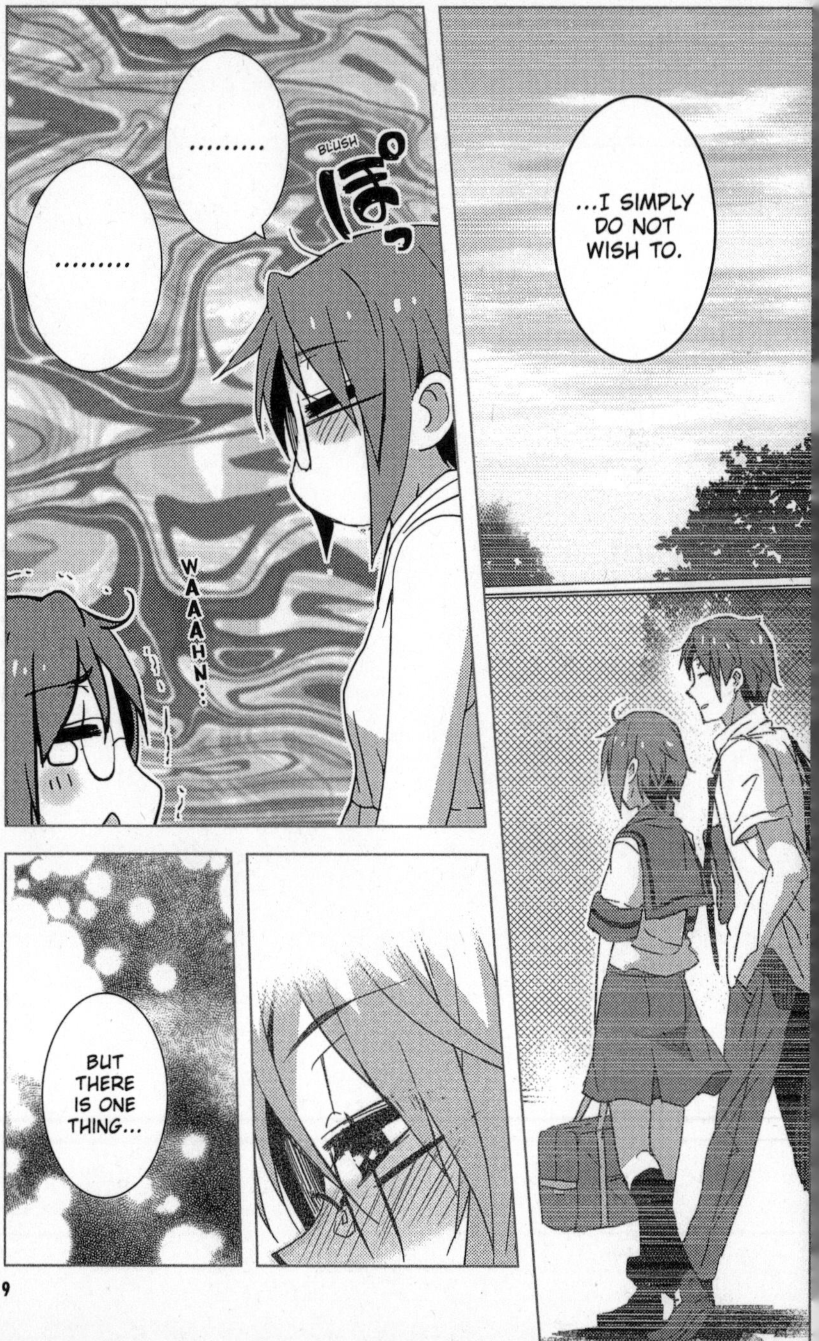

...I SIMPLY DO NOT WISH TO.
ぽっ
BLUSH
....
....
WAAAAHN...
BUT THERE IS ONE THING...

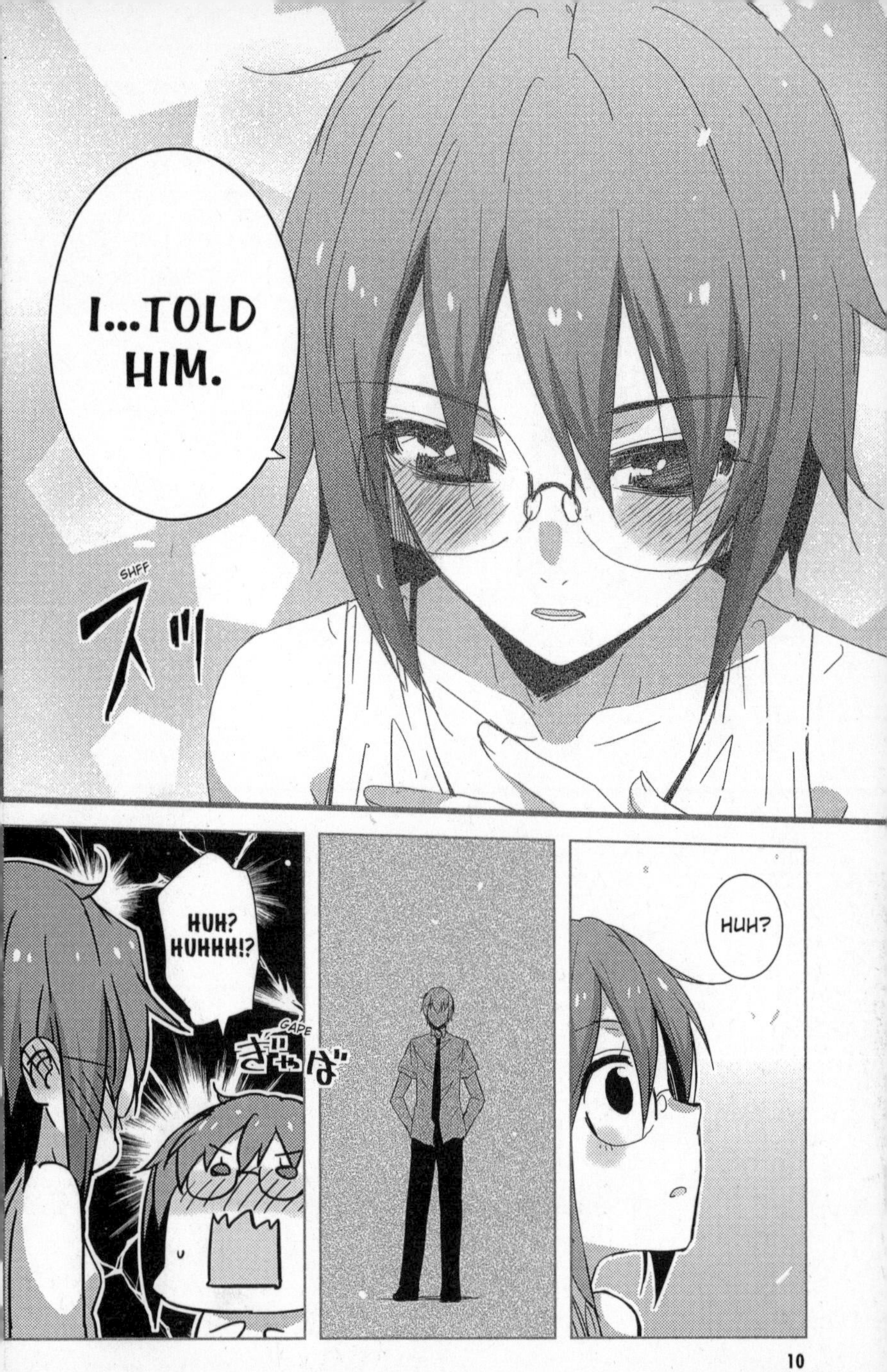
I...TOLD HIM.
SHFF
HUH?
HUH? HUHHH!?
GAPE

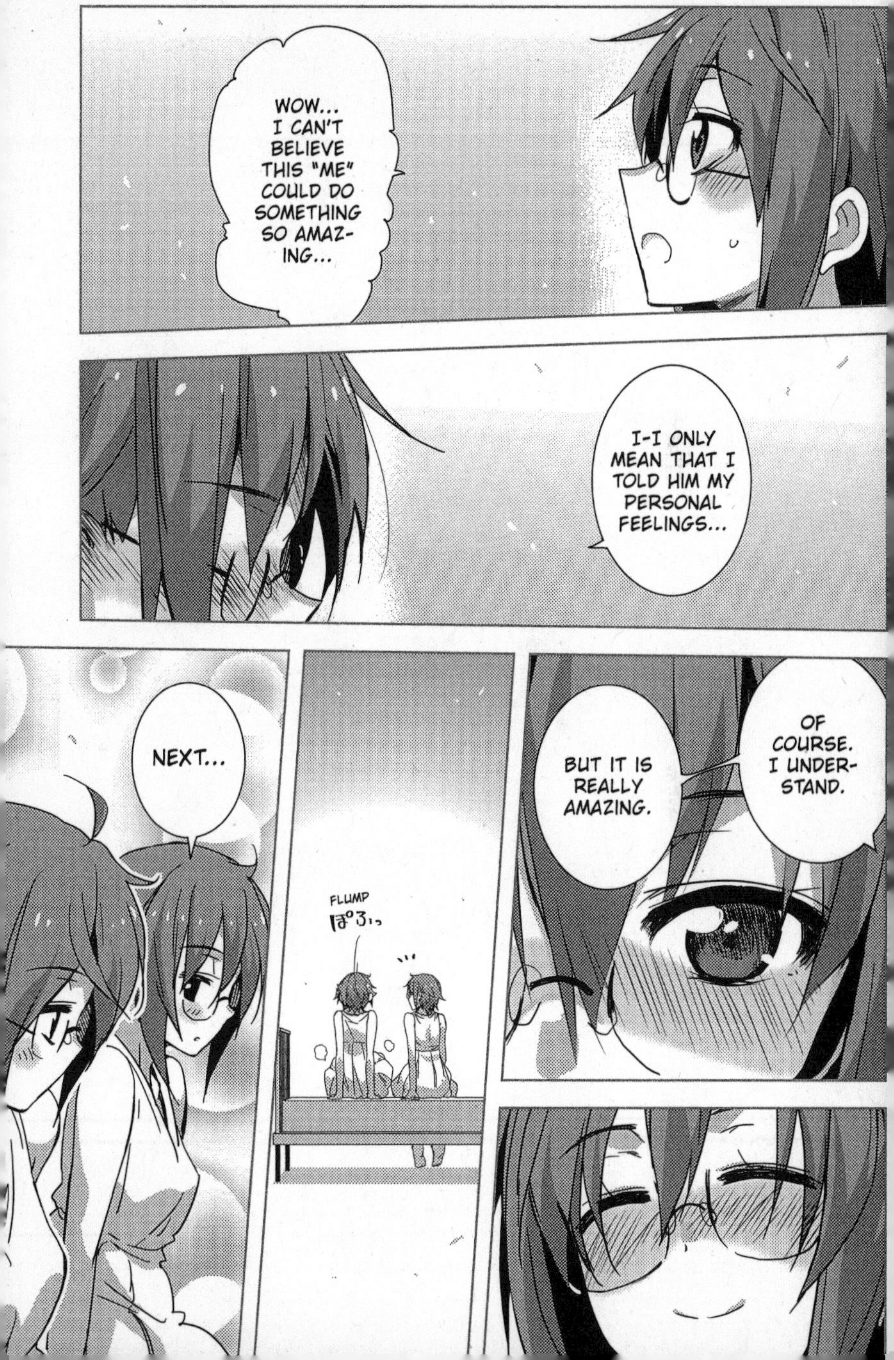
WOW... I CAN'T BELIEVE THIS "ME" COULD DO SOMETHING SO AMAZ-ING...
I-I ONLY MEAN THAT I TOLD HIM MY PERSONAL FEELINGS...
OF COURSE. I UNDER-STAND.
BUT IT IS REALLY AMAZING.
FLUMP
ぽふっ
NEXT...

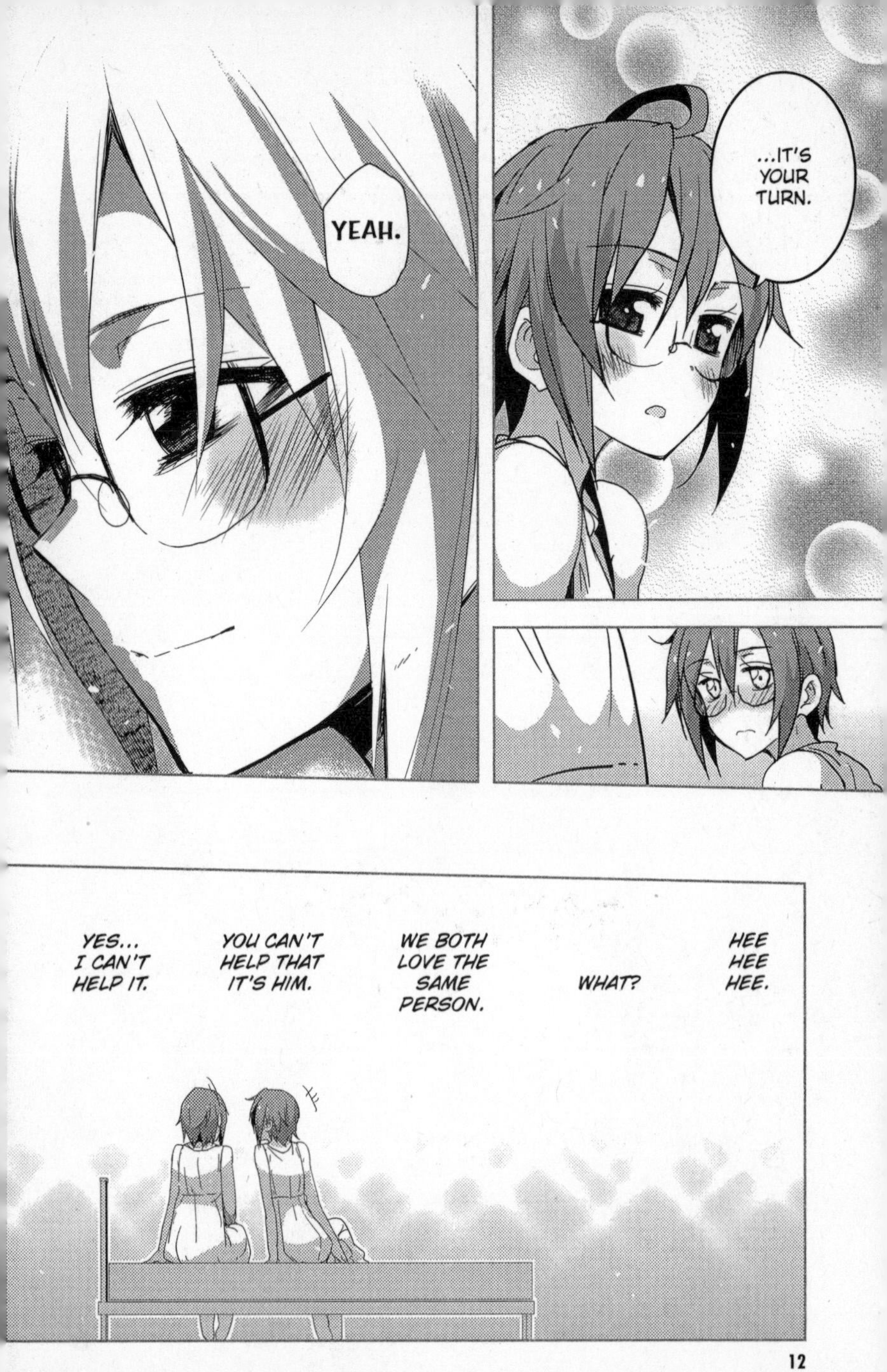
...IT'S YOUR TURN.
YEAH.
HEE HEE HEE.
WHAT?
WE BOTH LOVE THE SAME PERSON.
YOU CAN'T HELP THAT IT'S HIM.
YES... I CAN'T HELP IT.

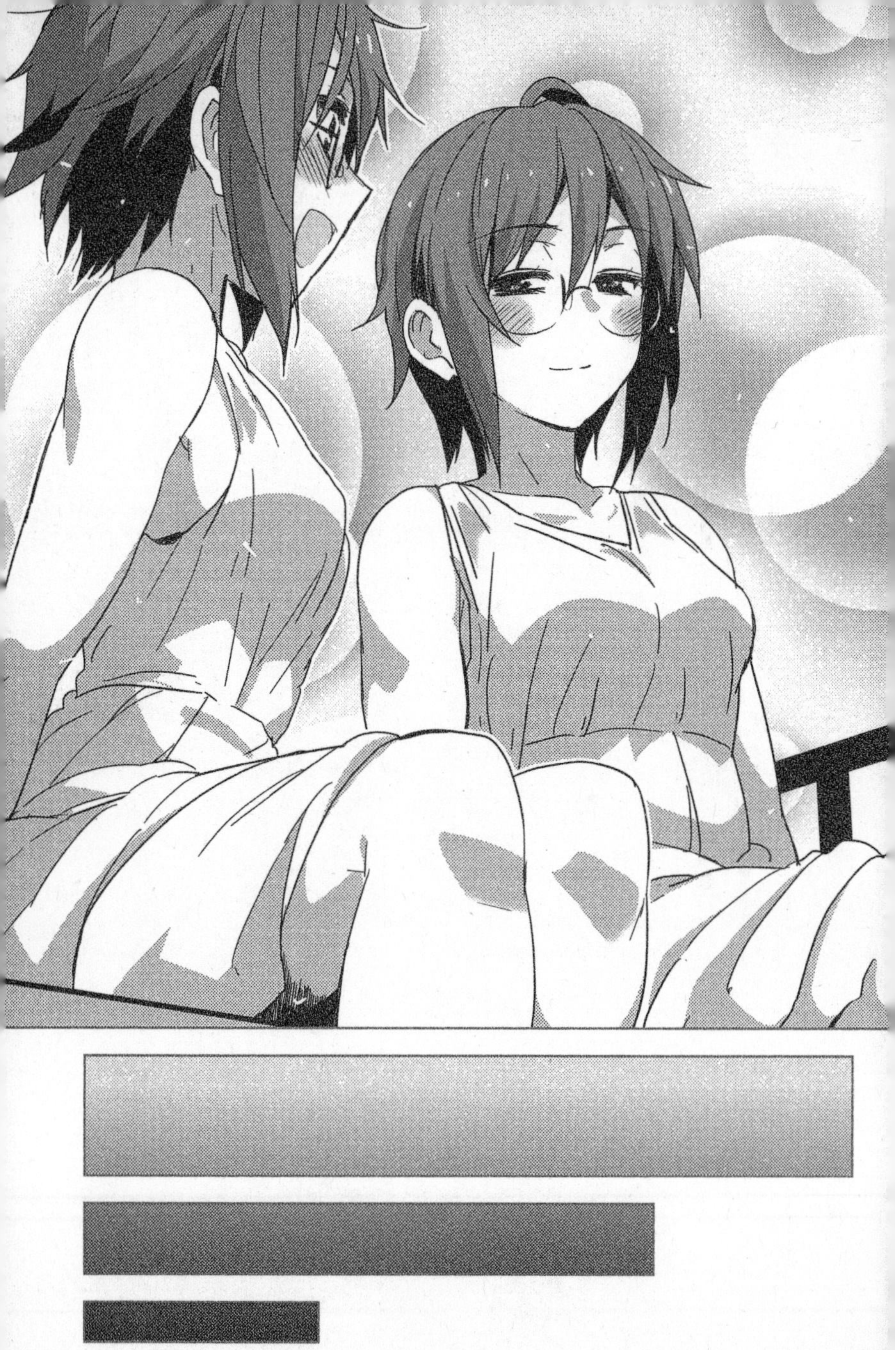

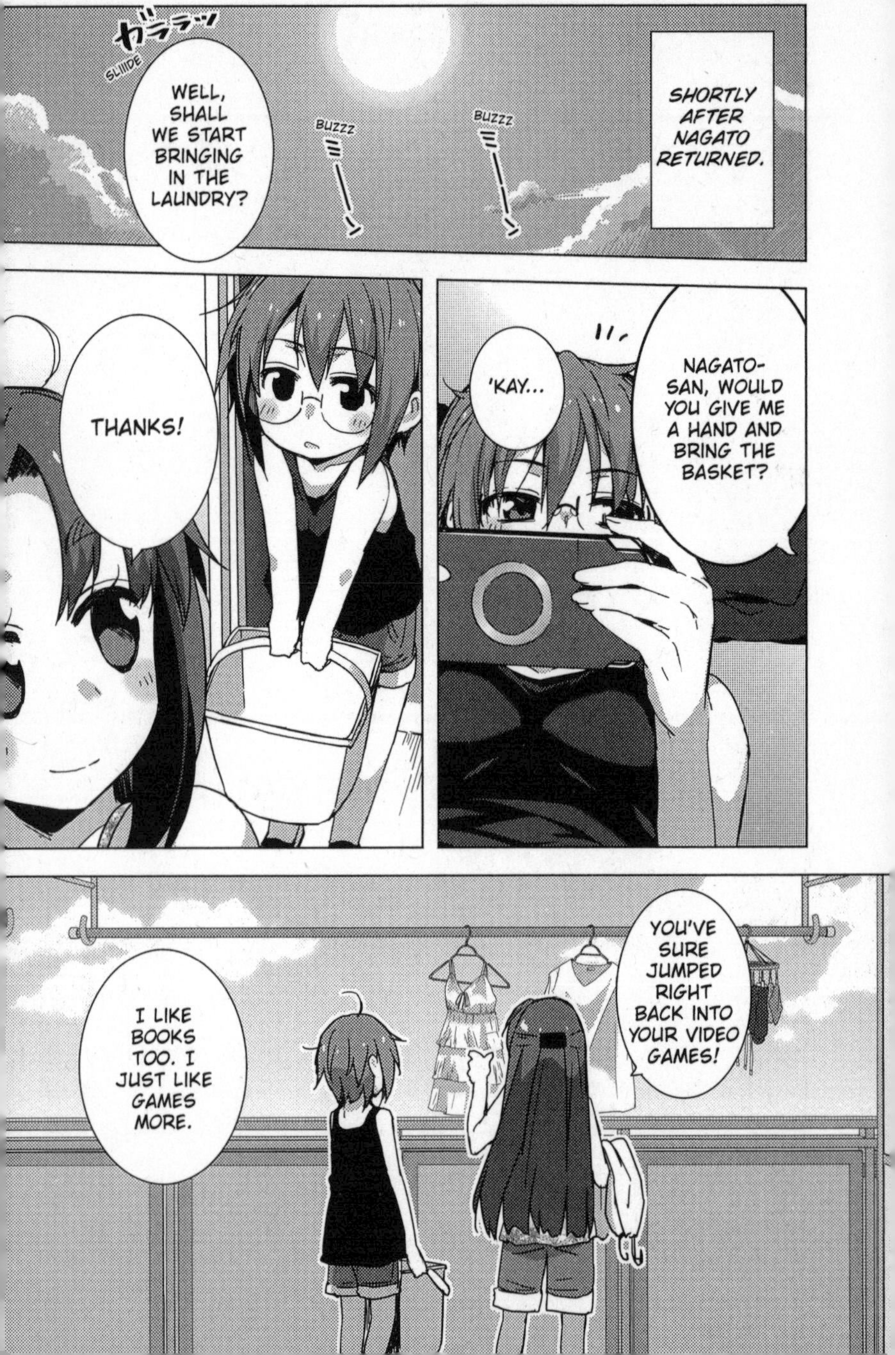
SHORTLY AFTER NAGATO RETURNED.
BUZZZ
BUZZZ
SLIIIDE
WELL, SHALL WE START BRINGING IN THE LAUNDRY?
NAGATO-SAN, WOULD YOU GIVE ME A HAND AND BRING THE BASKET?
'KAY...
THANKS!
YOU'VE SURE JUMPED RIGHT BACK INTO YOUR VIDEO GAMES!
I LIKE BOOKS TOO. I JUST LIKE GAMES MORE.

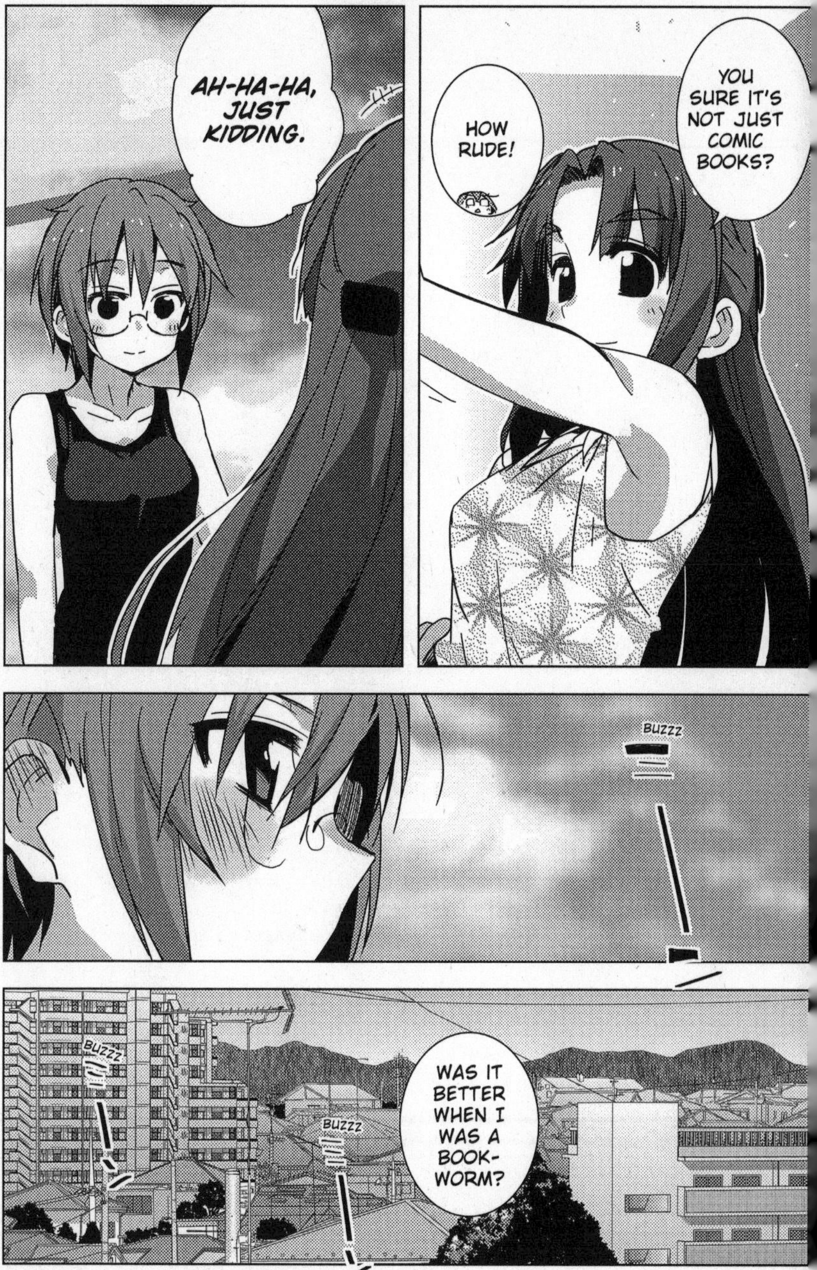
YOU SURE IT'S NOT JUST COMIC BOOKS?
HOW RUDE!
AH-HA-HA, JUST KIDDING.
BUZZZ
WAS IT BETTER WHEN I WAS A BOOK-WORM?
BUZZZ
BUZZZ

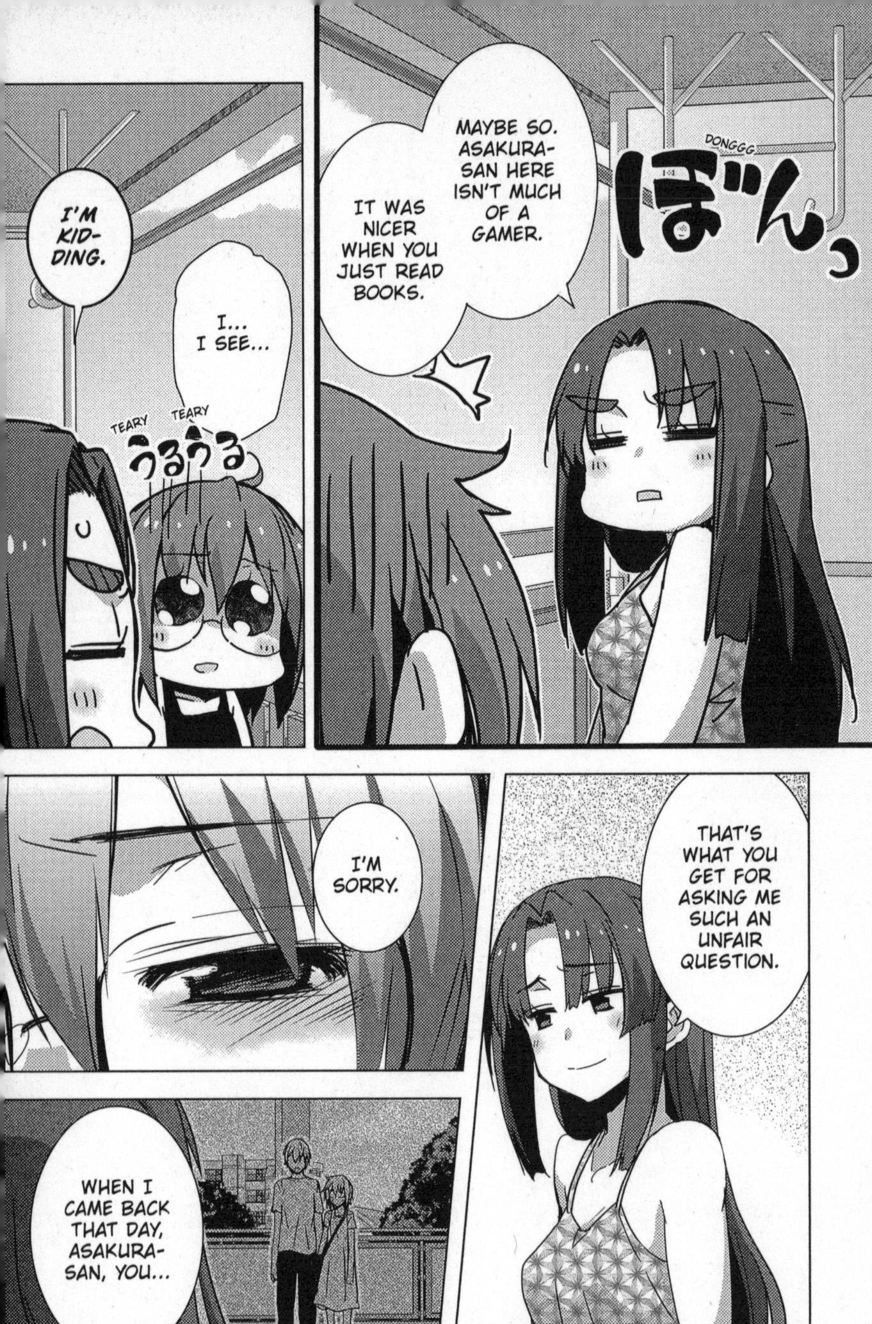

DONGGG
ぼんっ
MAYBE SO. ASAKURA-SAN HERE ISN'T MUCH OF A GAMER.
IT WAS NICER WHEN YOU JUST READ BOOKS.
I... I SEE...
TEARY TEARY
うるうる
I'M KIDDING.
THAT'S WHAT YOU GET FOR ASKING ME SUCH AN UNFAIR QUESTION.
I'M SORRY.
WHEN I CAME BACK THAT DAY, ASAKURA-SAN, YOU...

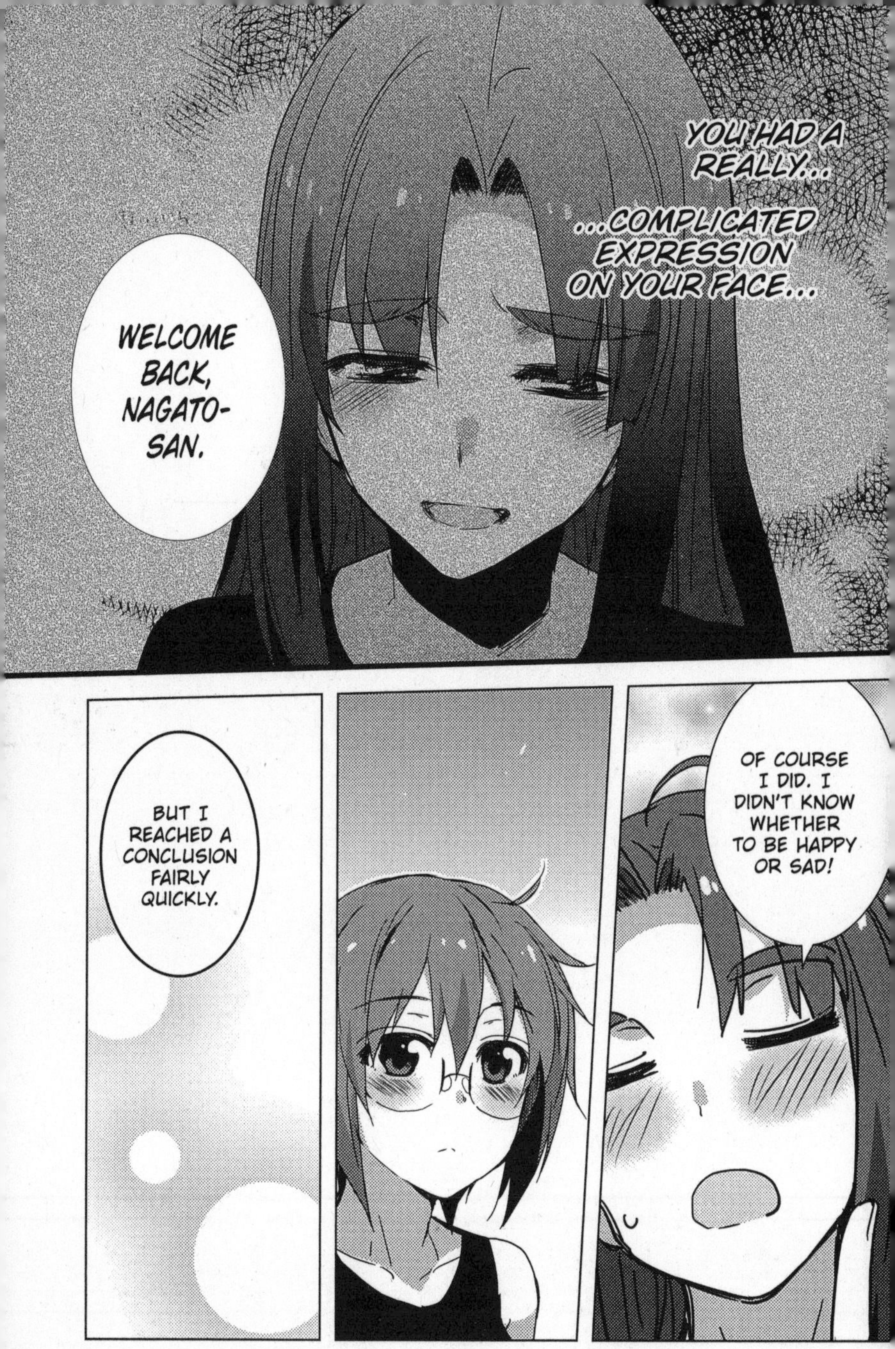
YOU HAD A REALLY...
...COMPLICATED EXPRESSION ON YOUR FACE...
WELCOME BACK, NAGATO-SAN.
OF COURSE I DID. I DIDN'T KNOW WHETHER TO BE HAPPY OR SAD!
BUT I REACHED A CONCLUSION FAIRLY QUICKLY.

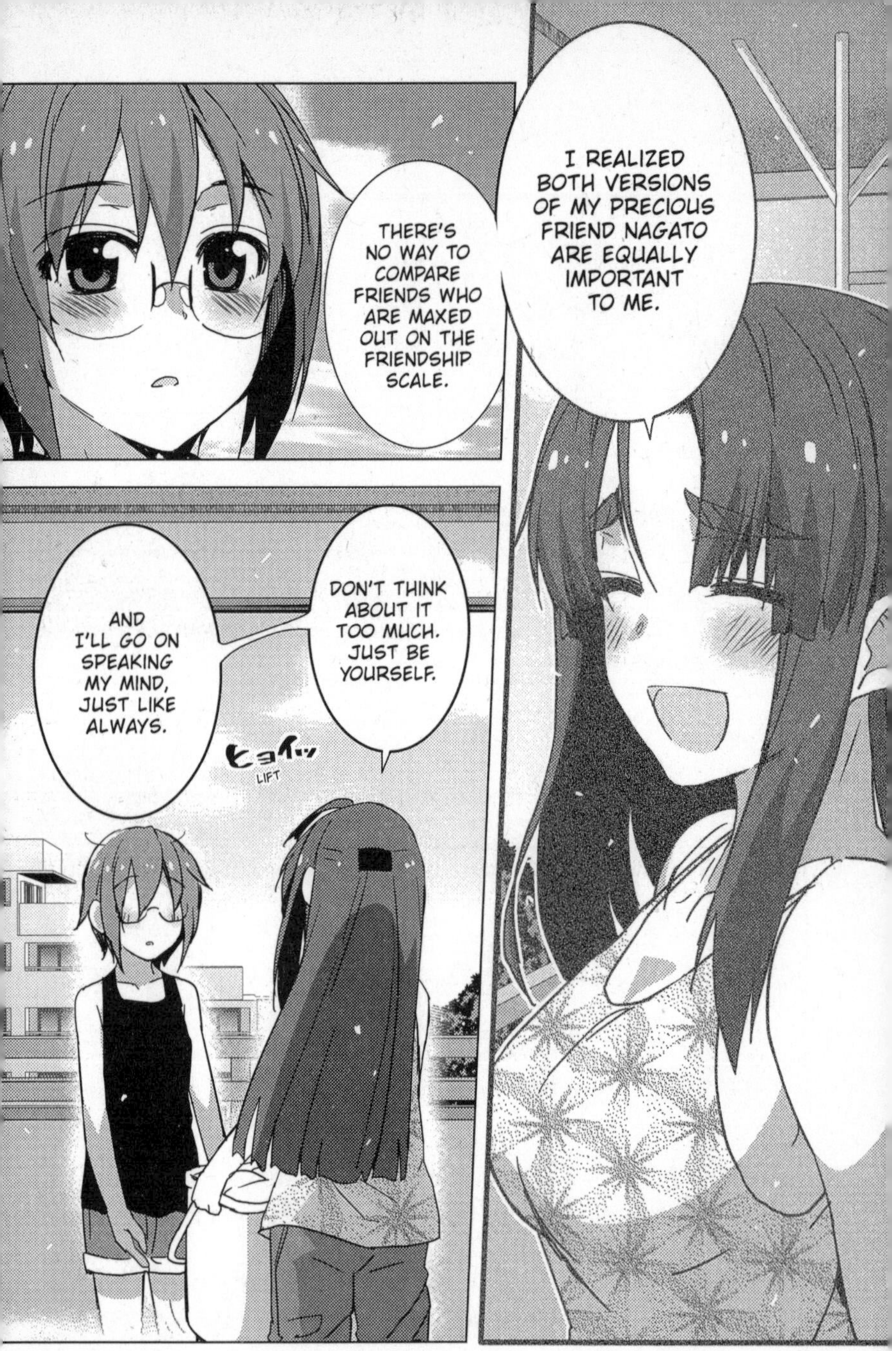
I REALIZED BOTH VERSIONS OF MY PRECIOUS FRIEND NAGATO ARE EQUALLY IMPORTANT TO ME.
THERE'S NO WAY TO COMPARE FRIENDS WHO ARE MAXED OUT ON THE FRIENDSHIP SCALE.
DON'T THINK ABOUT IT TOO MUCH. JUST BE YOURSELF.
AND I'LL GO ON SPEAKING MY MIND, JUST LIKE ALWAYS.
ヒョイッ
LIFT

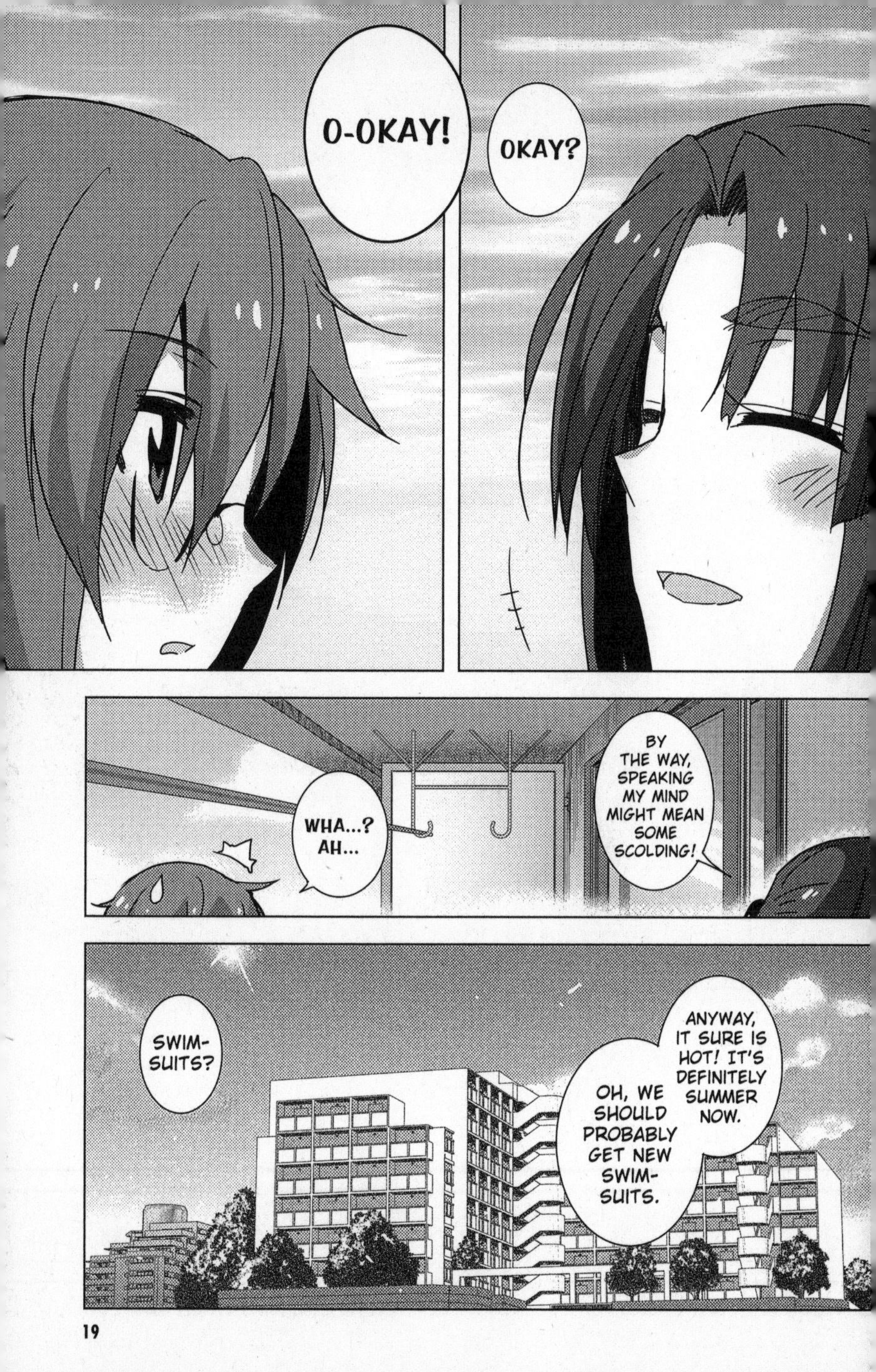
OKAY?
O-OKAY!
BY THE WAY, SPEAKING MY MIND MIGHT MEAN SOME SCOLDING!
WHA...? AH...
ANYWAY, IT SURE IS HOT! IT'S DEFINITELY SUMMER NOW.
OH, WE SHOULD PROBABLY GET NEW SWIM-SUITS.
SWIM-SUITS?

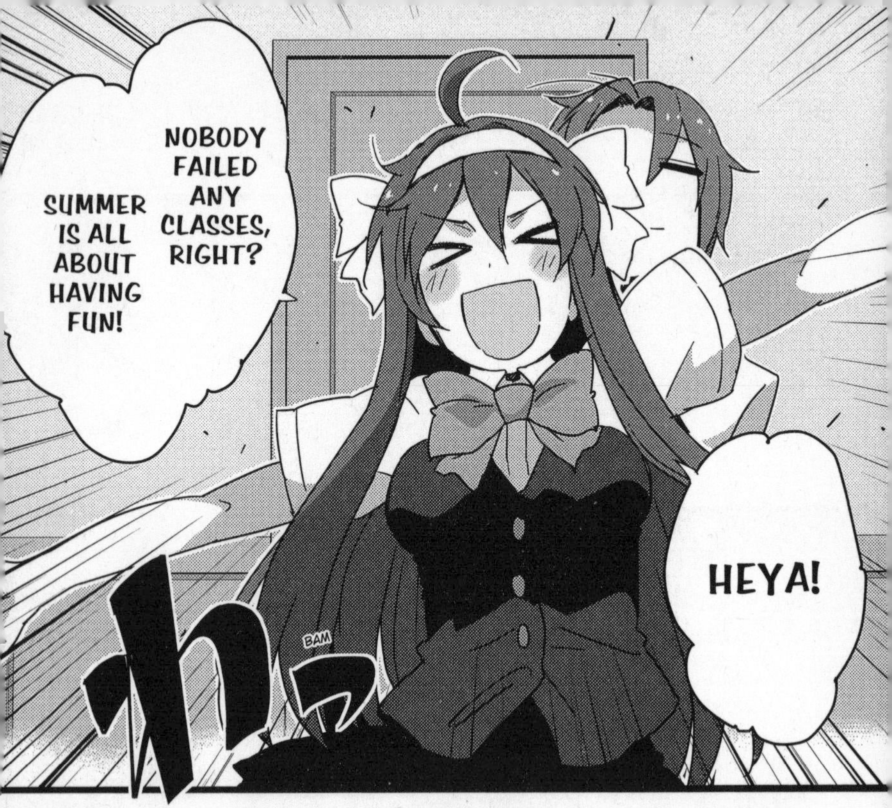
HEYA!
NOBODY FAILED ANY CLASSES, RIGHT?
SUMMER IS ALL ABOUT HAVING FUN!
BAM

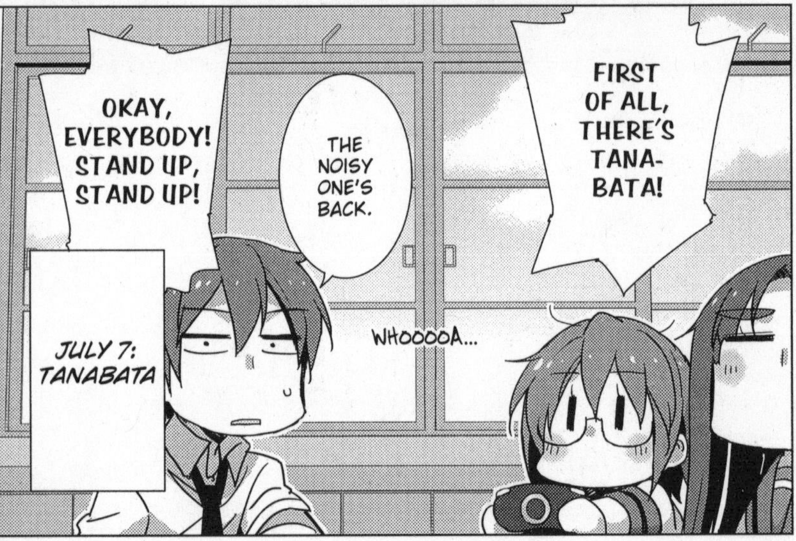
FIRST OF ALL, THERE'S TANA-BATA!
THE NOISY ONE'S BACK.
OKAY, EVERYBODY! STAND UP, STAND UP!
WHOOOOA...
JULY 7: TANABATA

I FEEL LIKE
I'VE BEEN
GONE FOR A
WHOLE
VOLUME!!

ALL RIGHT! LET'S GO!!
GO WHERE!?

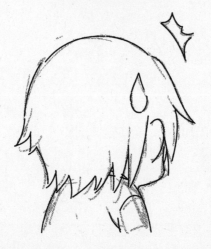

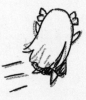

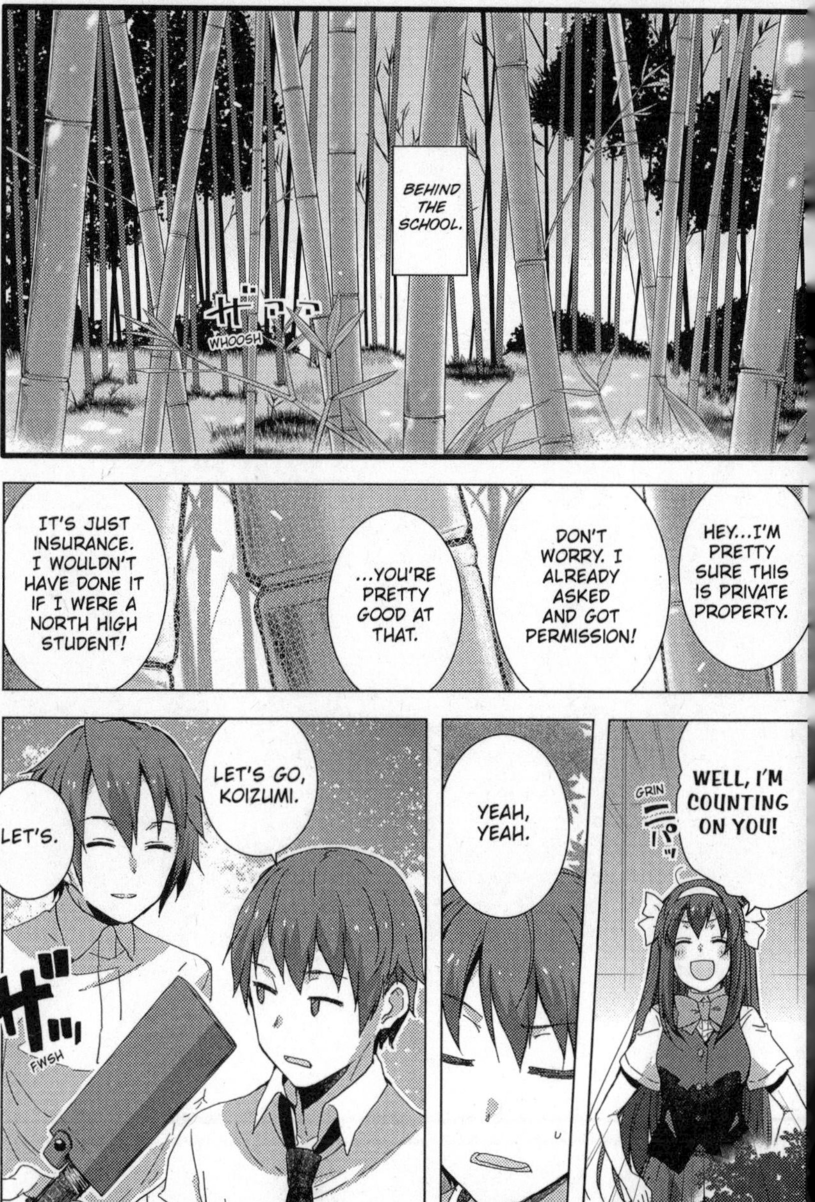
BEHIND THE SCHOOL.
WHOOSH
HEY...I'M PRETTY SURE THIS IS PRIVATE PROPERTY.
DON'T WORRY. I ALREADY ASKED AND GOT PERMISSION!
...YOU'RE PRETTY GOOD AT THAT.
IT'S JUST INSURANCE. I WOULDN'T HAVE DONE IT IF I WERE A NORTH HIGH STUDENT!
GRIN
WELL, I'M COUNTING ON YOU!
YEAH, YEAH.
LET'S GO, KOIZUMI.
LET'S.
FWSH

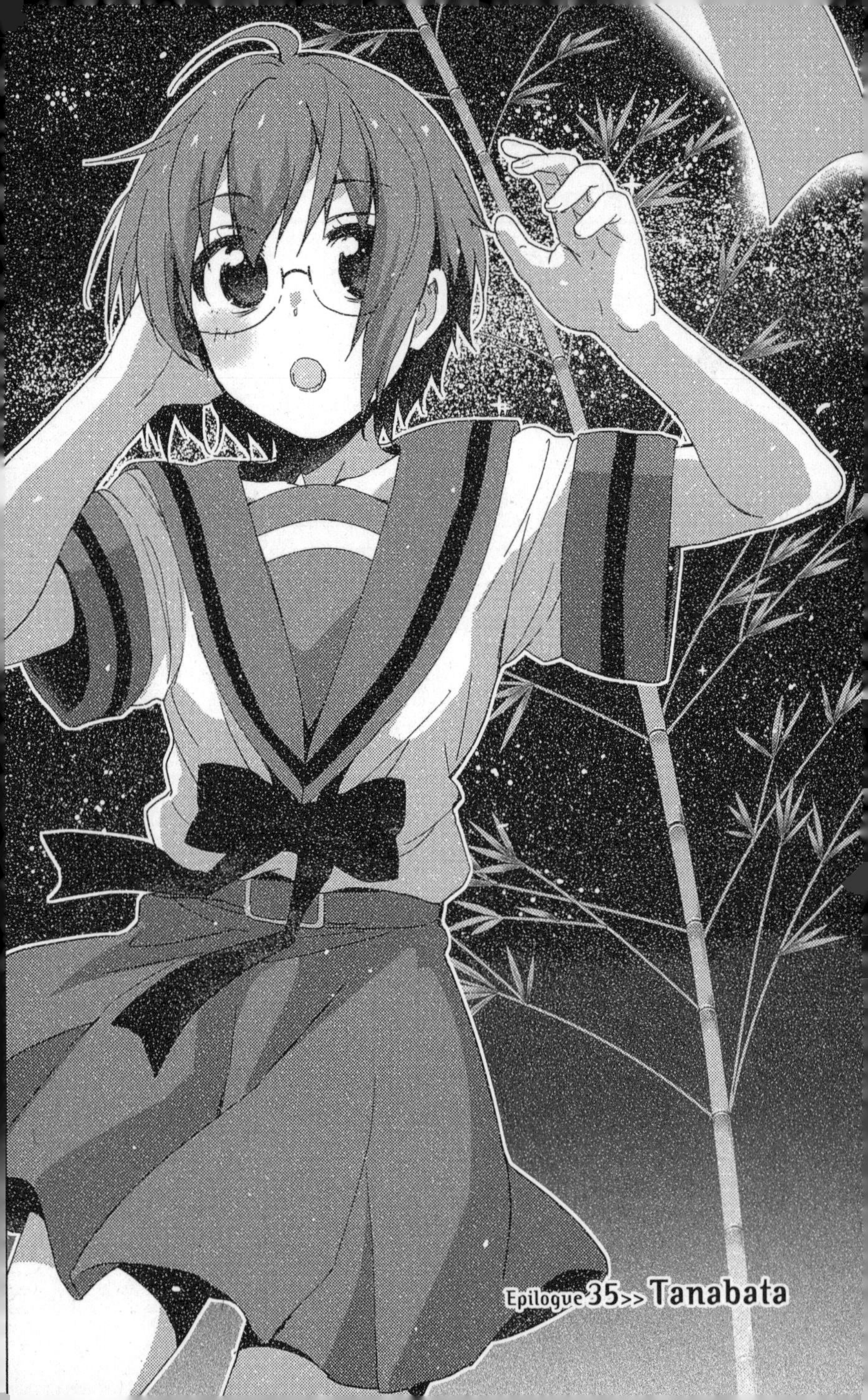
Epilogue 35>> Tanabata

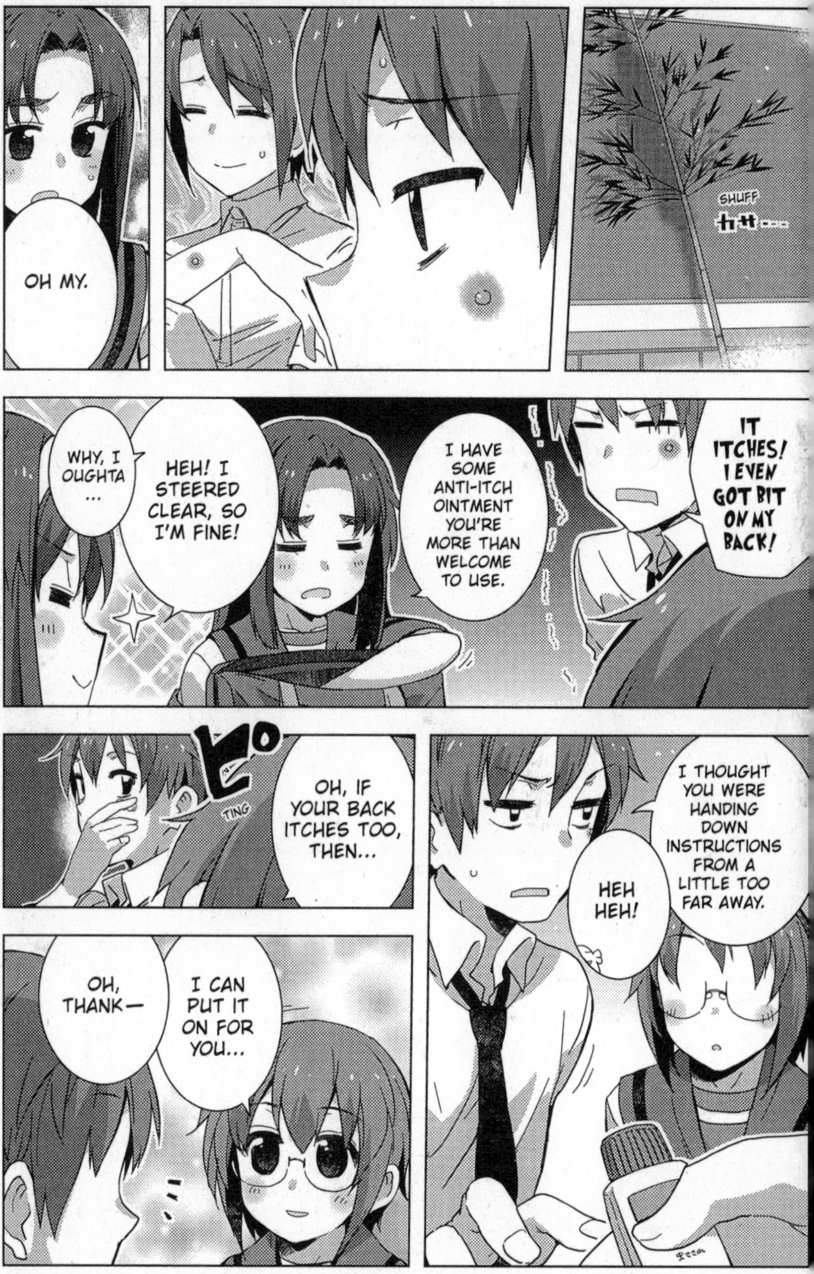
SHUFF
OH MY.
IT ITCHES! I EVEN GOT BIT ON MY BACK!
I HAVE SOME ANTI-ITCH OINTMENT YOU'RE MORE THAN WELCOME TO USE.
HEH! I STEERED CLEAR, SO I'M FINE!
WHY, I OUGHTA ...
I THOUGHT YOU WERE HANDING DOWN INSTRUCTIONS FROM A LITTLE TOO FAR AWAY.
HEH HEH!
OH, IF YOUR BACK ITCHES TOO, THEN...
TING
I CAN PUT IT ON FOR YOU...
OH, THANK—

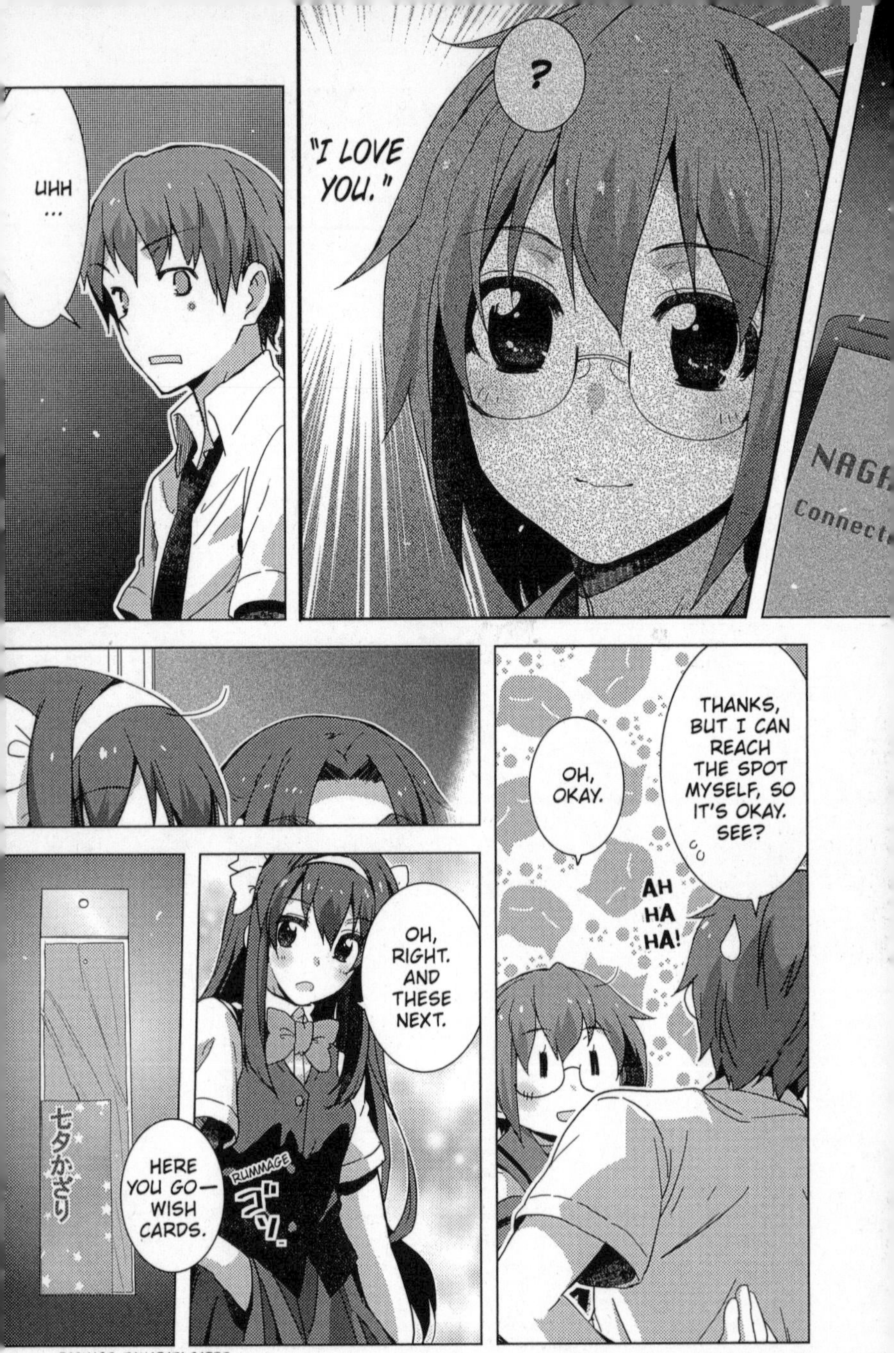
?
"I LOVE YOU."
UHH ...
THANKS, BUT I CAN REACH THE SPOT MYSELF, SO IT'S OKAY. SEE?
OH, OKAY.
AH HA HA!
OH, RIGHT. AND THESE NEXT.
RUMMAGE
HERE YOU GO— WISH CARDS.
七夕かざり

PACKAGE: TANABATA CARDS

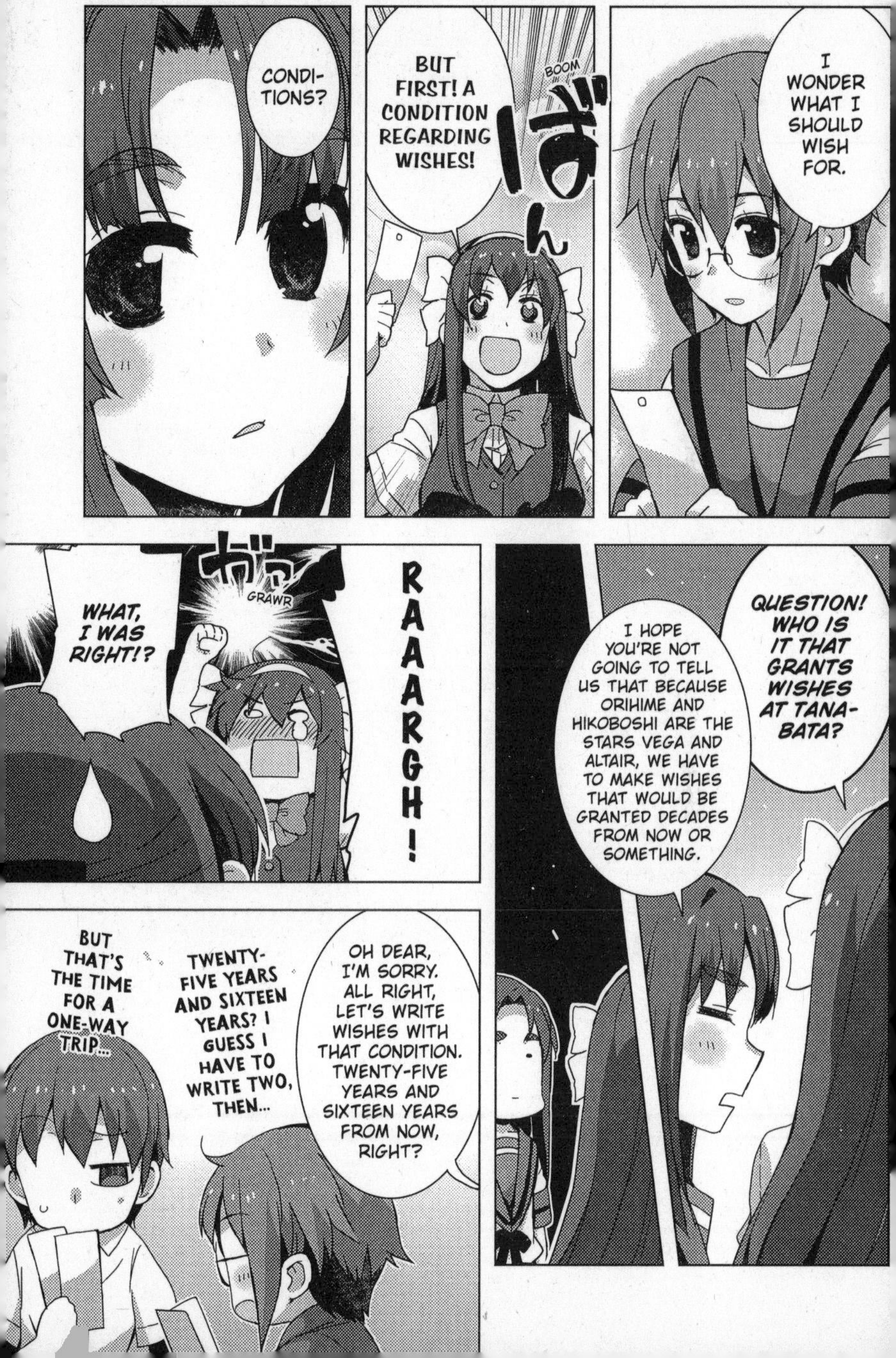
I WONDER WHAT I SHOULD WISH FOR.
BOOM
ばん
BUT FIRST! A CONDITION REGARDING WISHES!
CONDI-TIONS?
QUESTION! WHO IS IT THAT GRANTS WISHES AT TANA-BATA?
I HOPE YOU'RE NOT GOING TO TELL US THAT BECAUSE ORIHIME AND HIKOBOSHI ARE THE STARS VEGA AND ALTAIR, WE HAVE TO MAKE WISHES THAT WOULD BE GRANTED DECADES FROM NOW OR SOMETHING.
RAAAARGH!
GRAWR
WHAT, I WAS RIGHT!?
OH DEAR, I'M SORRY. ALL RIGHT, LET'S WRITE WISHES WITH THAT CONDITION. TWENTY-FIVE YEARS AND SIXTEEN YEARS FROM NOW, RIGHT?
TWENTY-FIVE YEARS AND SIXTEEN YEARS? I GUESS I HAVE TO WRITE TWO, THEN...
BUT THAT'S THE TIME FOR A ONE-WAY TRIP...

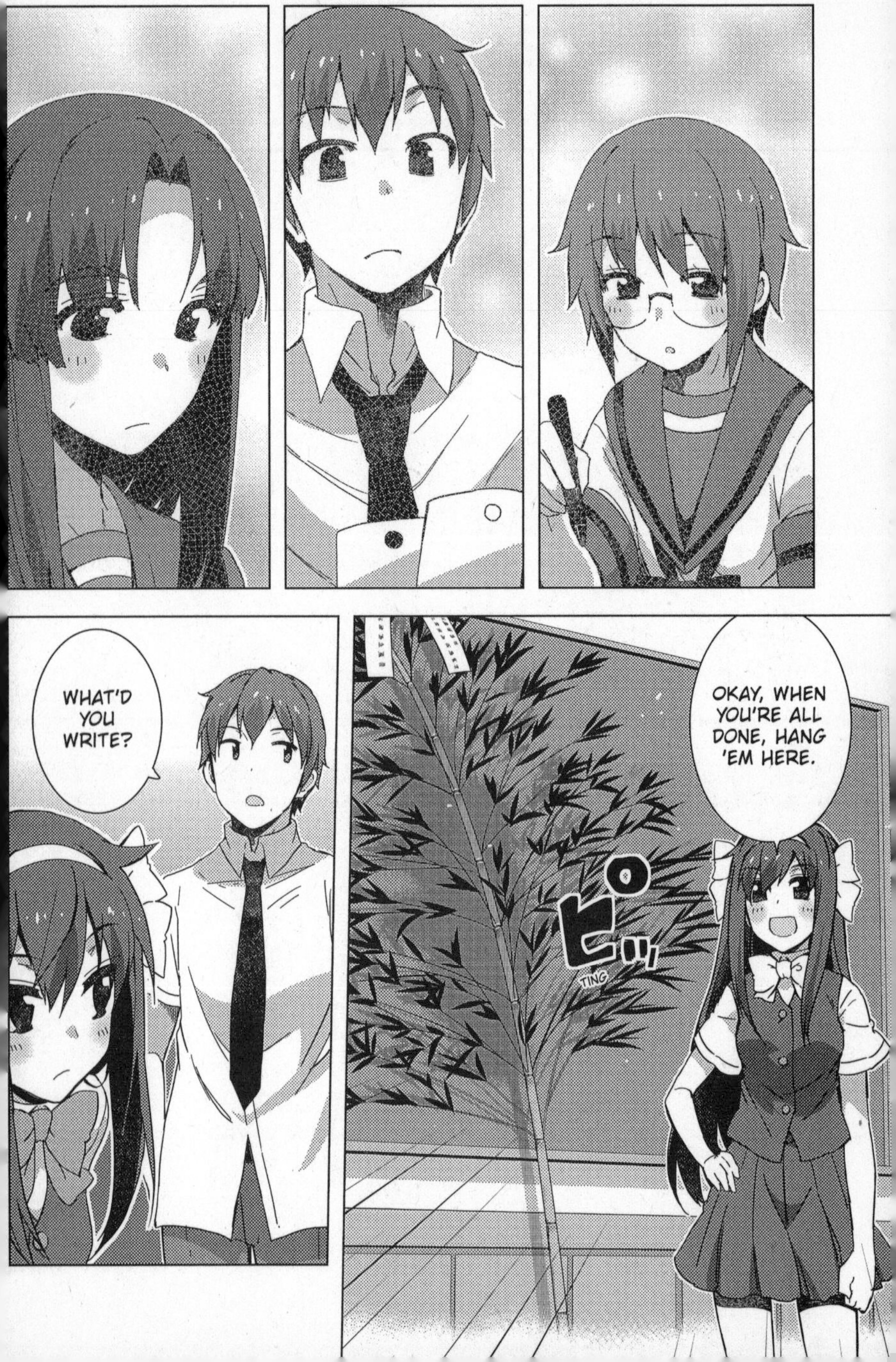
OKAY, WHEN YOU'RE ALL DONE, HANG 'EM HERE.
TING
WHAT'D YOU WRITE?

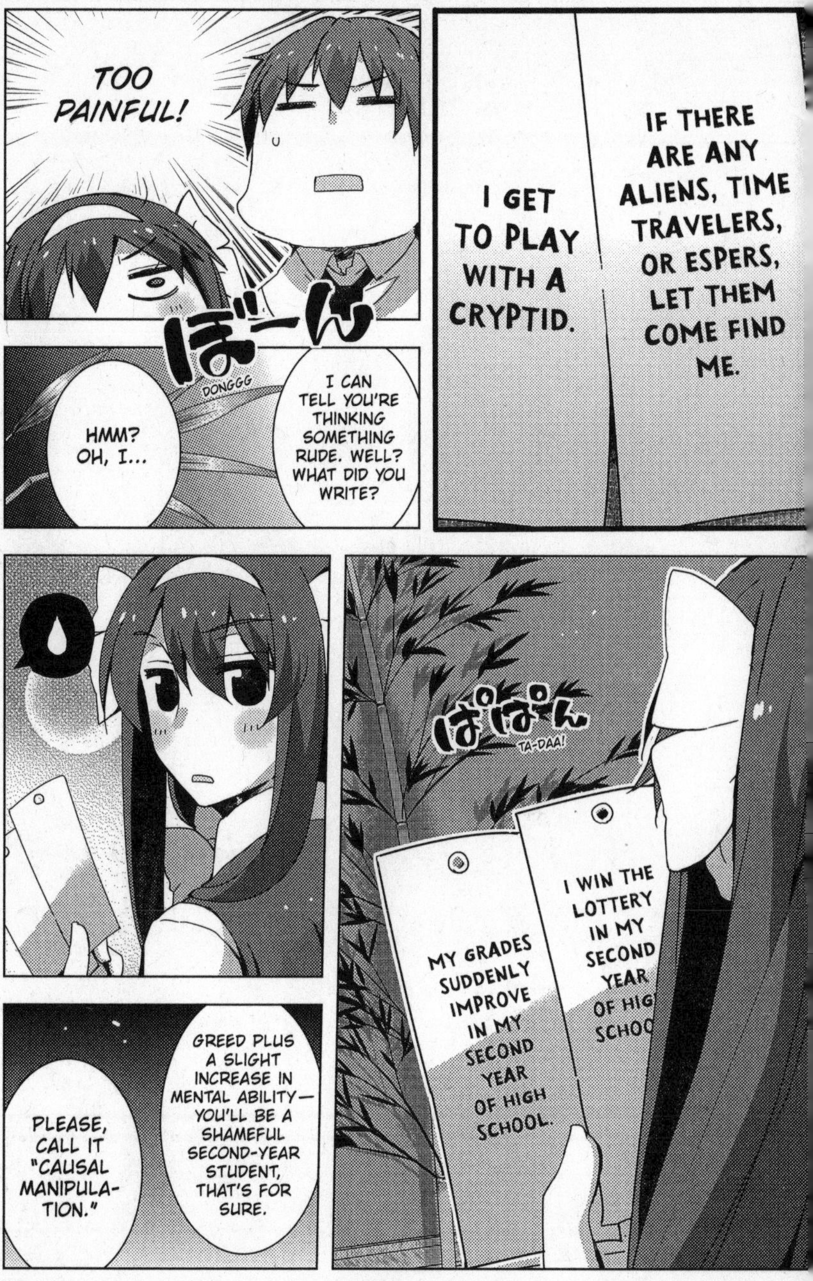
IF THERE ARE ANY ALIENS, TIME TRAVELERS, OR ESPERS, LET THEM COME FIND ME.
I GET TO PLAY WITH A CRYPTID.
TOO PAINFUL!
ぼーん
DONGGG
I CAN TELL YOU'RE THINKING SOMETHING RUDE. WELL? WHAT DID YOU WRITE?
HMM? OH, I...
ぱぱん
TA-DAA!
I WIN THE LOTTERY IN MY SECOND YEAR OF HIG SCHOO
MY GRADES SUDDENLY IMPROVE IN MY SECOND YEAR OF HIGH SCHOOL.
GREED PLUS A SLIGHT INCREASE IN MENTAL ABILITY— YOU'LL BE A SHAMEFUL SECOND-YEAR STUDENT, THAT'S FOR SURE.
PLEASE, CALL IT "CAUSAL MANIPULATION."

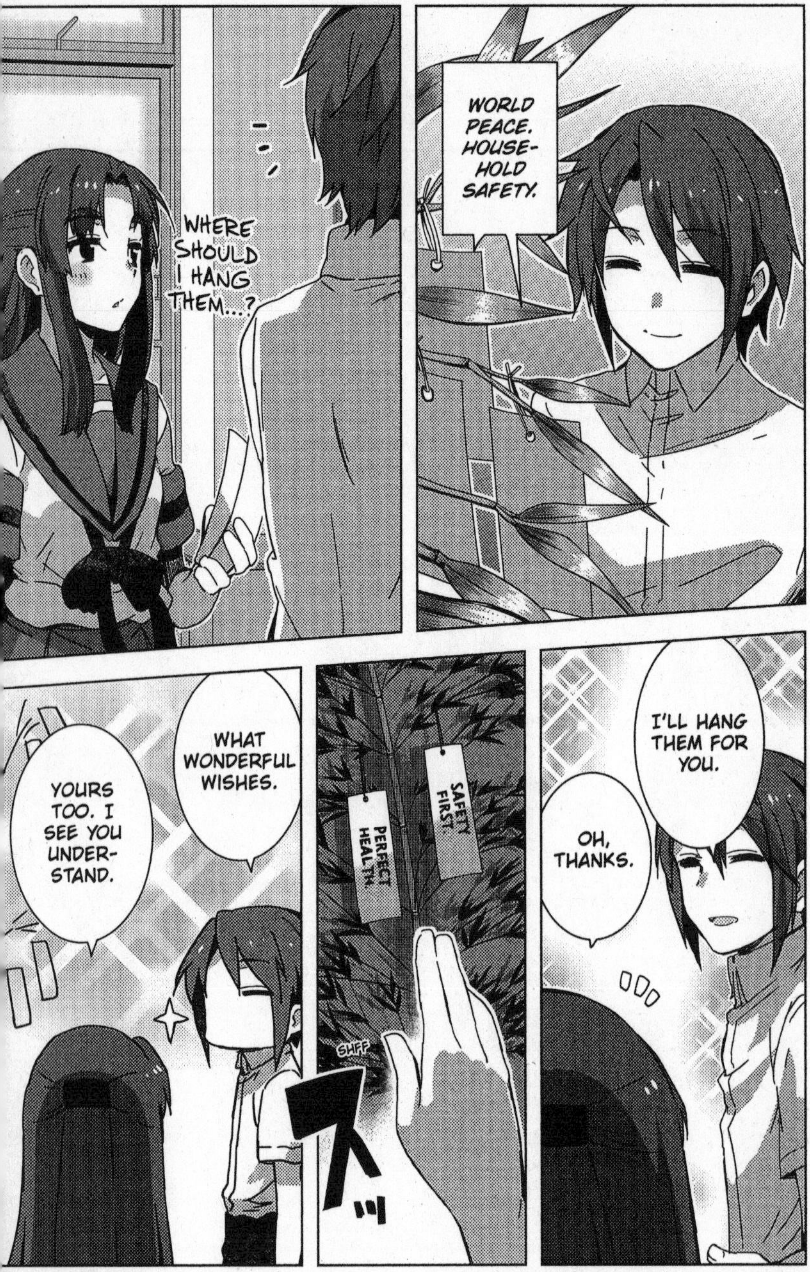
WORLD PEACE. HOUSE-HOLD SAFETY.
…
WHERE SHOULD I HANG THEM…?
I'LL HANG THEM FOR YOU.
OH, THANKS.
SAFETY FIRST
PERFECT HEALTH
SHFF
WHAT WONDERFUL WISHES.
YOURS TOO. I SEE YOU UNDER-STAND.

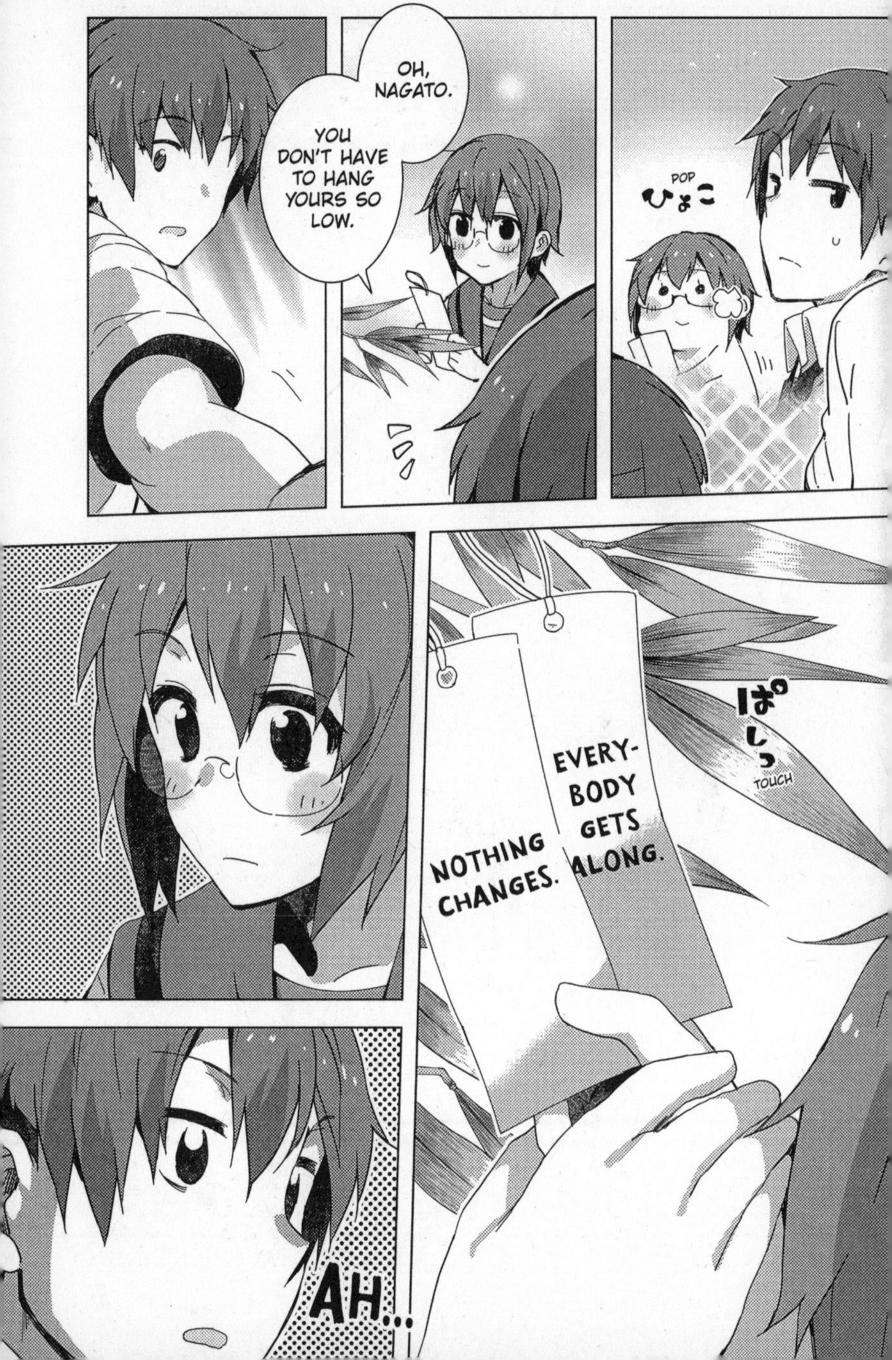
ひょこ
POP
OH, NAGATO.
YOU DON'T HAVE TO HANG YOURS SO LOW.
ぱしっ
TOUCH
EVERY-BODY GETS ALONG.
NOTHING CHANGES.
AH...

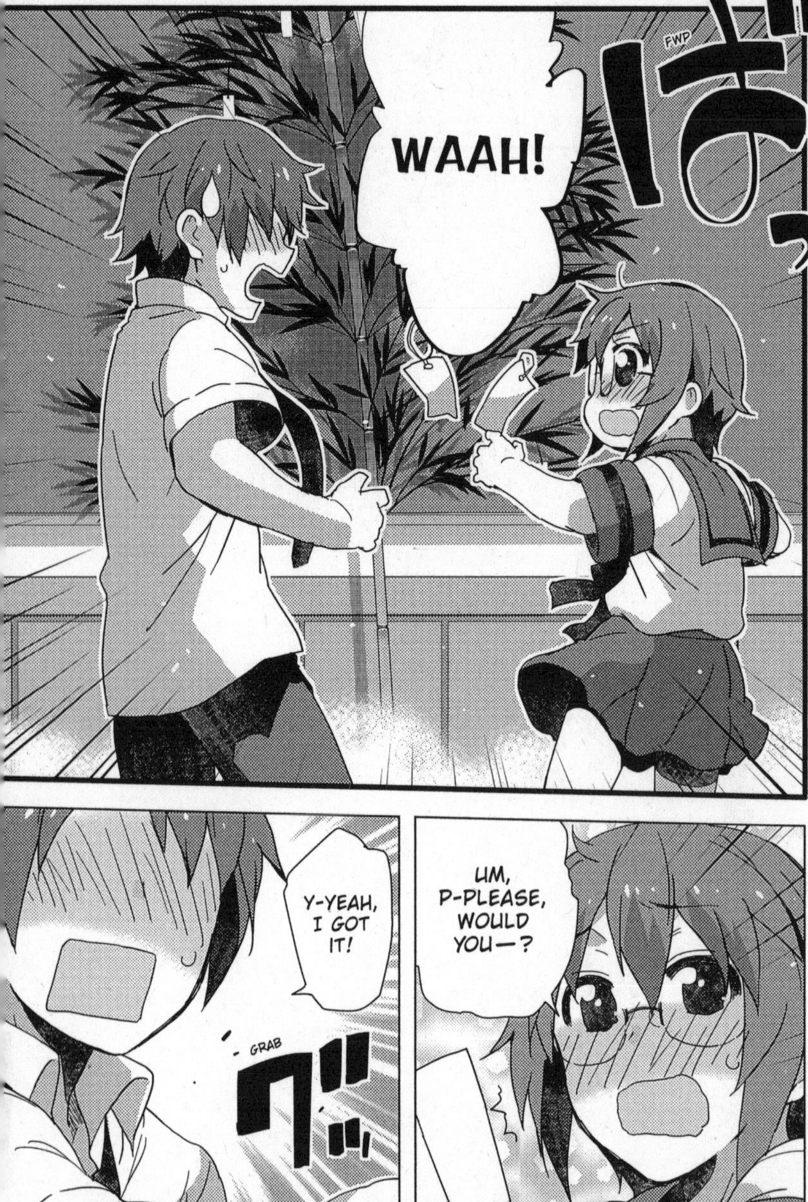
ばっ
FWP
WAAH!
UM, P-PLEASE, WOULD YOU—?
Y-YEAH, I GOT IT!
グッ
GRAB

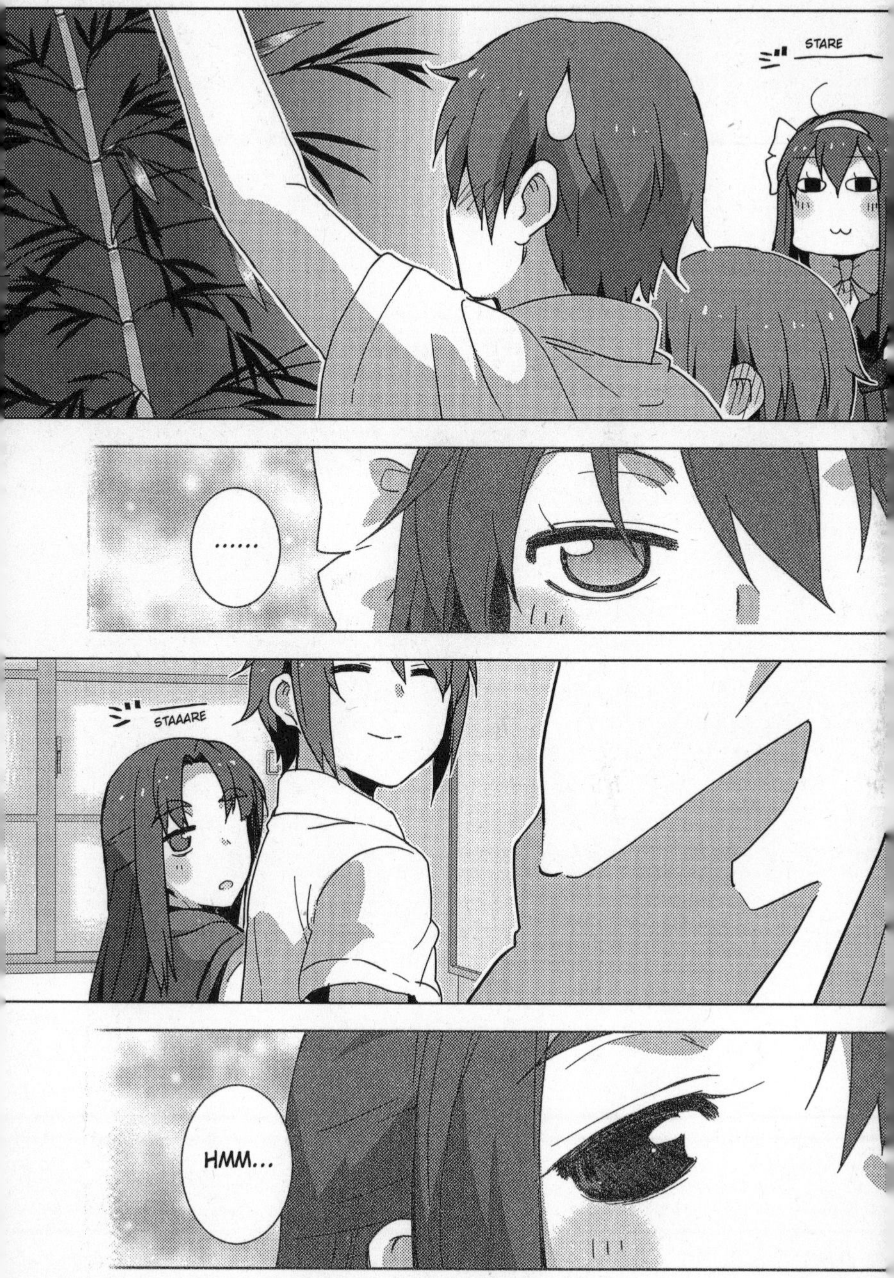
STARE
......
STAAARE
HMM...

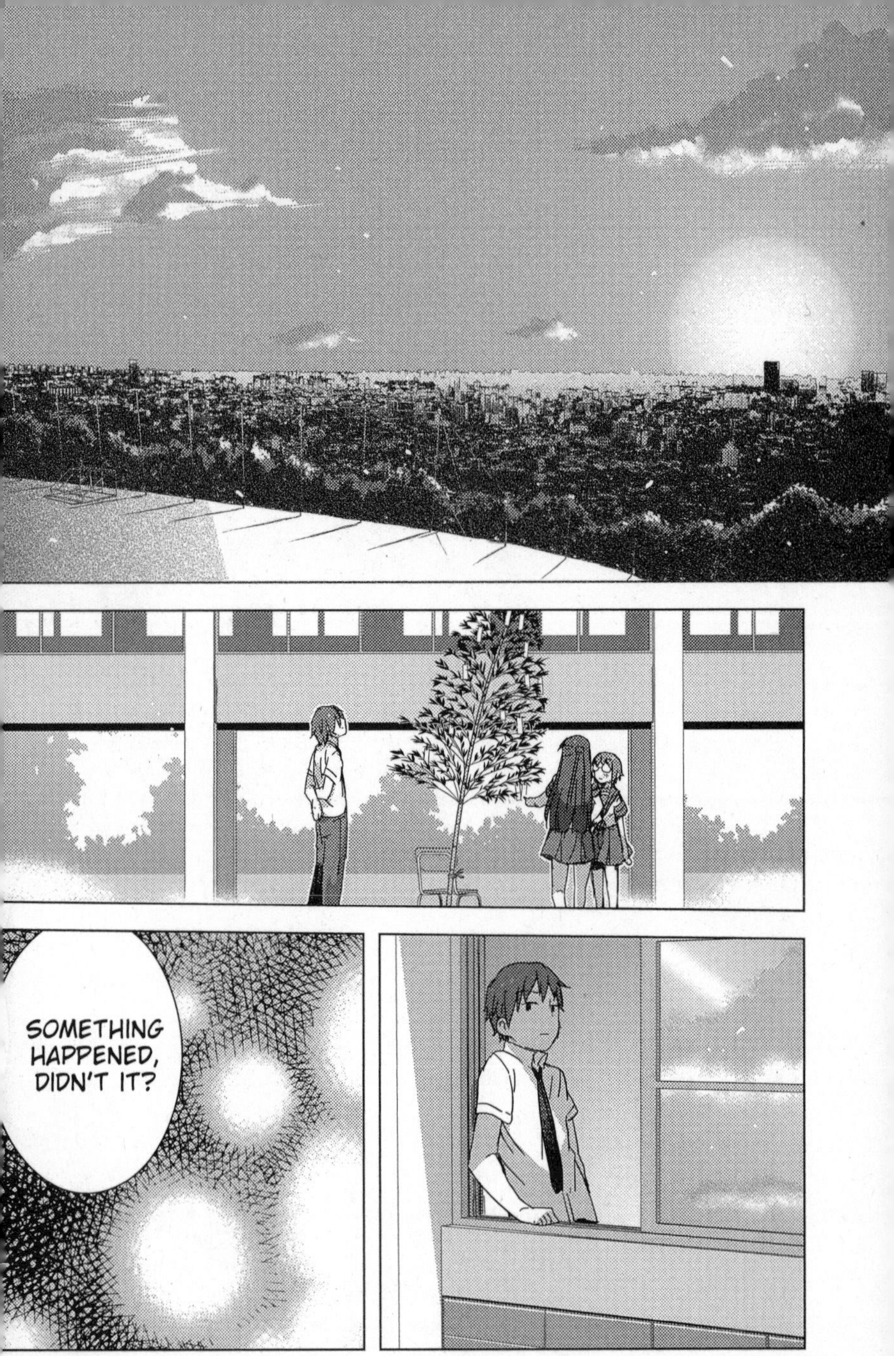
SOMETHING HAPPENED, DIDN'T IT?

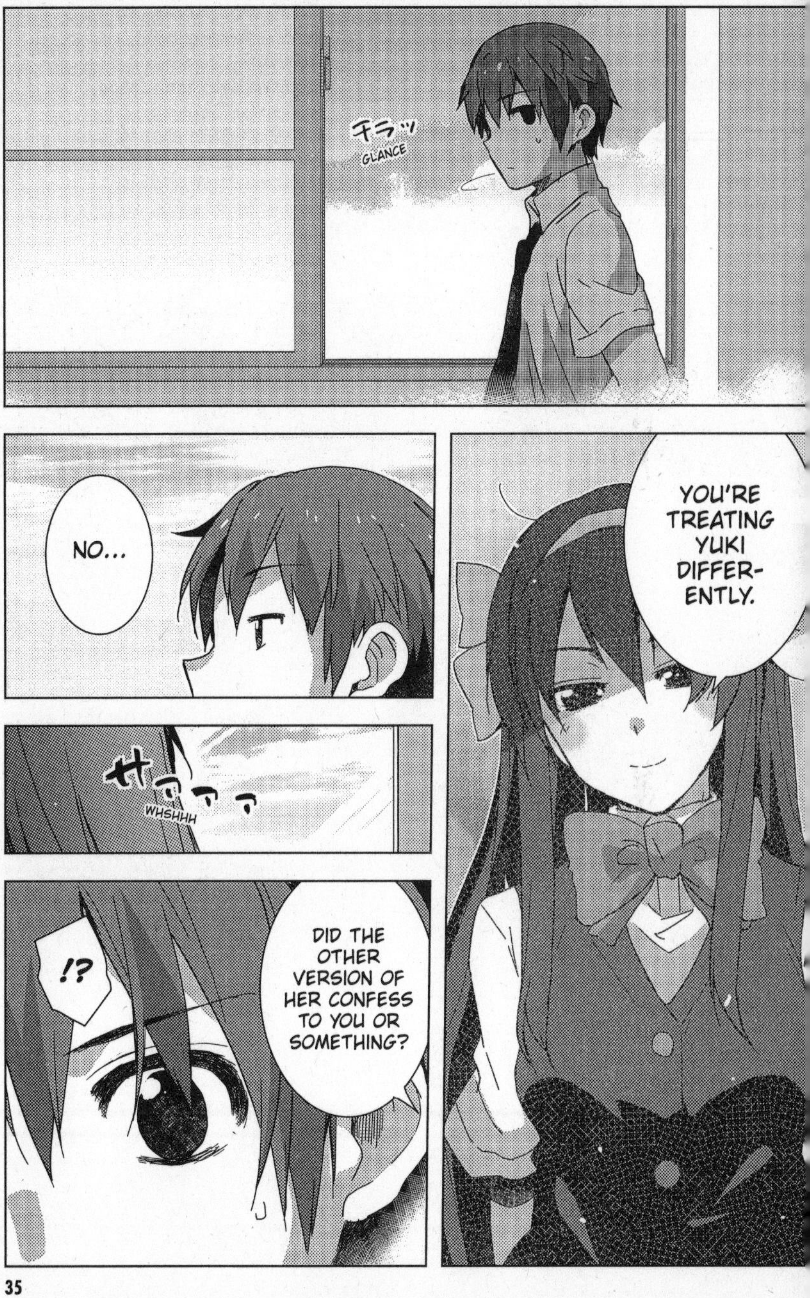
チラッ
GLANCE
YOU'RE TREATING YUKI DIFFER-ENTLY.
NO...
WHSHHH
!?
DID THE OTHER VERSION OF HER CONFESS TO YOU OR SOMETHING?

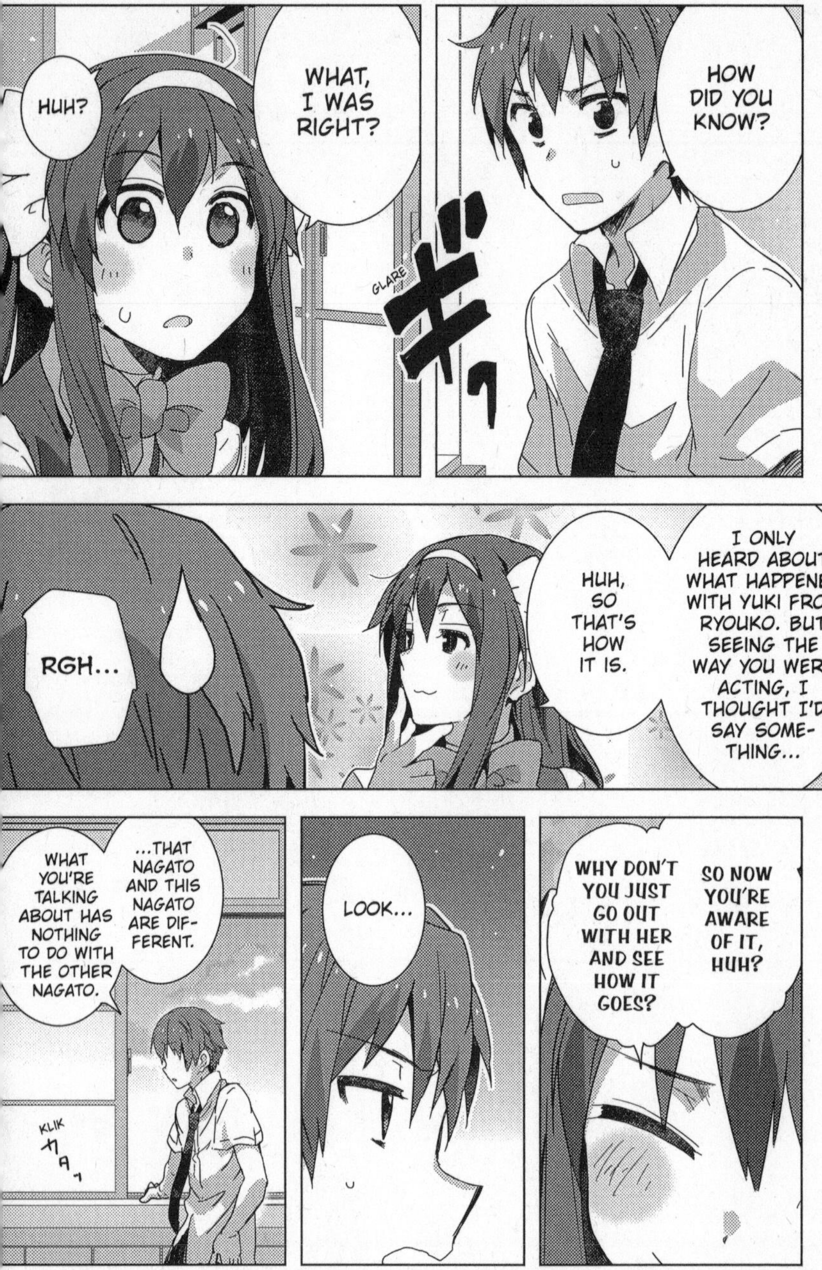
HOW DID YOU KNOW?
GLARE
HUH?
WHAT, I WAS RIGHT?
I ONLY HEARD ABOUT WHAT HAPPENED WITH YUKI FROM RYOUKO. BUT SEEING THE WAY YOU WERE ACTING, I THOUGHT I'D SAY SOME-THING...
HUH, SO THAT'S HOW IT IS.
RGH...
SO NOW YOU'RE AWARE OF IT, HUH?
WHY DON'T YOU JUST GO OUT WITH HER AND SEE HOW IT GOES?
LOOK...
...THAT NAGATO AND THIS NAGATO ARE DIF-FERENT.
WHAT YOU'RE TALKING ABOUT HAS NOTHING TO DO WITH THE OTHER NAGATO.
KLIK

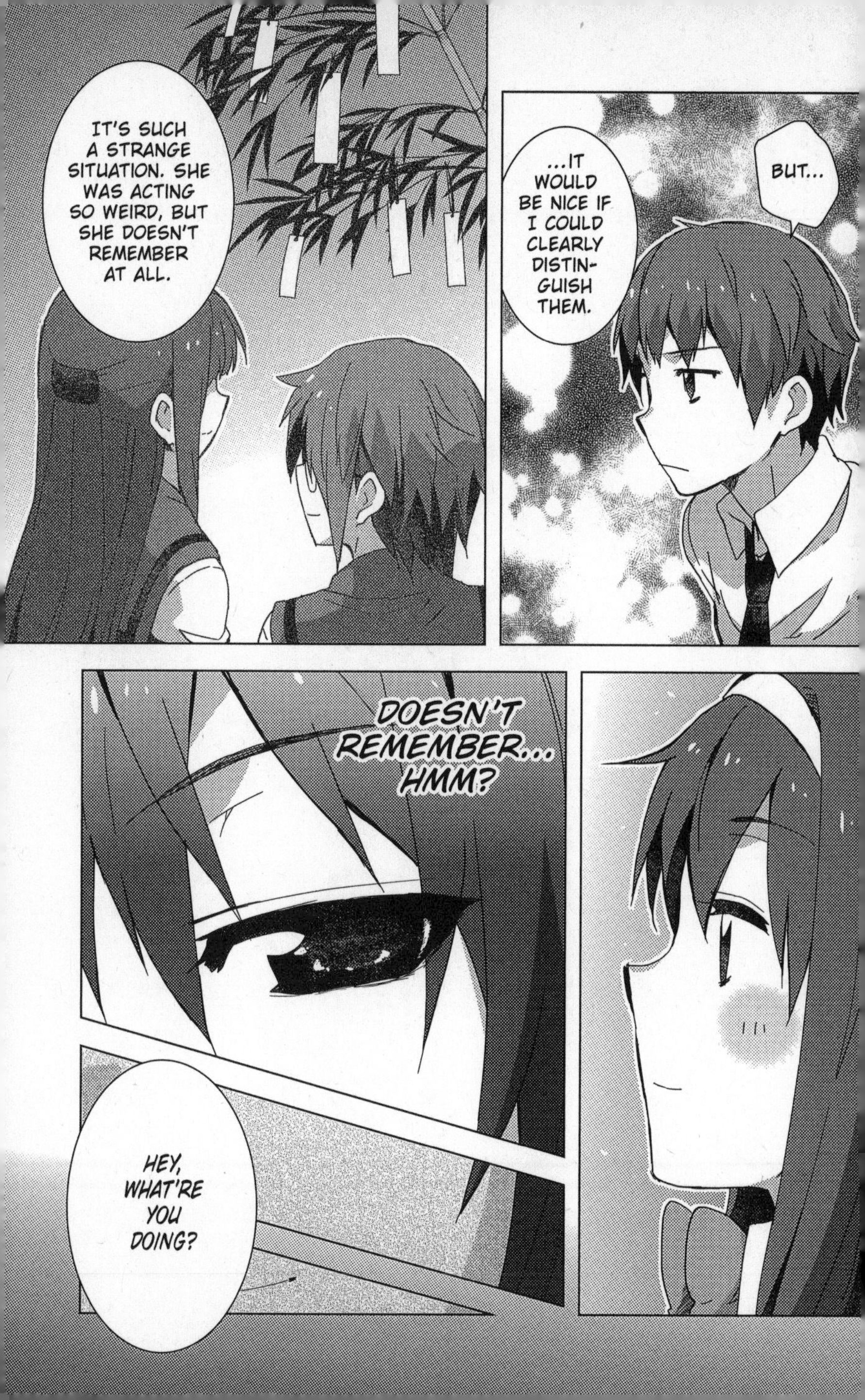
BUT...
...IT WOULD BE NICE IF I COULD CLEARLY DISTIN-GUISH THEM.
IT'S SUCH A STRANGE SITUATION. SHE WAS ACTING SO WEIRD, BUT SHE DOESN'T REMEMBER AT ALL.
DOESN'T REMEMBER... HMM?
HEY, WHAT'RE YOU DOING?

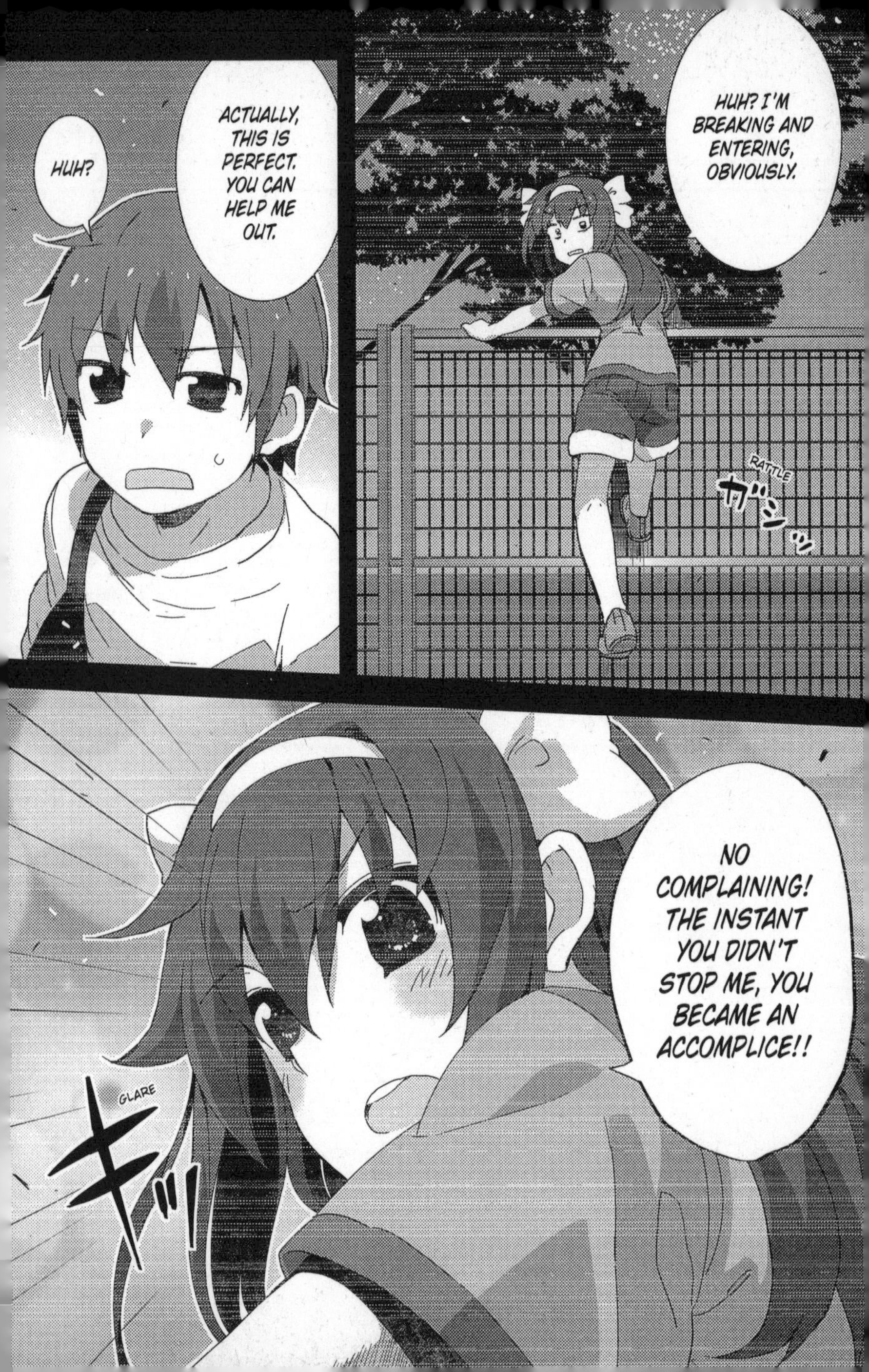
HUH? I'M BREAKING AND ENTERING, OBVIOUSLY.
RATTLE
HUH?
ACTUALLY, THIS IS PERFECT. YOU CAN HELP ME OUT.
NO COMPLAINING! THE INSTANT YOU DIDN'T STOP ME, YOU BECAME AN ACCOMPLICE!!
GLARE

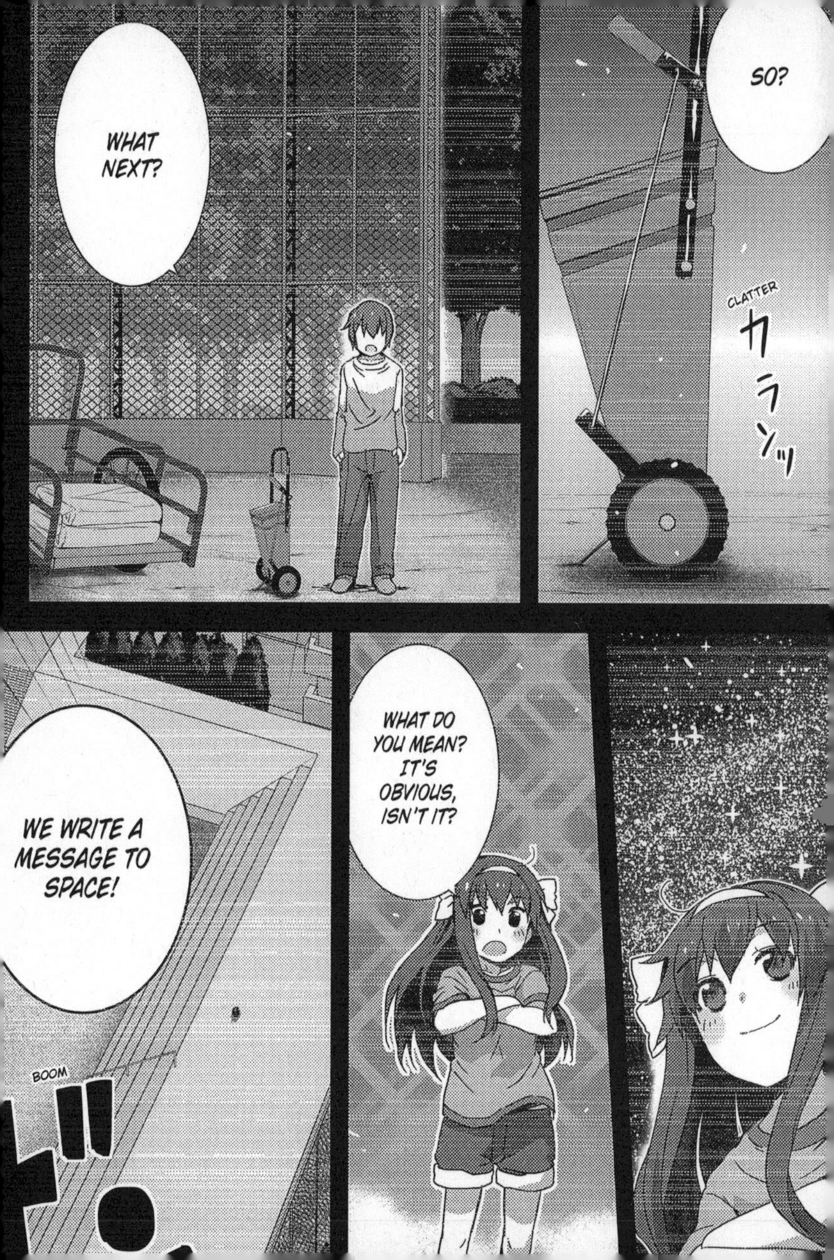
SO?
CLATTER
カランッ
WHAT NEXT?
WHAT DO YOU MEAN? IT'S OBVIOUS, ISN'T IT?
WE WRITE A MESSAGE TO SPACE!
BOOM

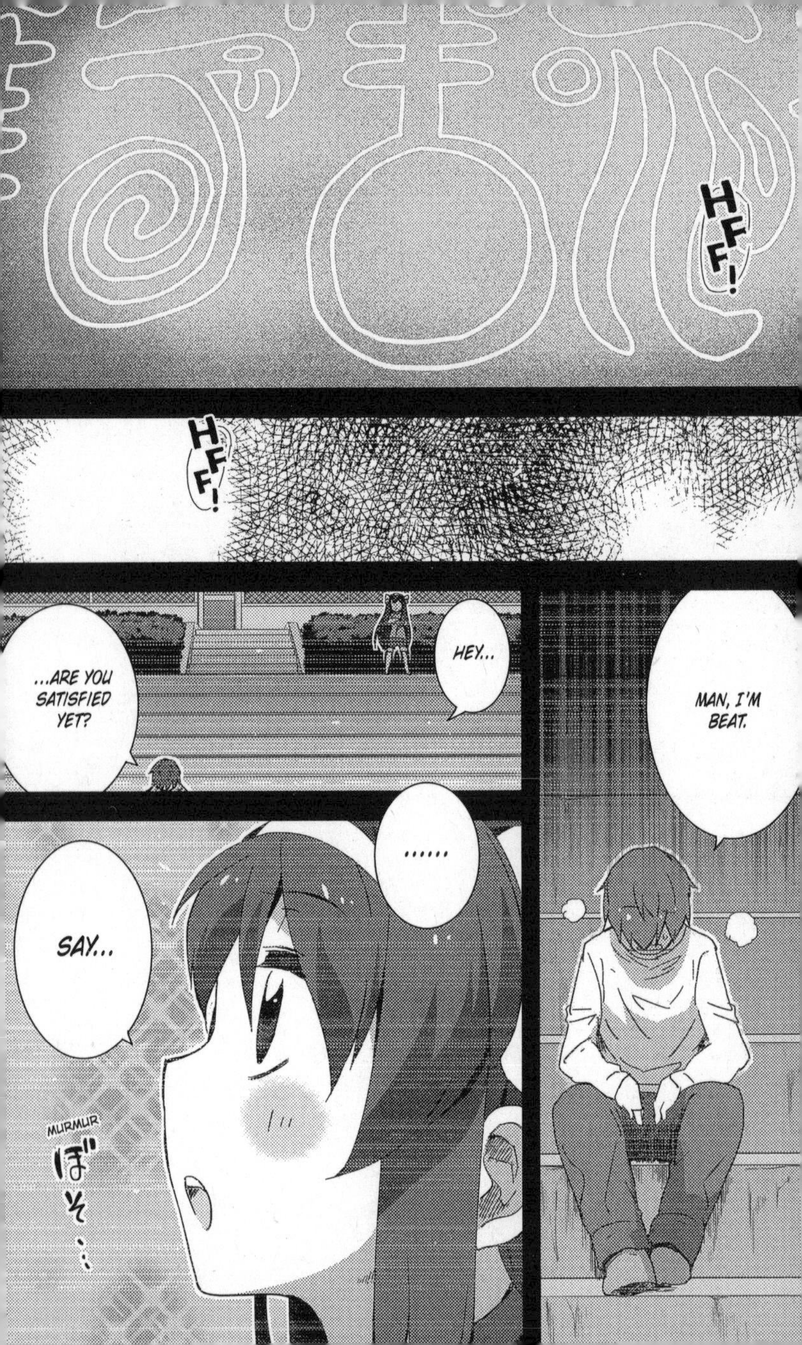
HFF!
HFF!
MAN, I'M BEAT.
HEY...
...ARE YOU SATISFIED YET?
......
SAY...
MURMUR
ぼそ…

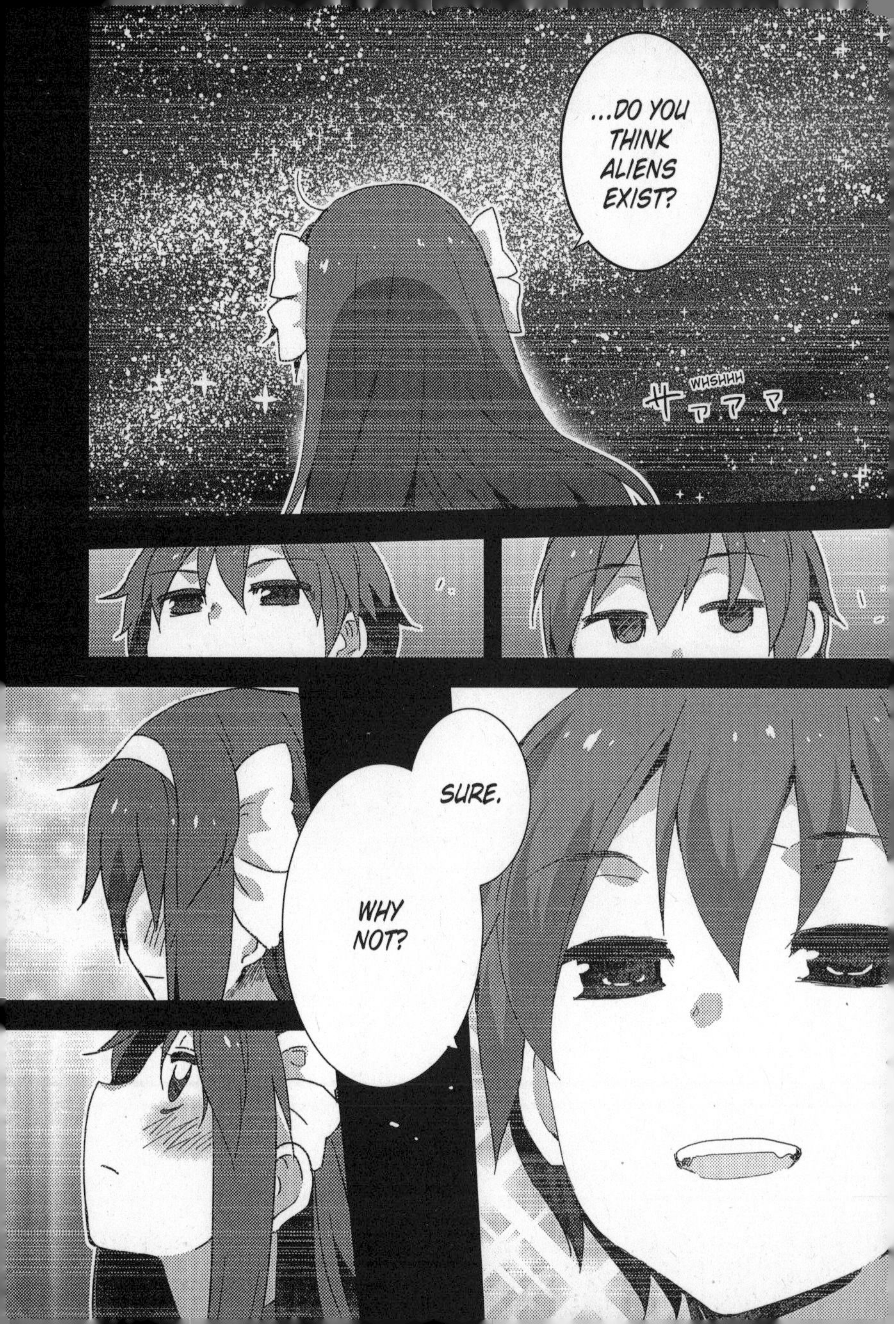
...DO YOU THINK ALIENS EXIST?
WHSHHH
SURE.
WHY NOT?

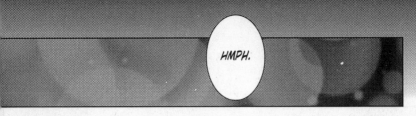

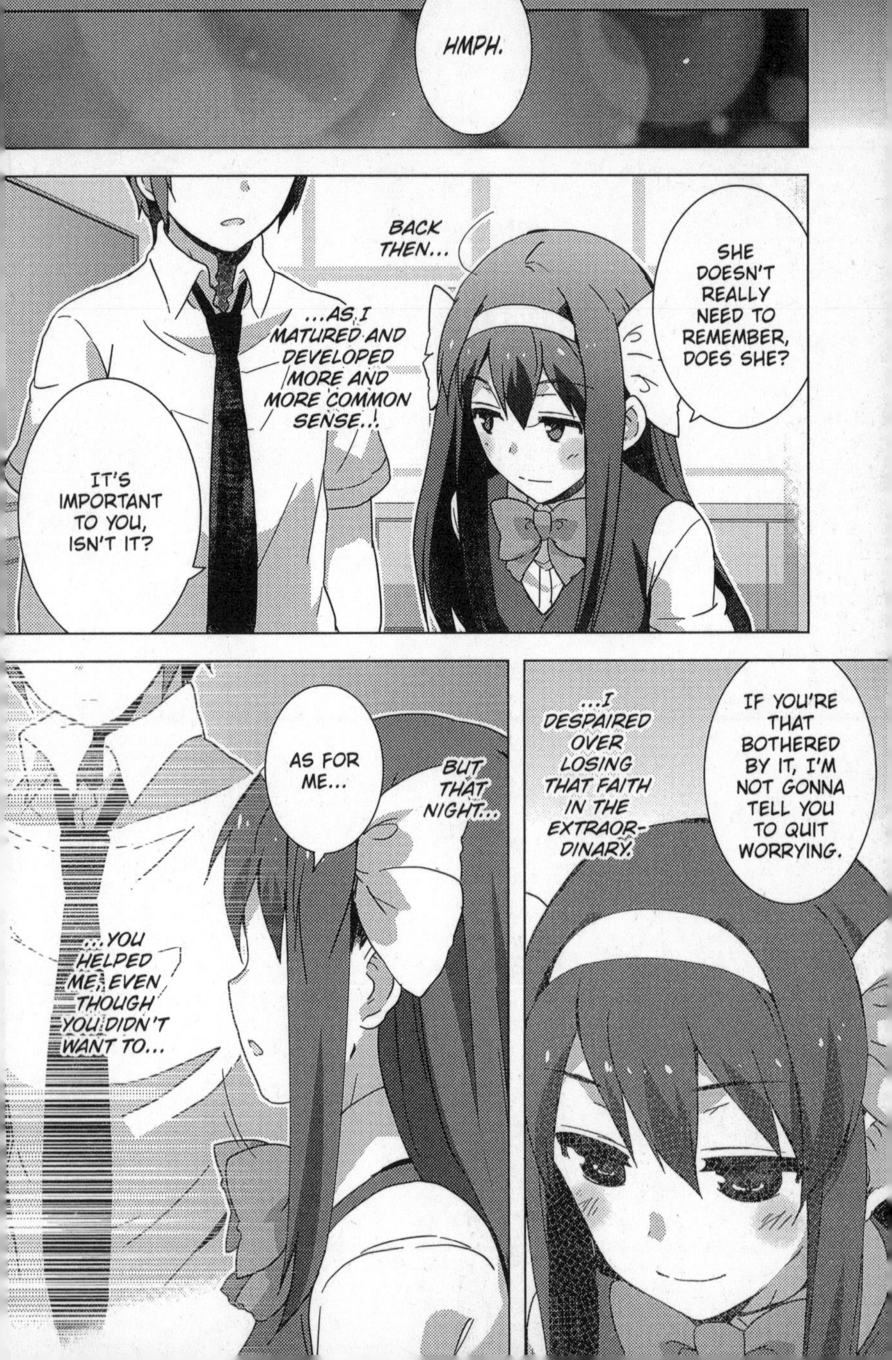
HMPH.
SHE DOESN'T REALLY NEED TO REMEMBER, DOES SHE?
BACK THEN...
...AS I MATURED AND DEVELOPED MORE AND MORE COMMON SENSE...
IT'S IMPORTANT TO YOU, ISN'T IT?
IF YOU'RE THAT BOTHERED BY IT, I'M NOT GONNA TELL YOU TO QUIT WORRYING.
...I DESPAIRED OVER LOSING THAT FAITH IN THE EXTRAOR-DINARY.
BUT THAT NIGHT...
AS FOR ME...
...YOU HELPED ME, EVEN THOUGH YOU DIDN'T WANT TO...

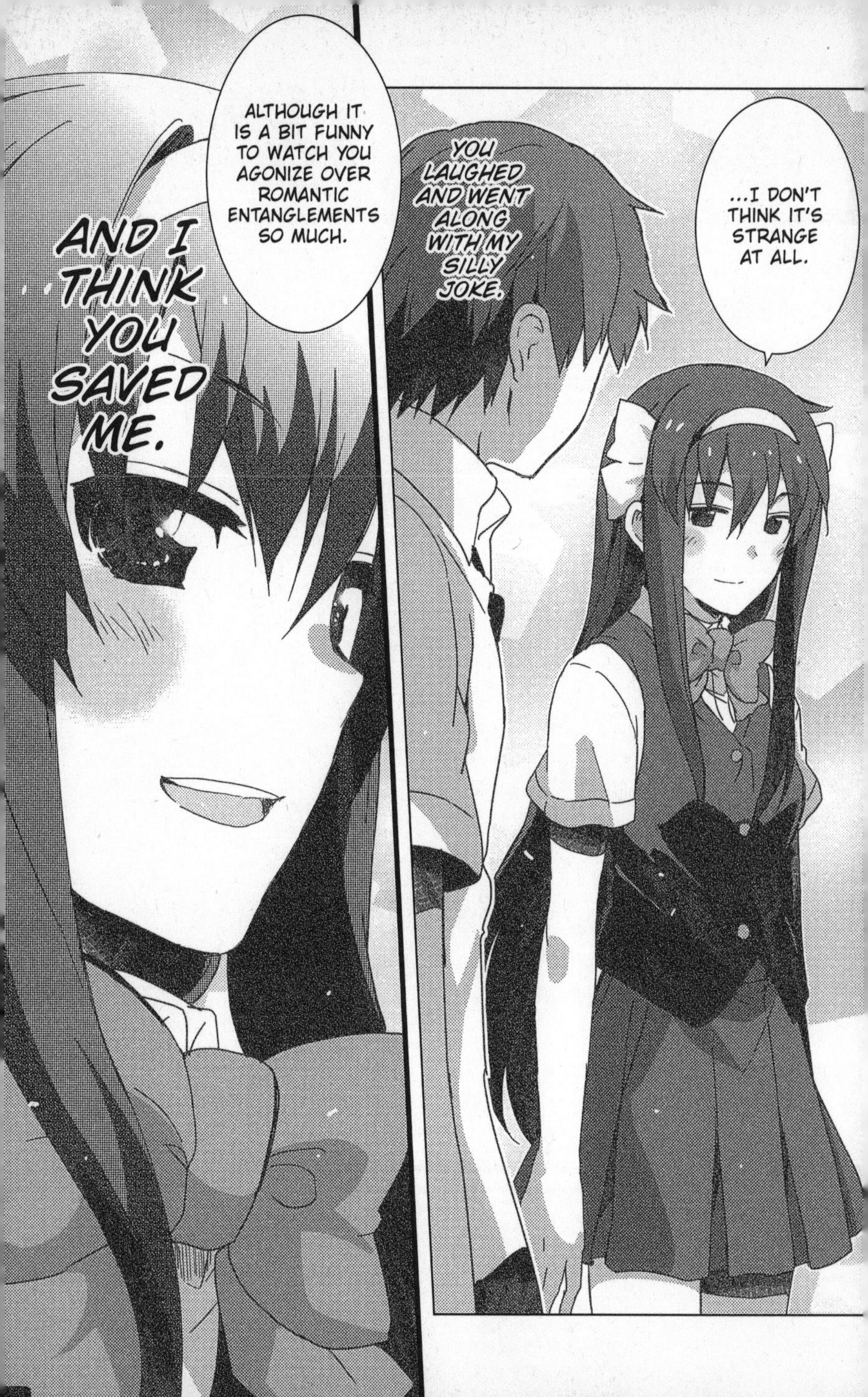
...I DON'T THINK IT'S STRANGE AT ALL.
YOU LAUGHED AND WENT ALONG WITH MY SILLY JOKE.
ALTHOUGH IT IS A BIT FUNNY TO WATCH YOU AGONIZE OVER ROMANTIC ENTANGLEMENTS SO MUCH.
AND I THINK YOU SAVED ME.

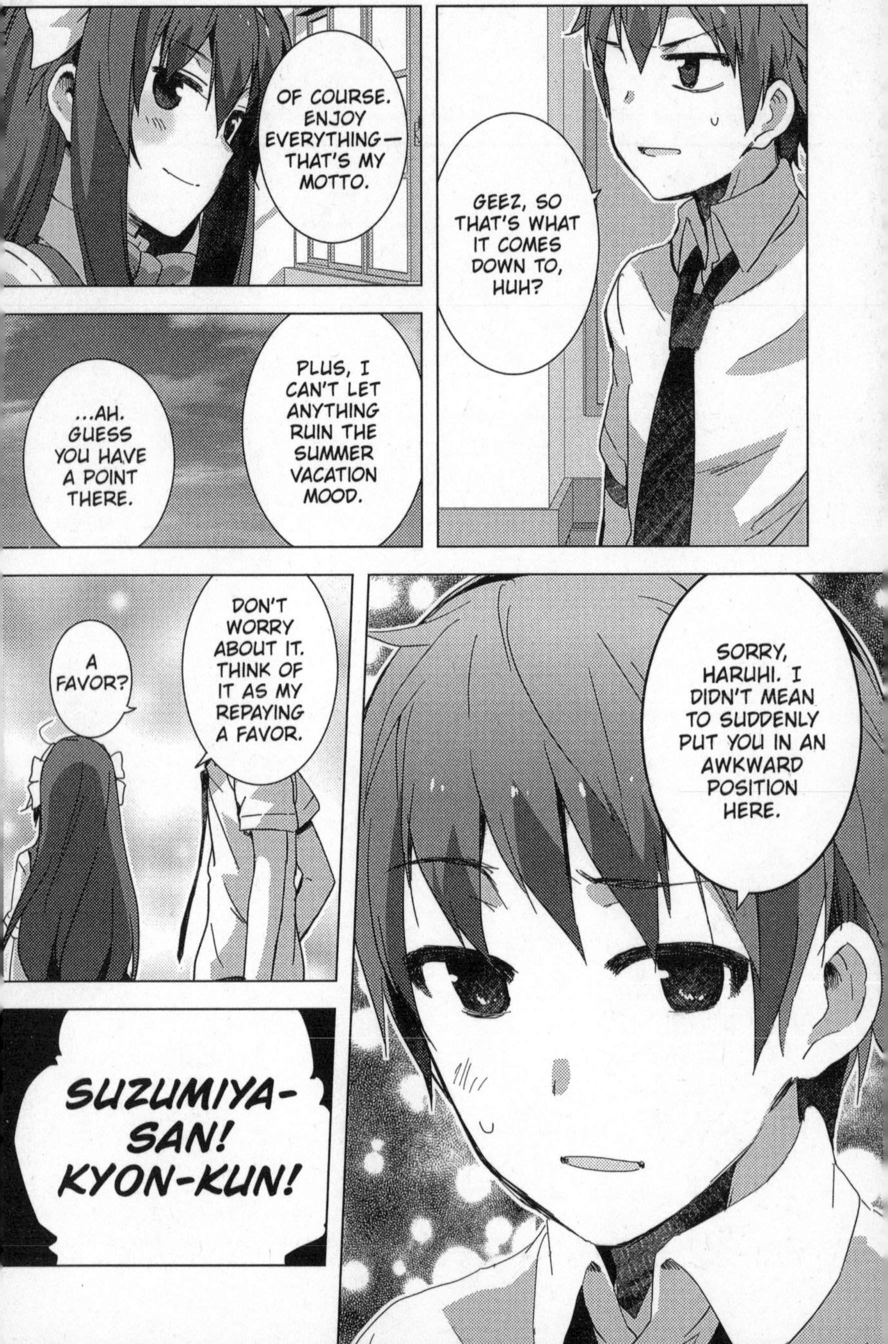
GEEZ, SO THAT'S WHAT IT COMES DOWN TO, HUH?
OF COURSE. ENJOY EVERYTHING— THAT'S MY MOTTO.
PLUS, I CAN'T LET ANYTHING RUIN THE SUMMER VACATION MOOD.
...AH. GUESS YOU HAVE A POINT THERE.
SORRY, HARUHI. I DIDN'T MEAN TO SUDDENLY PUT YOU IN AN AWKWARD POSITION HERE.
DON'T WORRY ABOUT IT. THINK OF IT AS MY REPAYING A FAVOR.
A FAVOR?
SUZUMIYA-SAN! KYON-KUN!

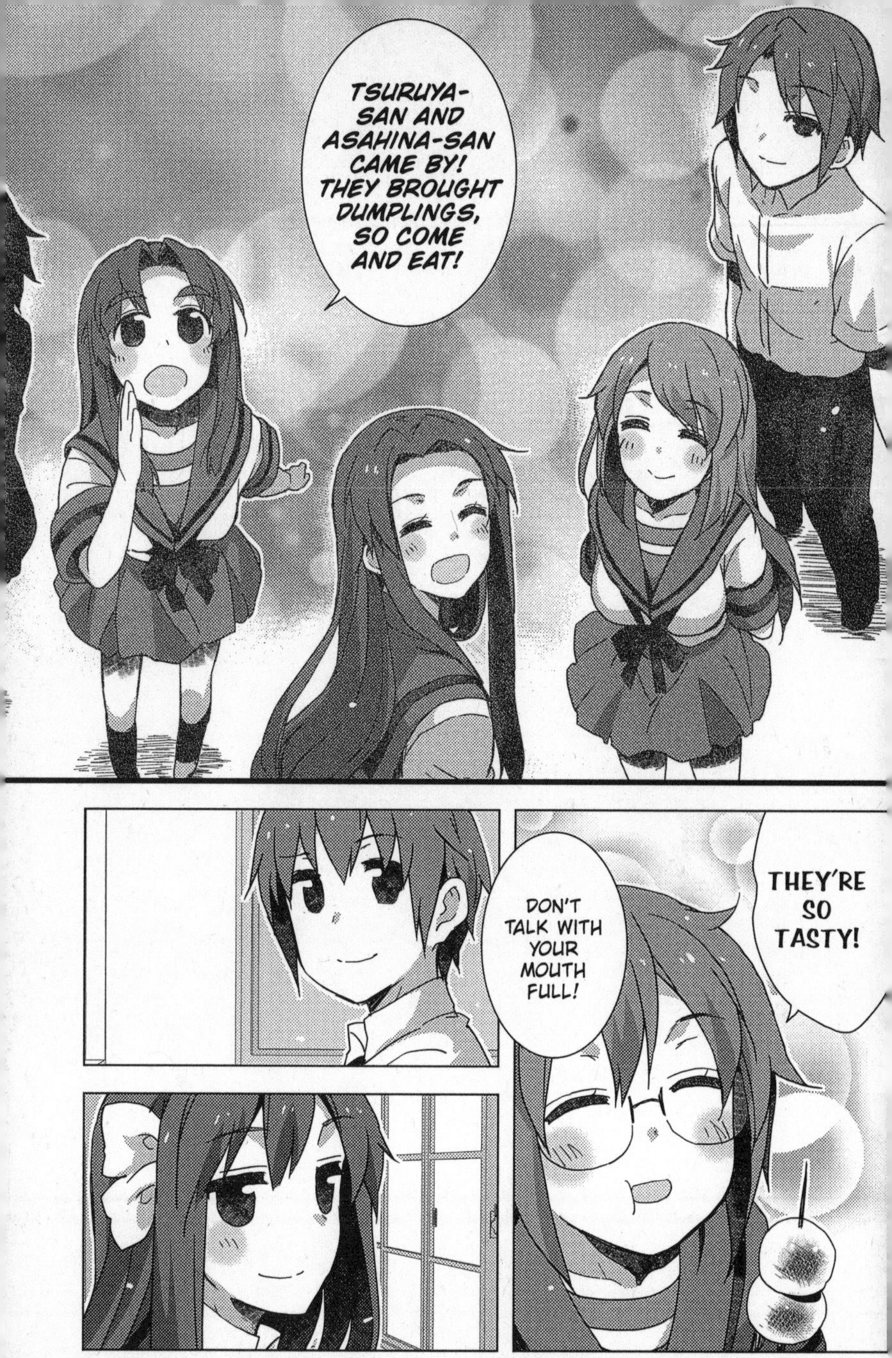
TSURUYA-SAN AND ASAHINA-SAN CAME BY! THEY BROUGHT DUMPLINGS, SO COME AND EAT!
THEY'RE SO TASTY!
DON'T TALK WITH YOUR MOUTH FULL!

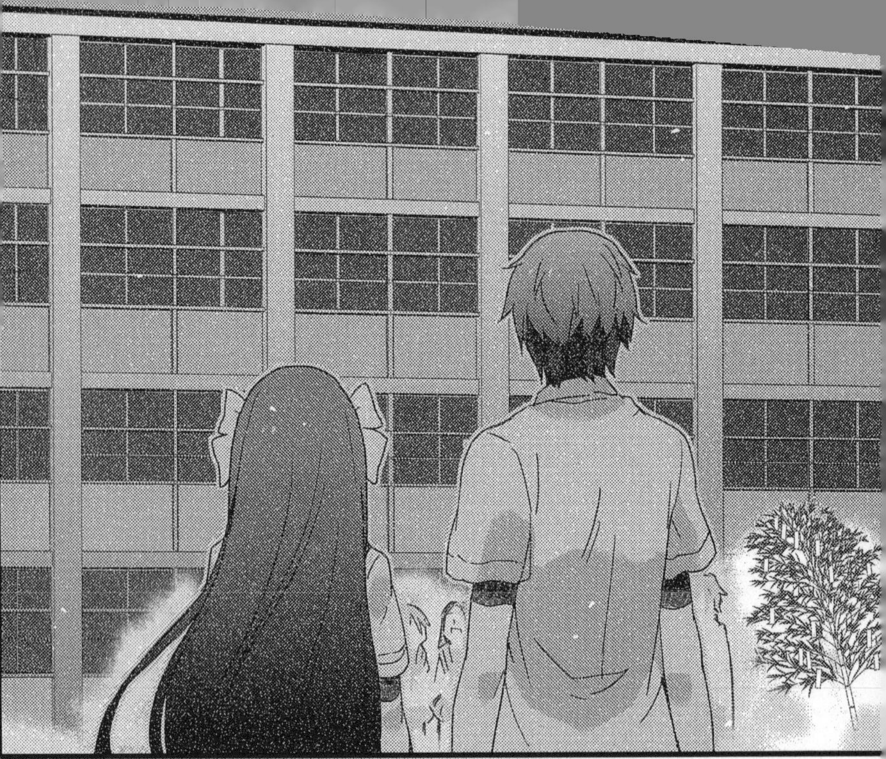
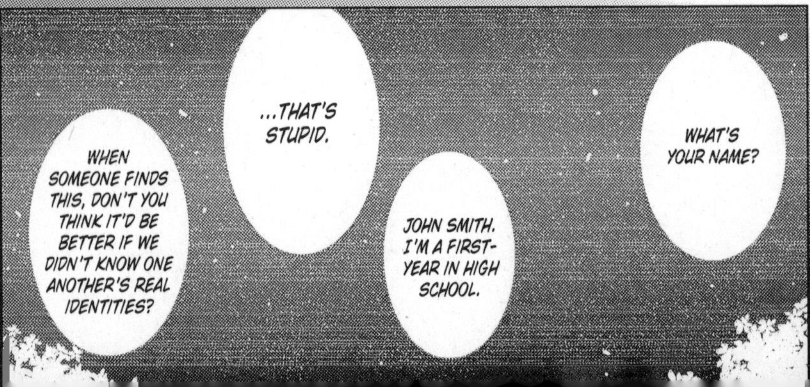
WHAT'S YOUR NAME?
JOHN SMITH. I'M A FIRST-YEAR IN HIGH SCHOOL.
...THAT'S STUPID.
WHEN SOMEONE FINDS THIS, DON'T YOU THINK IT'D BE BETTER IF WE DIDN'T KNOW ONE ANOTHER'S REAL IDENTITIES?

MIDDLE SCHOOL
STUDENTS

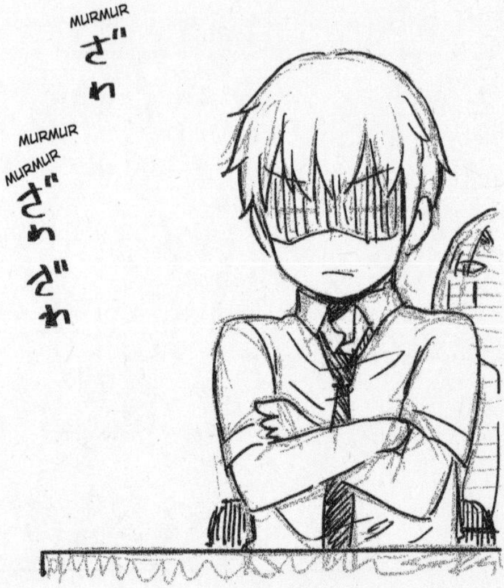
MURMUR
ざわ
MURMUR
MURMUR
ざわ ざわ

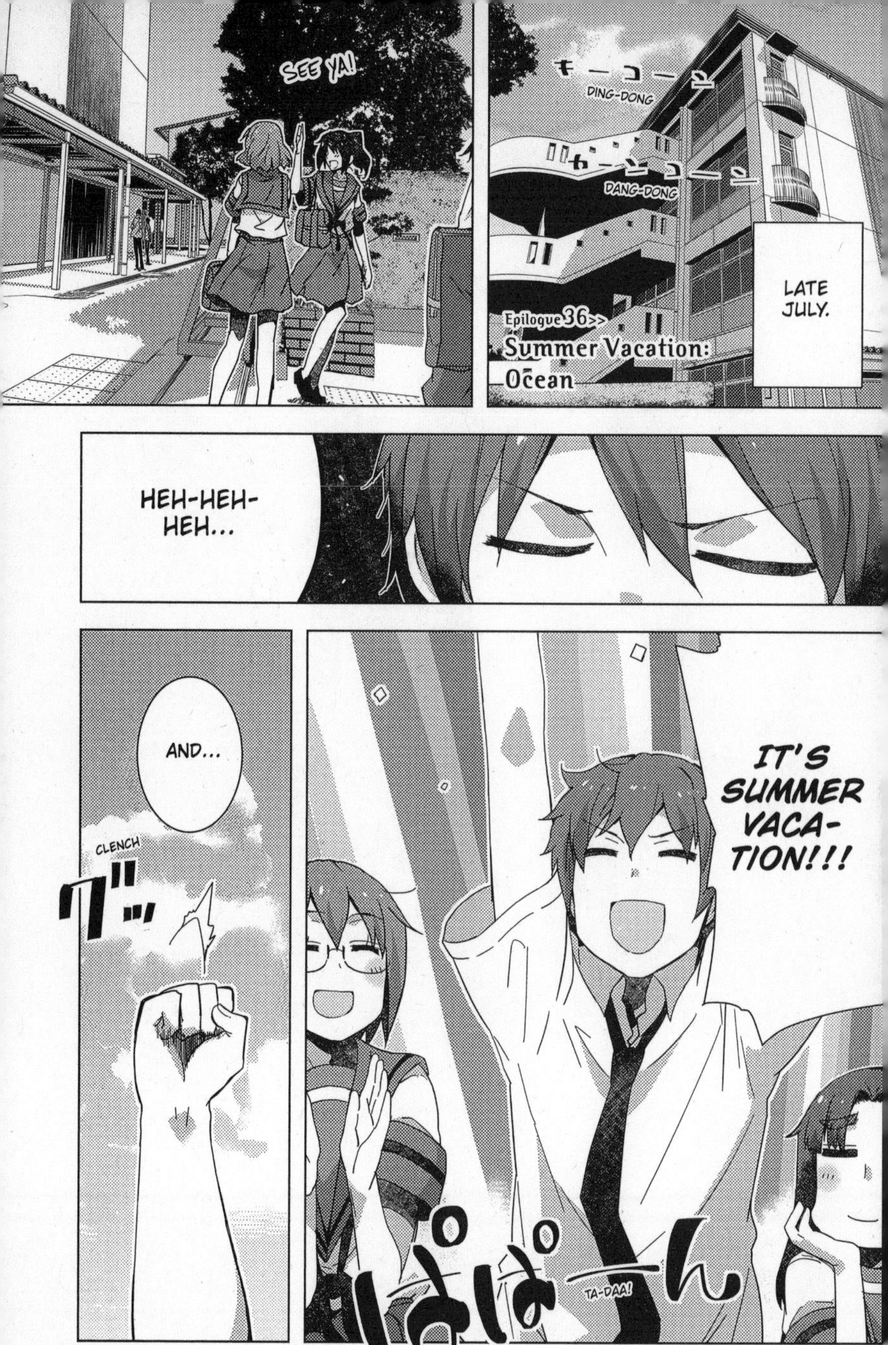

キーコーン
DING-DONG
カーンコーン
DANG-DONG
LATE JULY.
Epilogue 36>>
Summer Vacation: Ocean
SEE YA!
HEH-HEH-HEH...
IT'S SUMMER VACATION!!!
ぱぱーん
TA-DAA!
AND...
グッ
CLENCH

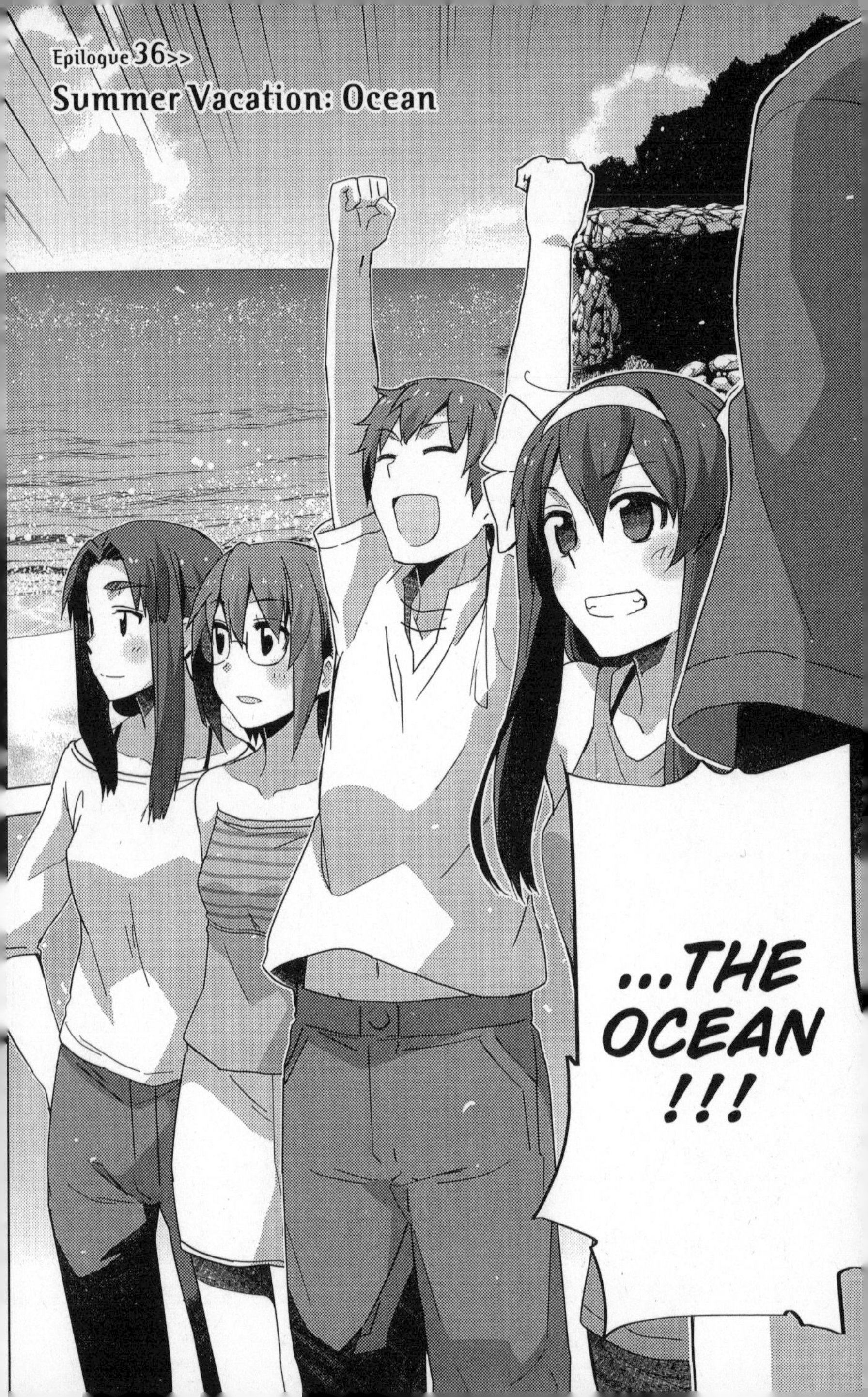
Epilogue 36>>
Summer Vacation: Ocean
...THE OCEAN !!!

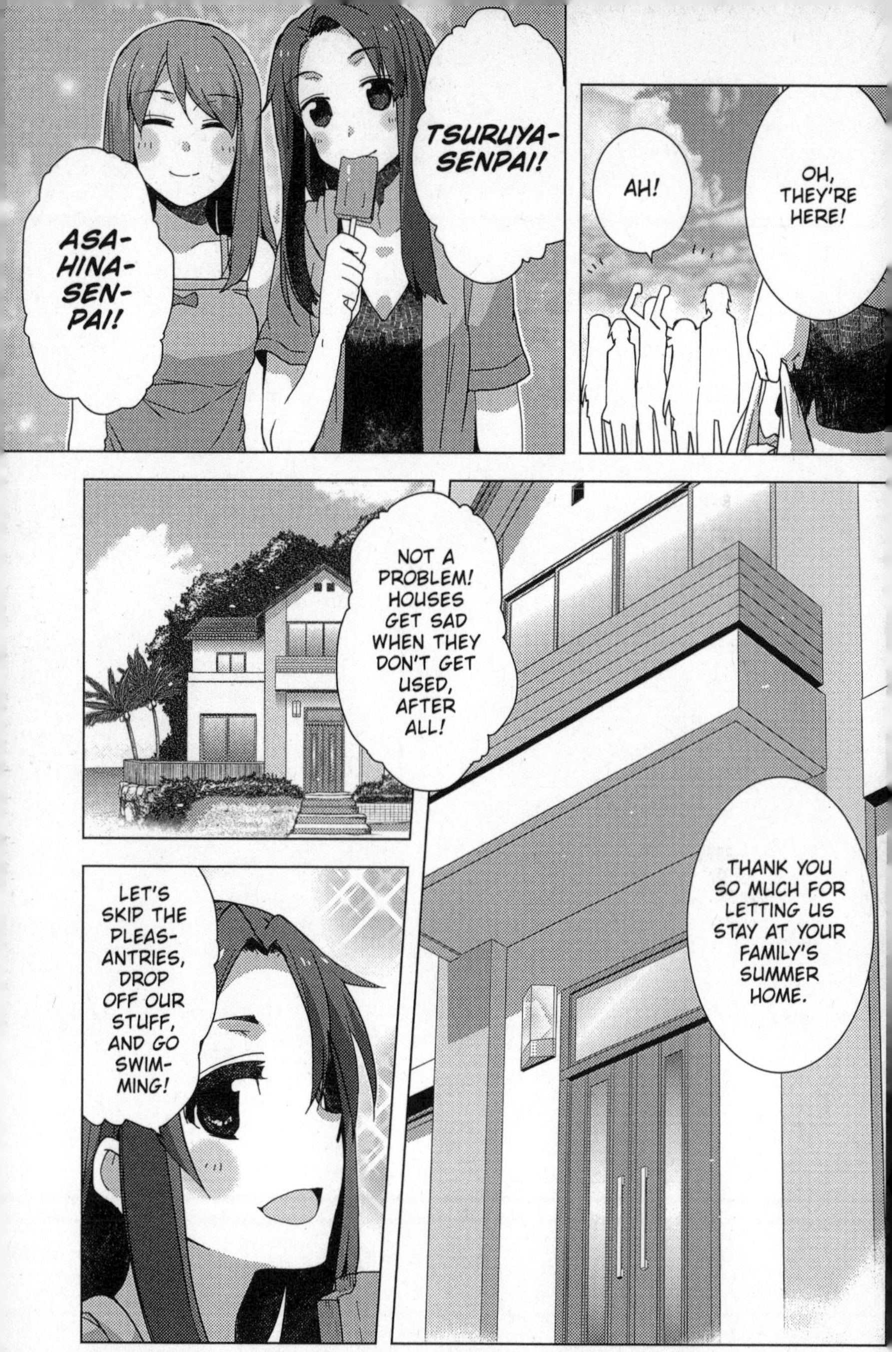
OH, THEY'RE HERE!
AH!
TSURUYA-SENPAI!
ASA-HINA-SEN-PAI!
THANK YOU SO MUCH FOR LETTING US STAY AT YOUR FAMILY'S SUMMER HOME.
NOT A PROBLEM! HOUSES GET SAD WHEN THEY DON'T GET USED, AFTER ALL!
LET'S SKIP THE PLEAS-ANTRIES, DROP OFF OUR STUFF, AND GO SWIM-MING!

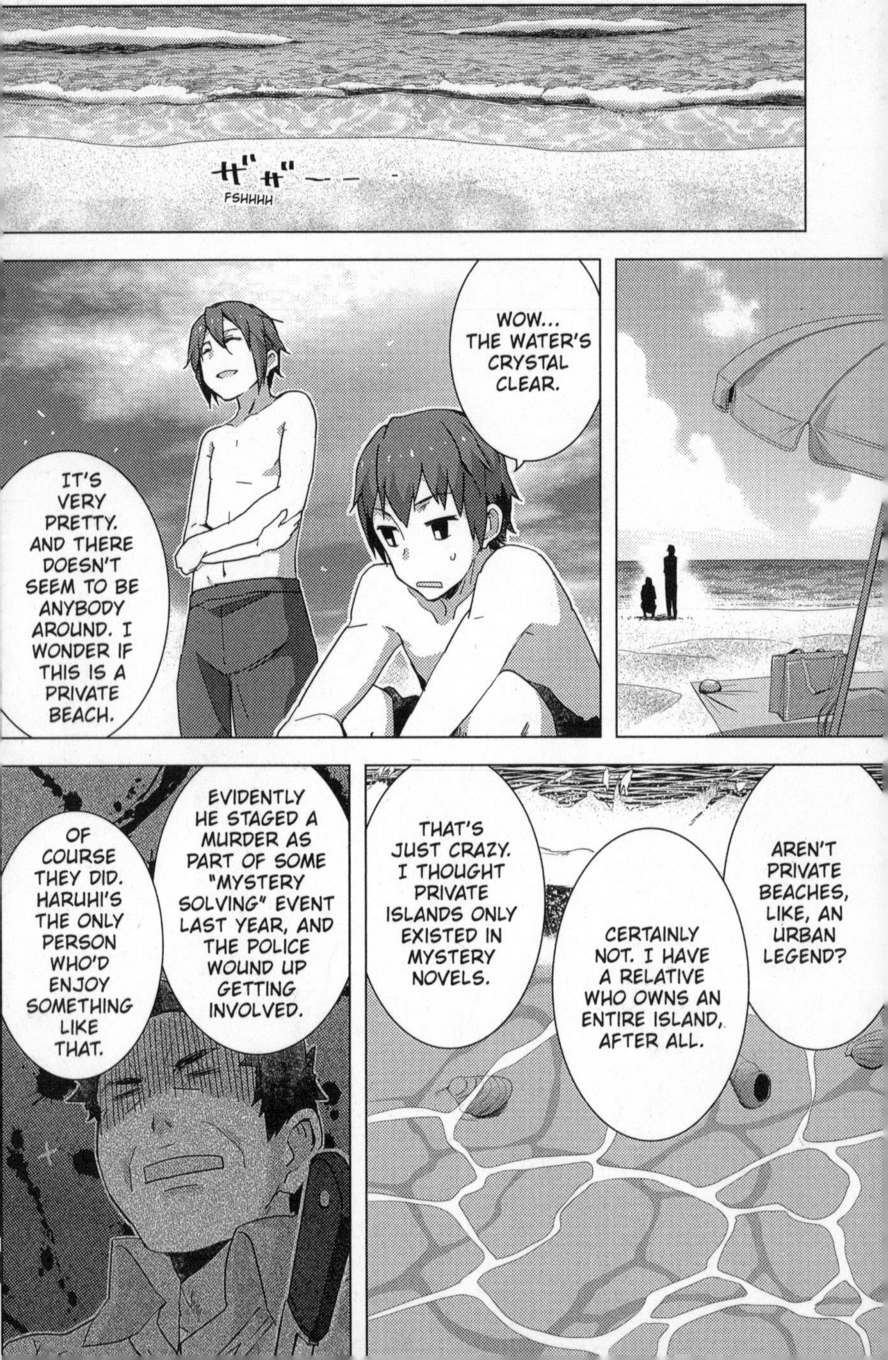
ザザー
FSHHHH
WOW... THE WATER'S CRYSTAL CLEAR.
IT'S VERY PRETTY. AND THERE DOESN'T SEEM TO BE ANYBODY AROUND. I WONDER IF THIS IS A PRIVATE BEACH.
AREN'T PRIVATE BEACHES, LIKE, AN URBAN LEGEND?
CERTAINLY NOT. I HAVE A RELATIVE WHO OWNS AN ENTIRE ISLAND, AFTER ALL.
THAT'S JUST CRAZY. I THOUGHT PRIVATE ISLANDS ONLY EXISTED IN MYSTERY NOVELS.
EVIDENTLY HE STAGED A MURDER AS PART OF SOME "MYSTERY SOLVING" EVENT LAST YEAR, AND THE POLICE WOUND UP GETTING INVOLVED.
OF COURSE THEY DID. HARUHI'S THE ONLY PERSON WHO'D ENJOY SOMETHING LIKE THAT.

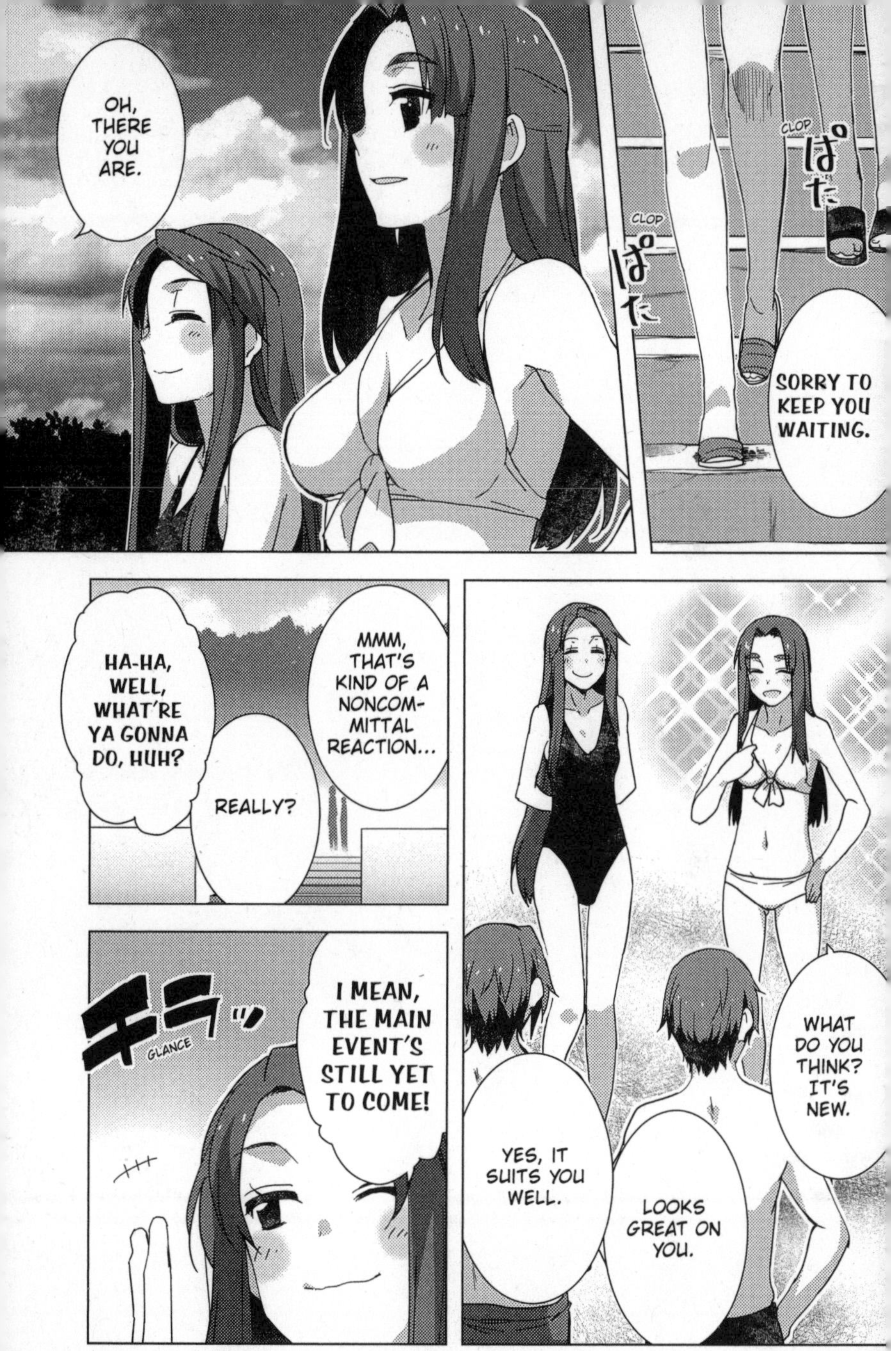
CLOP
ぱた
CLOP
ぱた
SORRY TO KEEP YOU WAITING.
OH, THERE YOU ARE.
WHAT DO YOU THINK? IT'S NEW.
LOOKS GREAT ON YOU.
YES, IT SUITS YOU WELL.
MMM, THAT'S KIND OF A NONCOMMITTAL REACTION...
REALLY?
HA-HA, WELL, WHAT'RE YA GONNA DO, HUH?
I MEAN, THE MAIN EVENT'S STILL YET TO COME!
チラッ
GLANCE

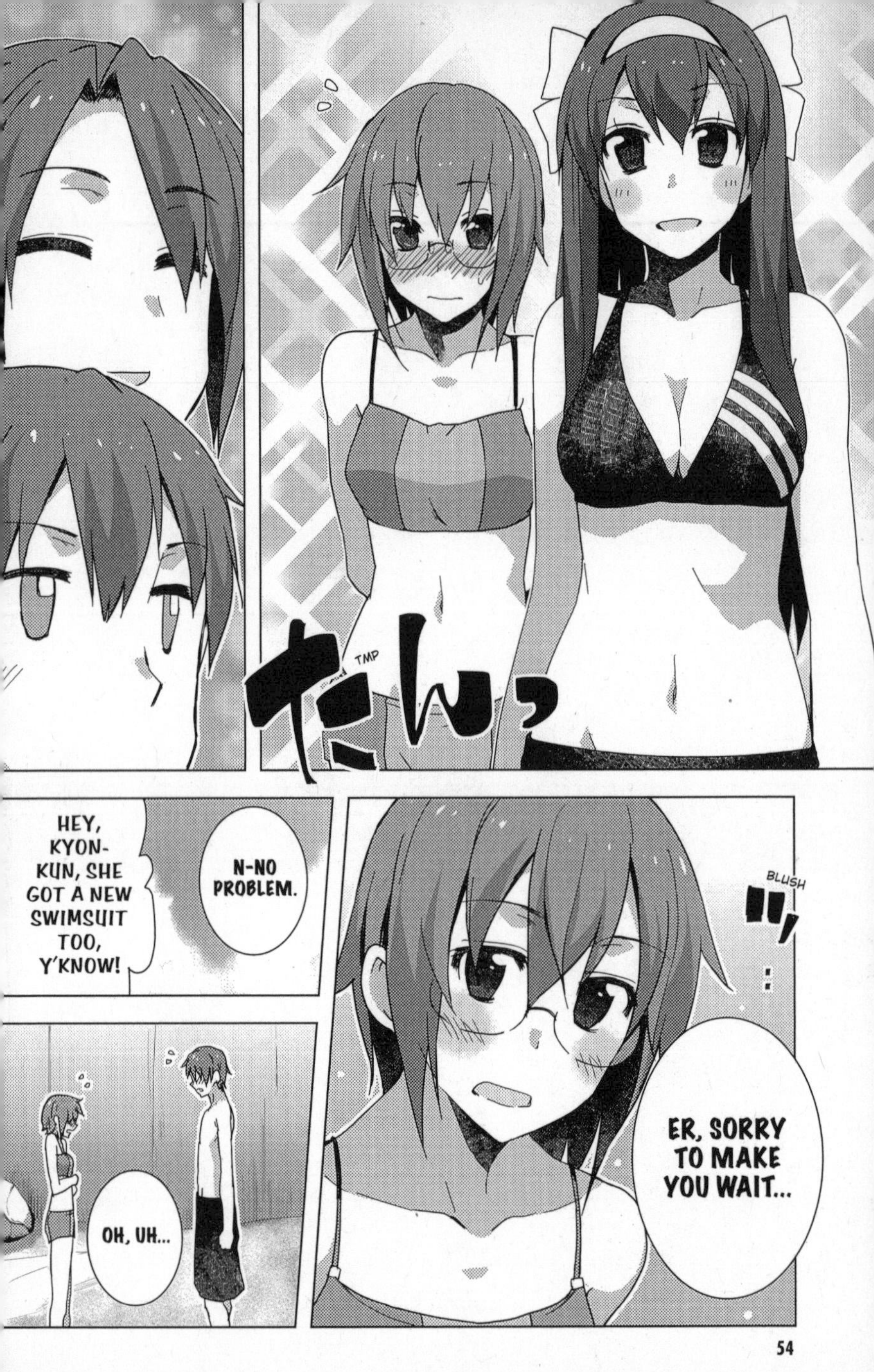
たんっ
TMP
BLUSH
ER, SORRY TO MAKE YOU WAIT...
N-NO PROBLEM.
HEY, KYON-KUN, SHE GOT A NEW SWIMSUIT TOO, Y'KNOW!
OH, UH...

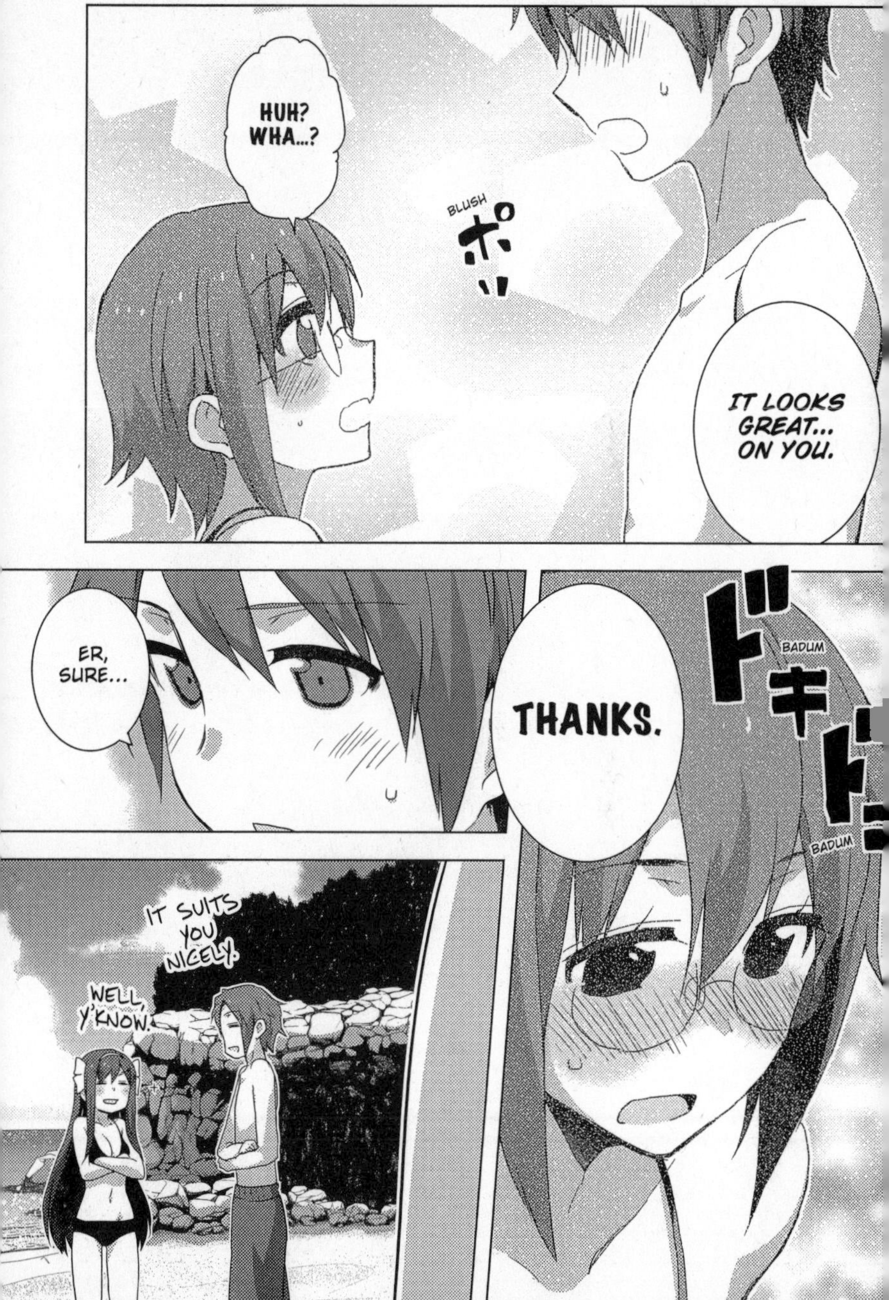
IT LOOKS GREAT... ON YOU.
BLUSH
HUH? WHA...?
THANKS.
BADUM
BADUM
ER, SURE...
IT SUITS YOU NICELY.
WELL, Y'KNOW.

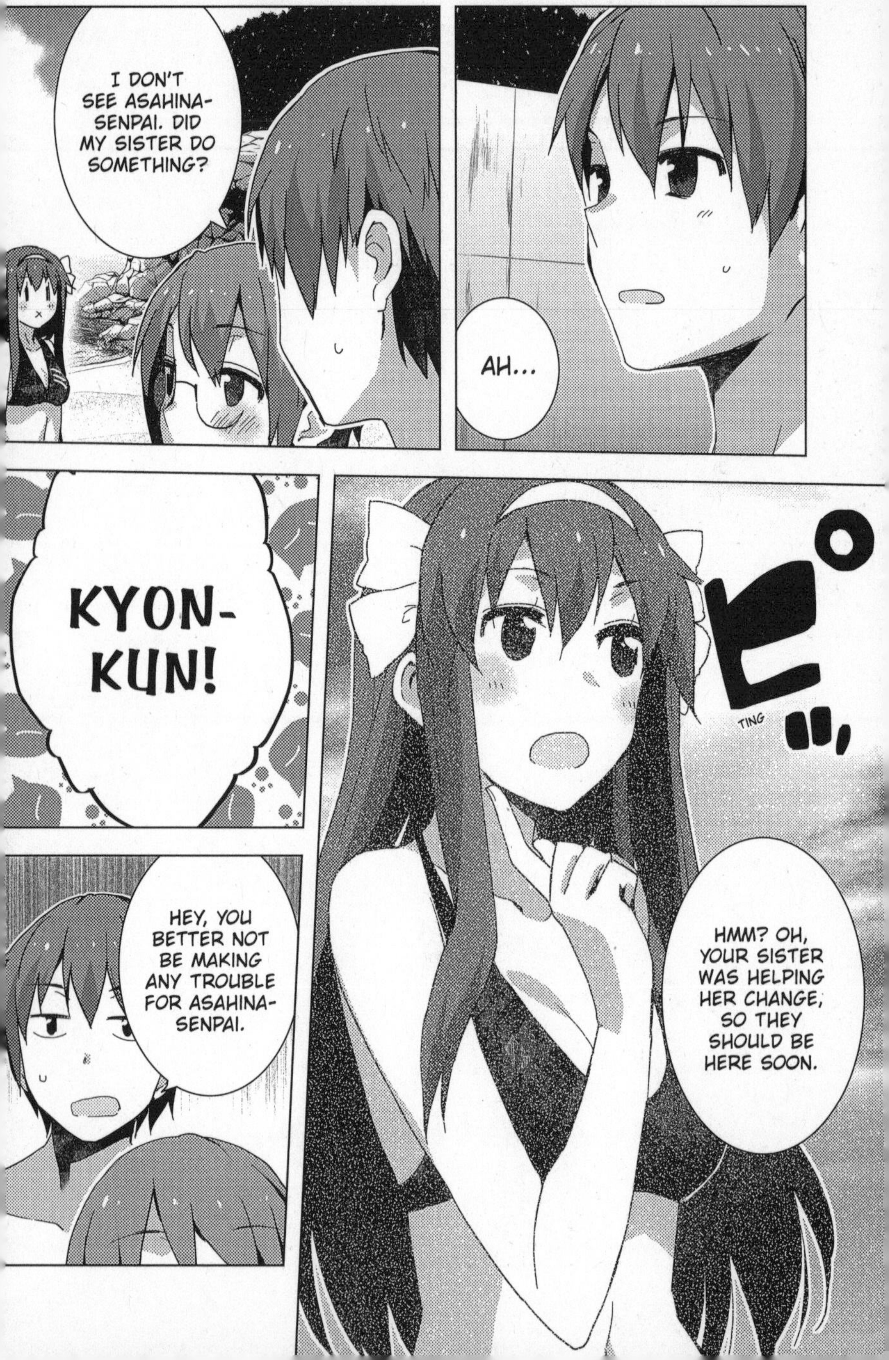
AH...
I DON'T SEE ASAHINA-SENPAI. DID MY SISTER DO SOMETHING?
TING
HMM? OH, YOUR SISTER WAS HELPING HER CHANGE, SO THEY SHOULD BE HERE SOON.
KYON-KUN!
HEY, YOU BETTER NOT BE MAKING ANY TROUBLE FOR ASAHINA-SENPAI.

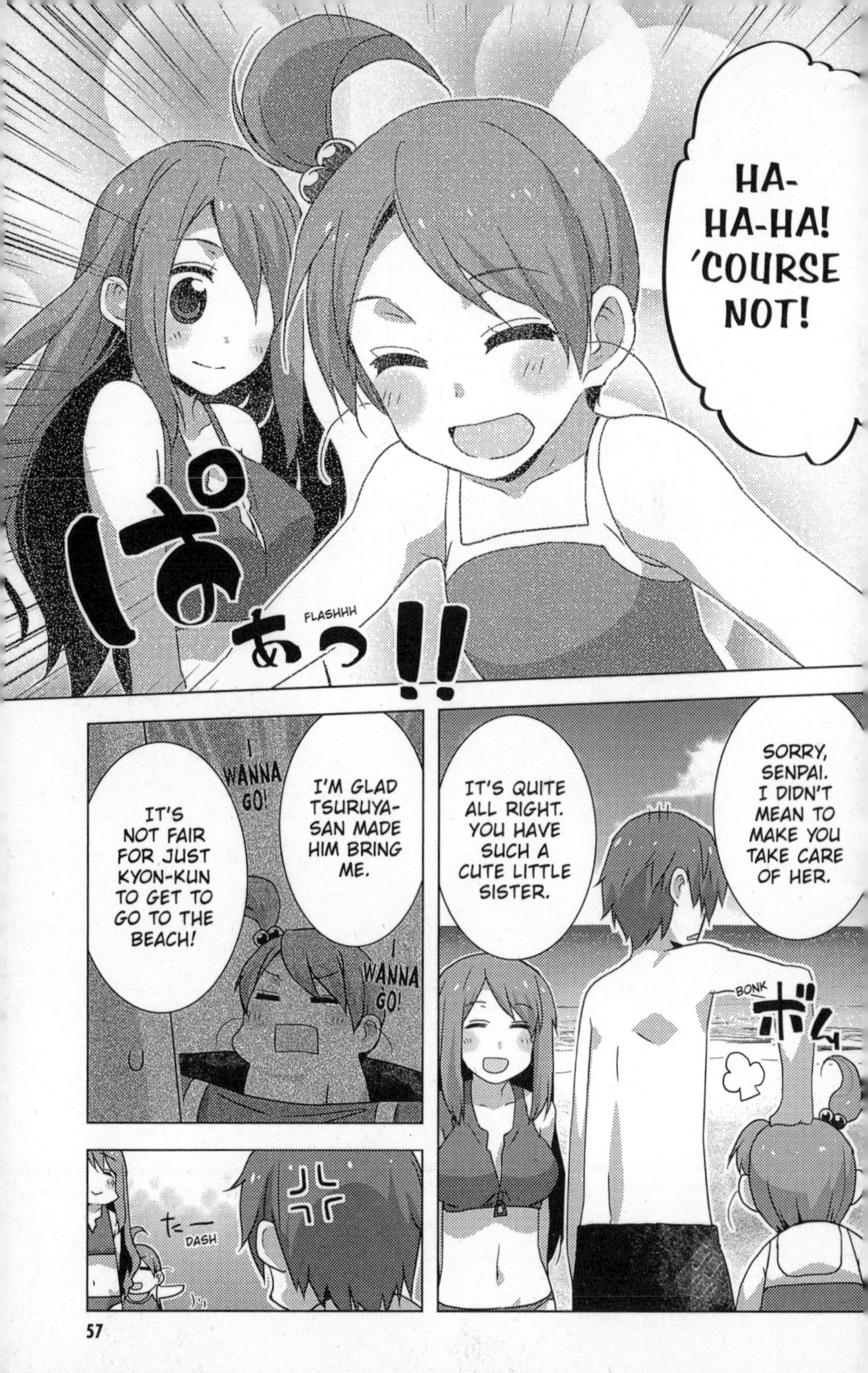
HA-HA-HA! 'COURSE NOT!
ぱあっ!!
FLASHHH
SORRY, SENPAI. I DIDN'T MEAN TO MAKE YOU TAKE CARE OF HER.
IT'S QUITE ALL RIGHT. YOU HAVE SUCH A CUTE LITTLE SISTER.
ボム
BONK
I'M GLAD TSURUYA-SAN MADE HIM BRING ME.
I WANNA GO!
IT'S NOT FAIR FOR JUST KYON-KUN TO GET TO GO TO THE BEACH!
I WANNA GO!
たー
DASH

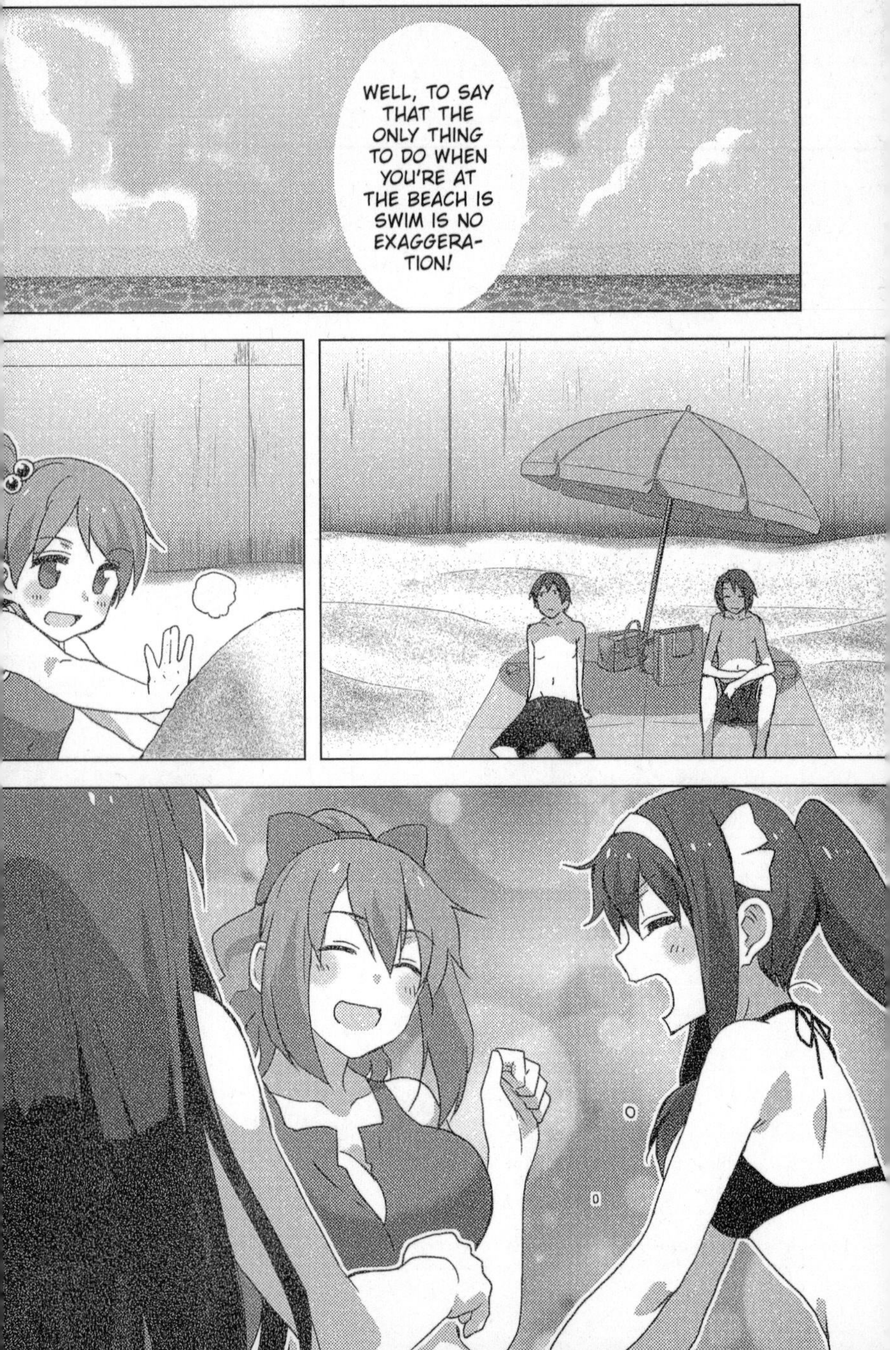
WELL, TO SAY THAT THE ONLY THING TO DO WHEN YOU'RE AT THE BEACH IS SWIM IS NO EXAGGERA-TION!

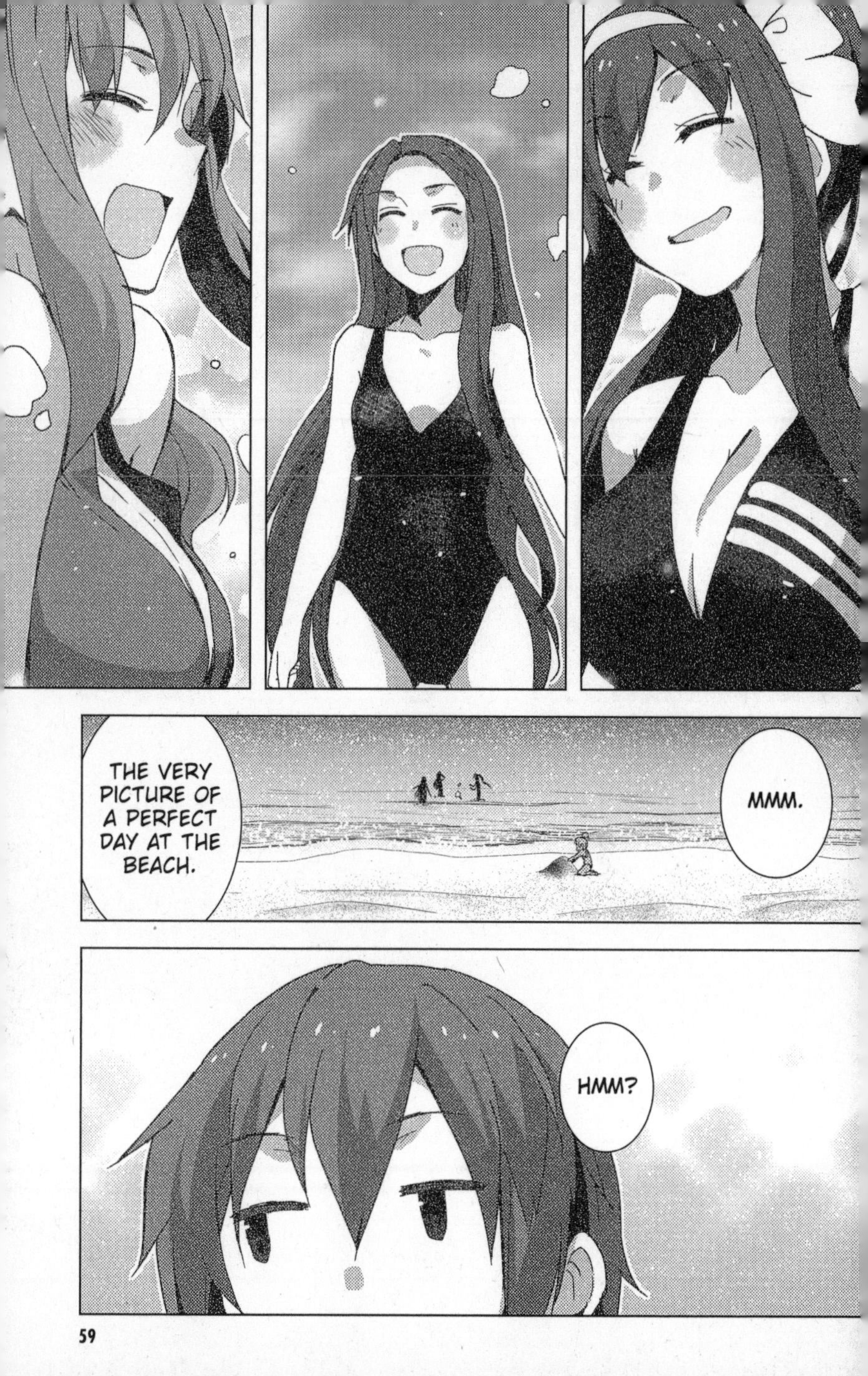
MMM.
THE VERY PICTURE OF A PERFECT DAY AT THE BEACH.
HMM?

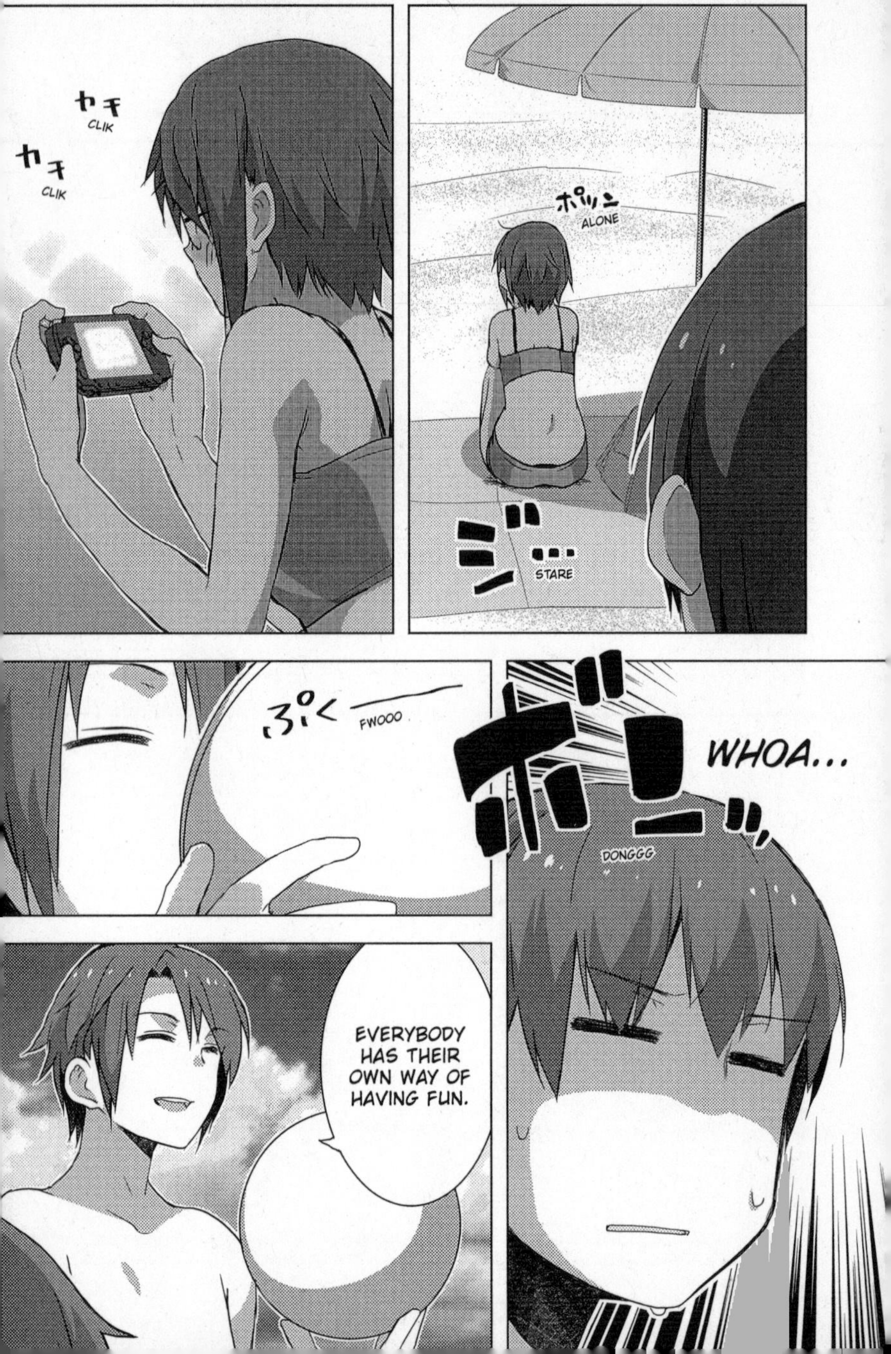
ALONE
STARE
カチ
CLIK
カチ
CLIK
DONGGG
WHOA...
ぷく
FWOOO
EVERYBODY HAS THEIR OWN WAY OF HAVING FUN.

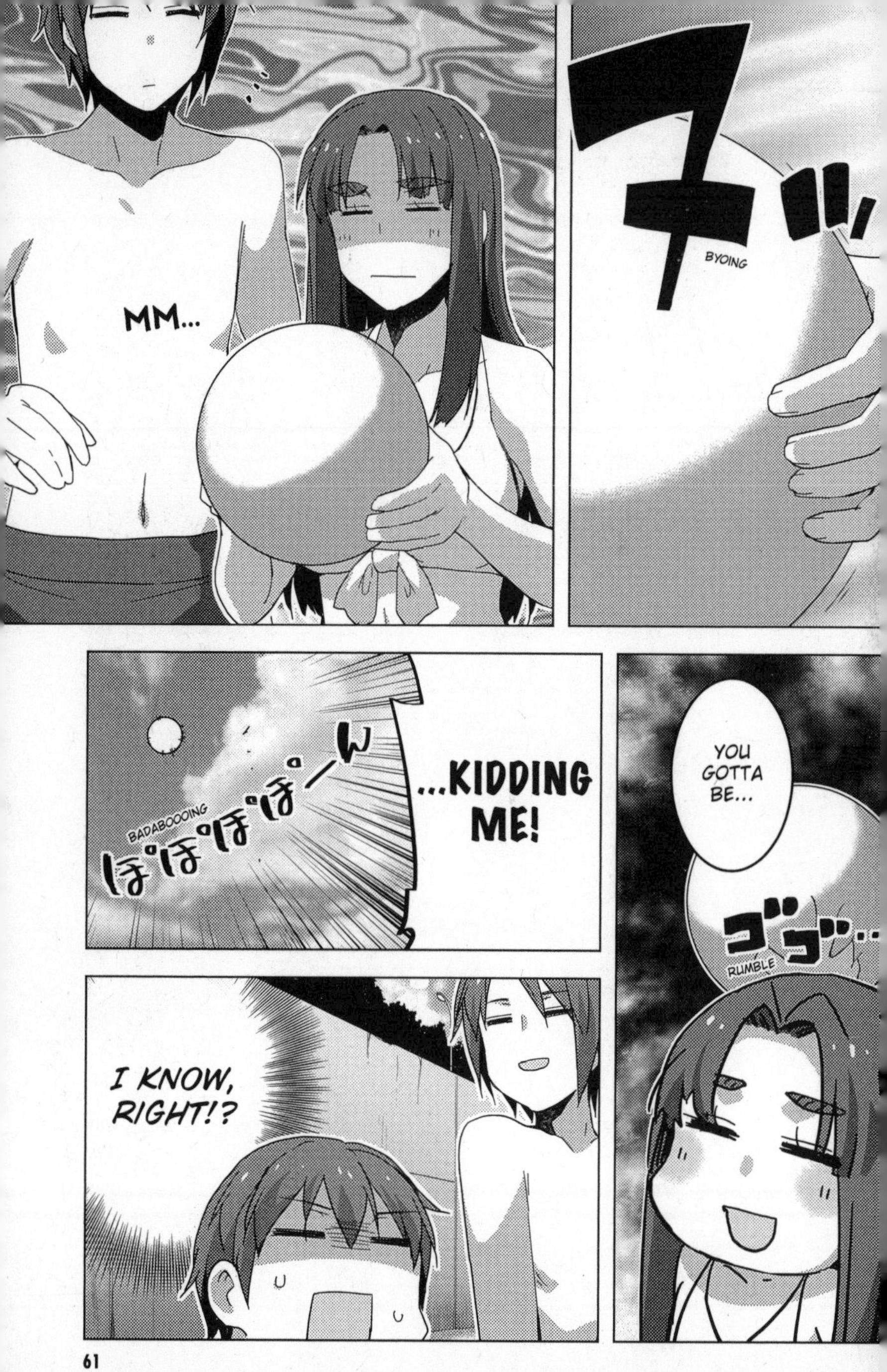
BYOING
MM...
YOU GOTTA BE...
ゴゴゴ...
RUMBLE
...KIDDING ME!
ぽぽぽぽーん
BADABOOOING
I KNOW, RIGHT!?

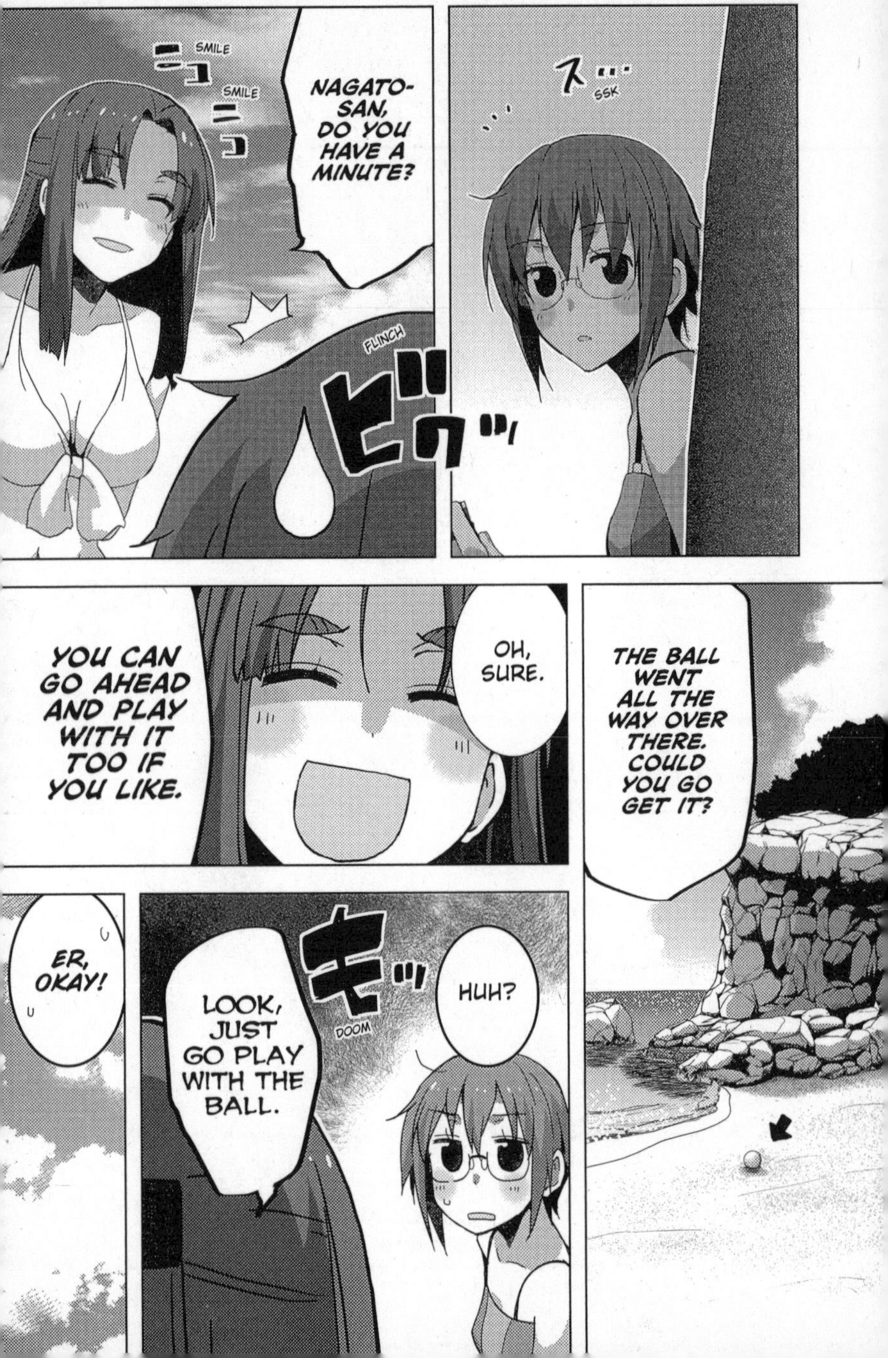
ス…
SSK
ニコ
SMILE
ニコ
SMILE
NAGATO-SAN, DO YOU HAVE A MINUTE?
ビクッ
FLINCH
THE BALL WENT ALL THE WAY OVER THERE. COULD YOU GO GET IT?
OH, SURE.
YOU CAN GO AHEAD AND PLAY WITH IT TOO IF YOU LIKE.
HUH?
キッ
DOOM
LOOK, JUST GO PLAY WITH THE BALL.
ER, OKAY!

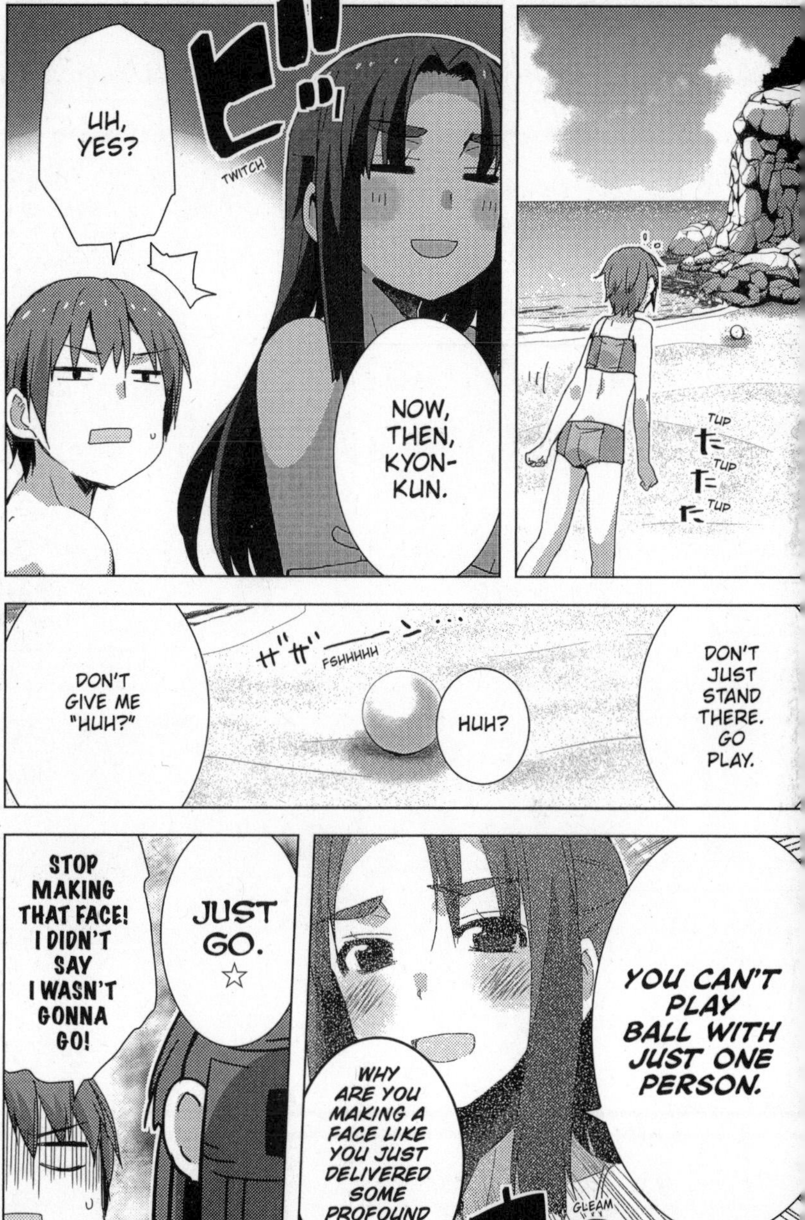
TUP
TUP
TUP
TWITCH
NOW, THEN, KYON-KUN.
UH, YES?
DON'T JUST STAND THERE. GO PLAY.
FSHHHHH
HUH?
DON'T GIVE ME "HUH?"
YOU CAN'T PLAY BALL WITH JUST ONE PERSON.
GLEAM
WHY ARE YOU MAKING A FACE LIKE YOU JUST DELIVERED SOME PROFOUND WISDOM?
JUST GO. ☆
STOP MAKING THAT FACE! I DIDN'T SAY I WASN'T GONNA GO!

S-SURE...

UM...
OKAY,
HERE
GOES.

SHFF

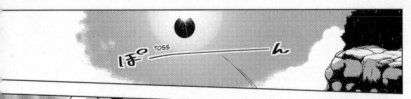

TOSS

GOT
IT!

HUP—

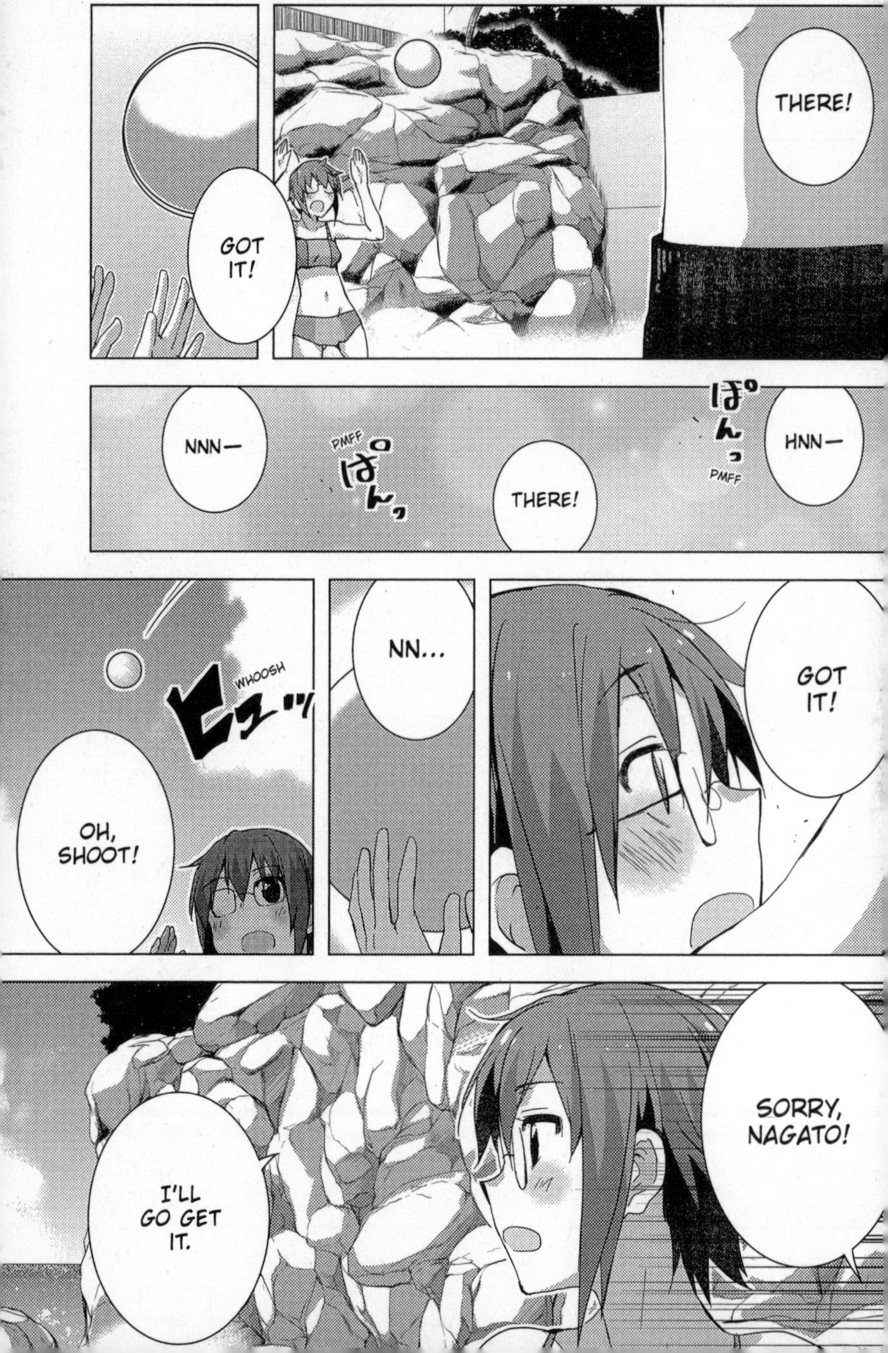
THERE!
GOT IT!
HNN—
ぽんっ
PMFF
THERE!
ぱんっ
PMFF
NNN—
GOT IT!
NN...
ヒュッ
WHOOSH
OH, SHOOT!
SORRY, NAGATO!
I'LL GO GET IT.

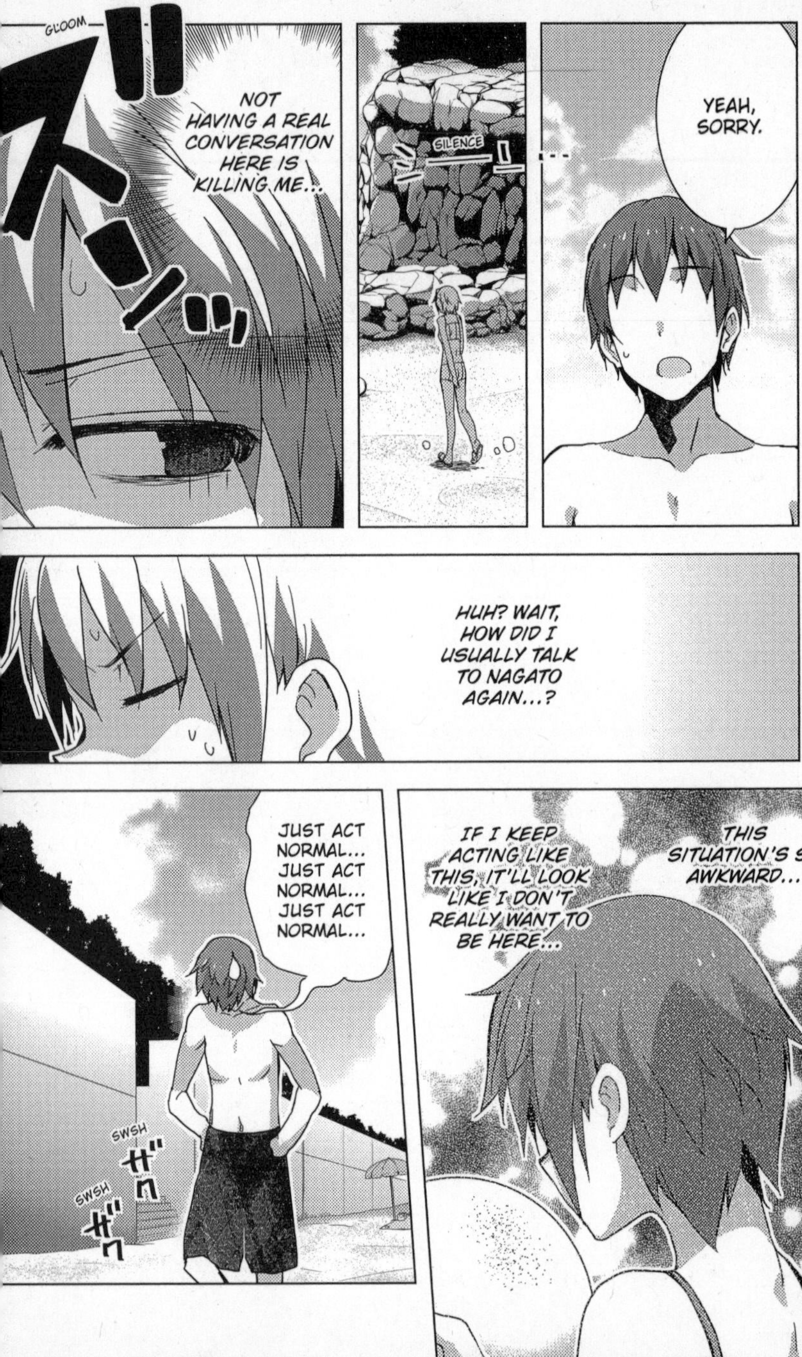
YEAH, SORRY.
...
SILENCE
GLOOM
NOT HAVING A REAL CONVERSATION HERE IS KILLING ME...
HUH? WAIT, HOW DID I USUALLY TALK TO NAGATO AGAIN...?
THIS SITUATION'S SO AWKWARD...
IF I KEEP ACTING LIKE THIS, IT'LL LOOK LIKE I DON'T REALLY WANT TO BE HERE...
JUST ACT NORMAL... JUST ACT NORMAL... JUST ACT NORMAL...
SWSH
SWSH

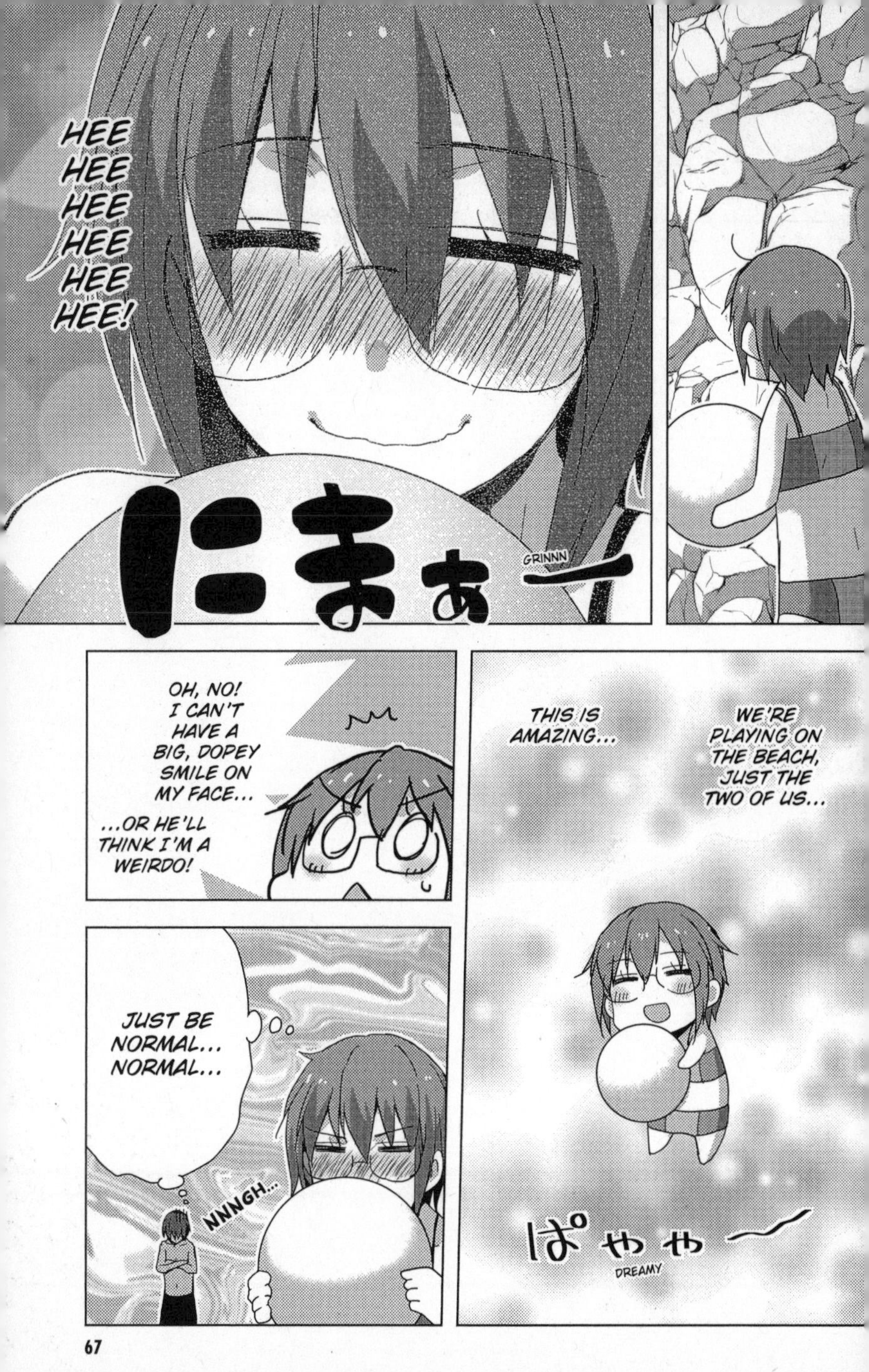
HEE HEE HEE HEE HEE HEE!
にまぁー
GRINNN
WE'RE PLAYING ON THE BEACH, JUST THE TWO OF US...
THIS IS AMAZING...
ぱややー
DREAMY
OH, NO! I CAN'T HAVE A BIG, DOPEY SMILE ON MY FACE...
...OR HE'LL THINK I'M A WEIRDO!
JUST BE NORMAL... NORMAL...
NNNGH...

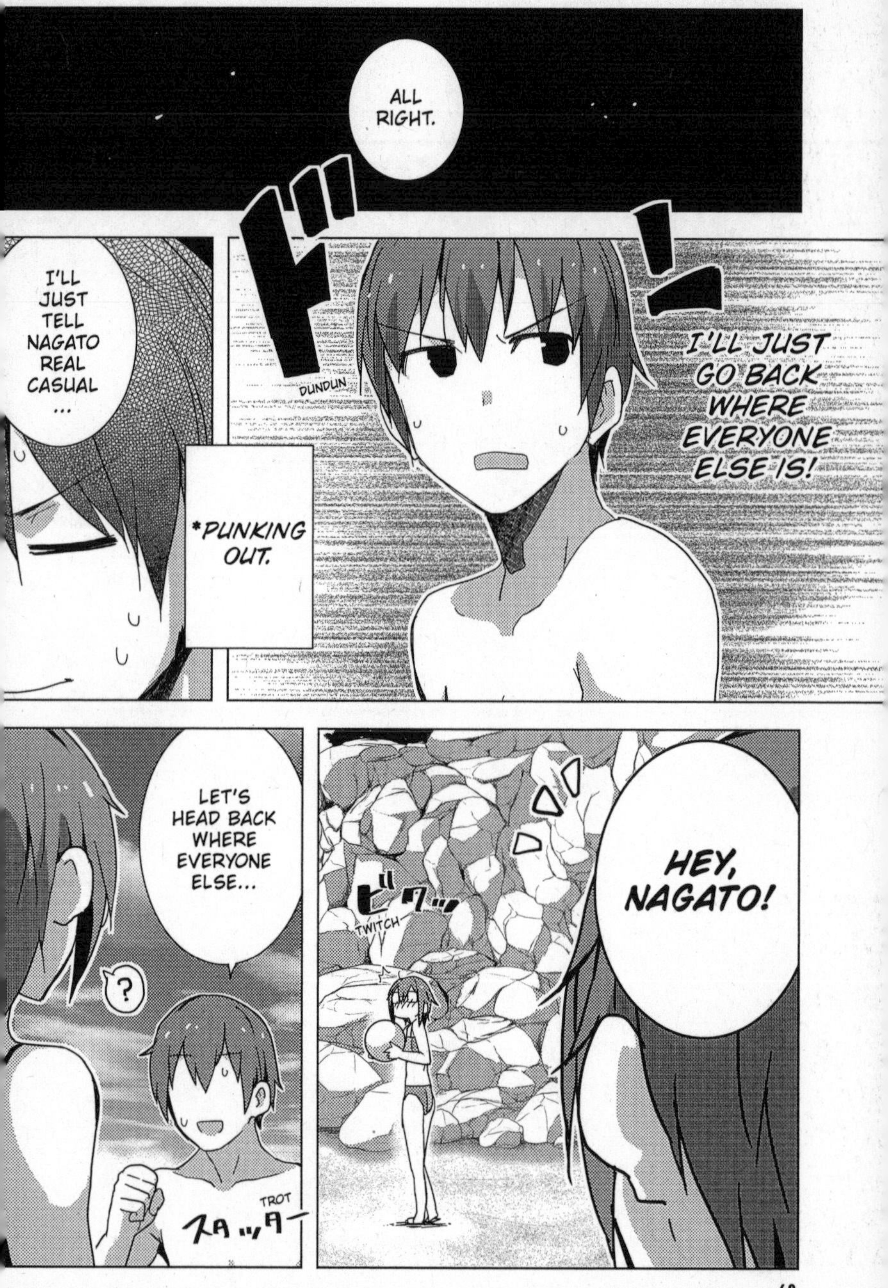
ALL RIGHT.
DUNDUN
I'LL JUST GO BACK WHERE EVERYONE ELSE IS!
*PUNKING OUT.
I'LL JUST TELL NAGATO REAL CASUAL...
HEY, NAGATO!
TWITCH
LET'S HEAD BACK WHERE EVERYONE ELSE...
?
TROT

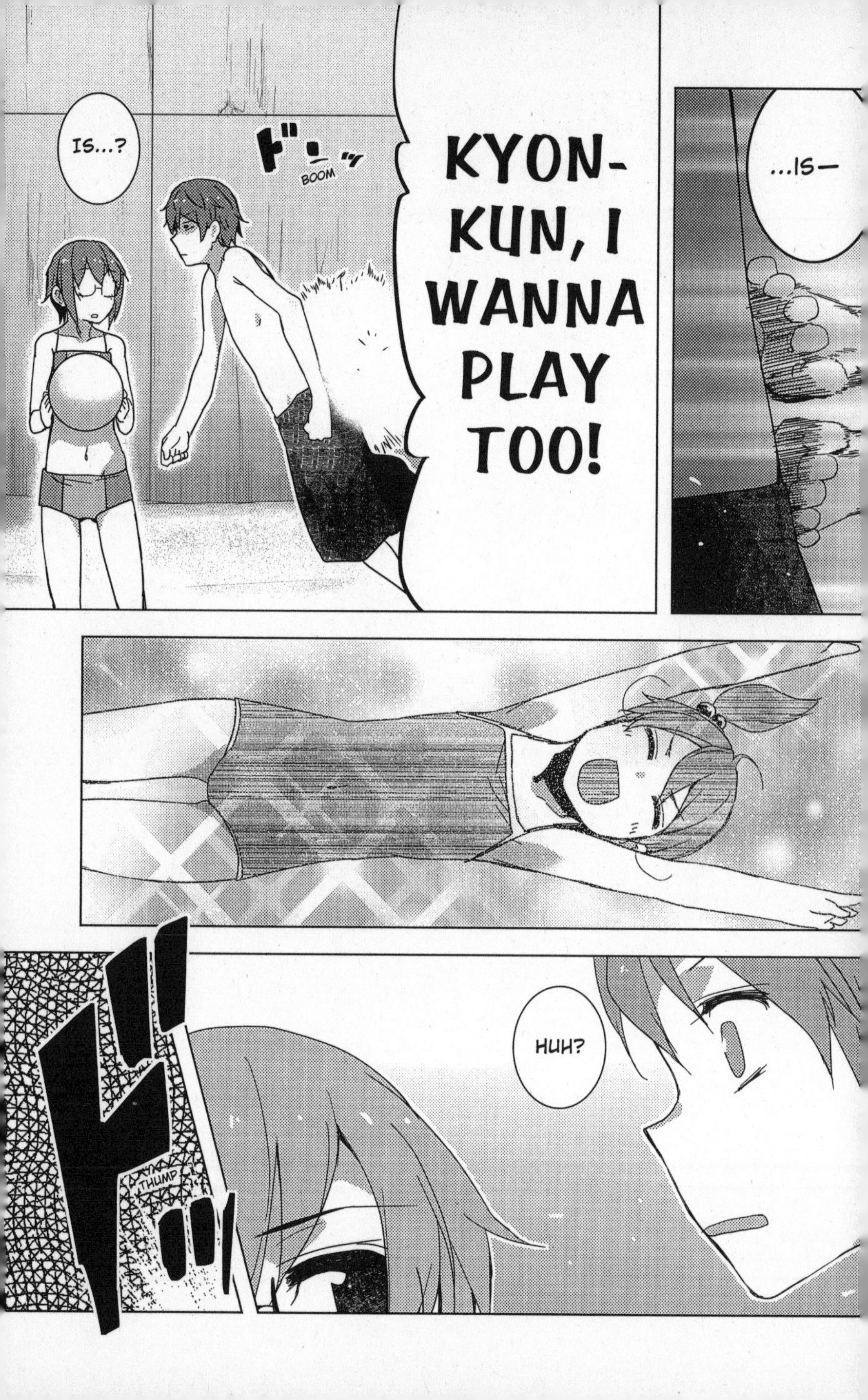
...IS—
KYON-KUN, I WANNA PLAY TOO!
BOOM
IS...?
HUH?
THUMP

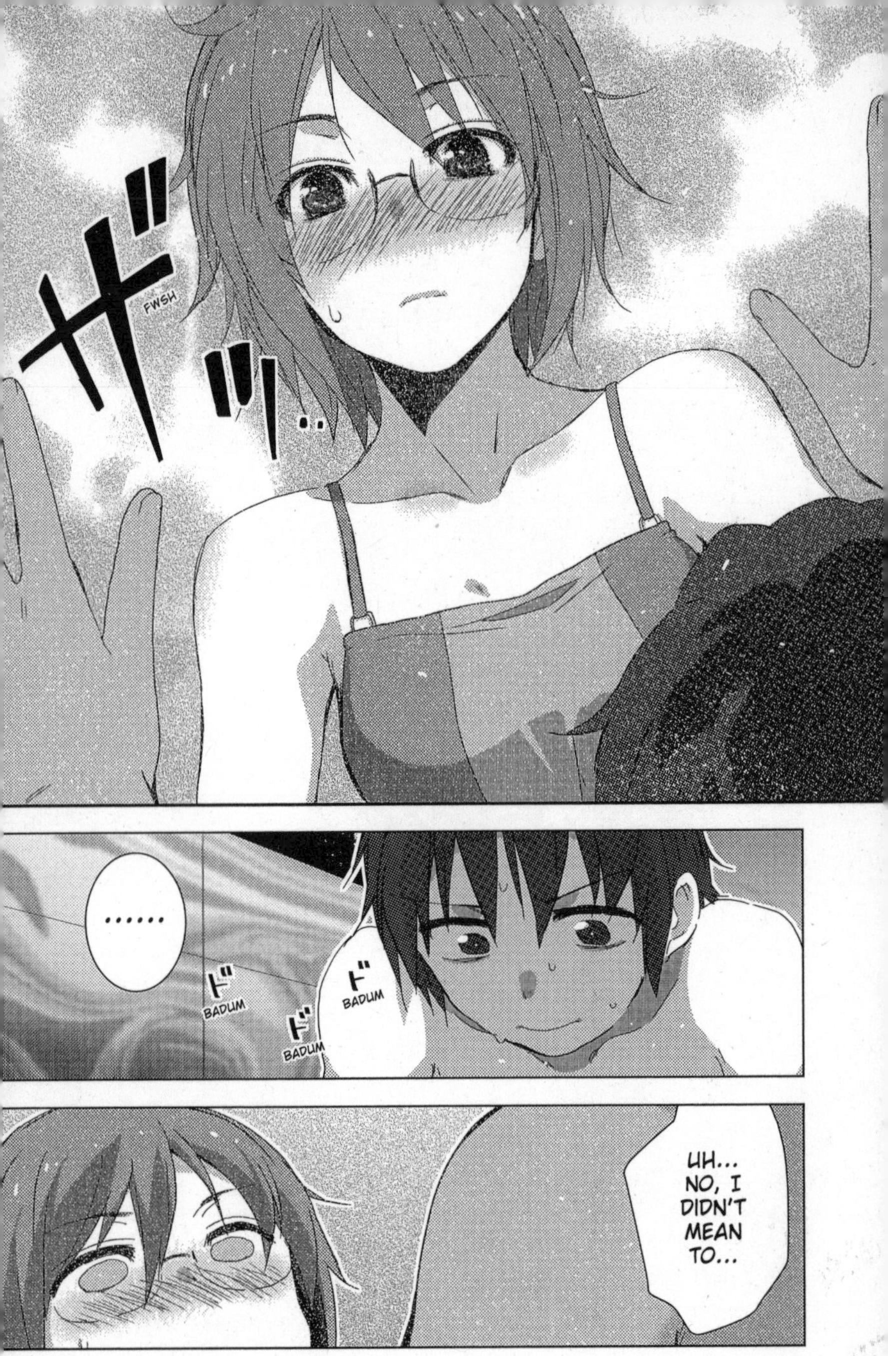
ザ
FWSH
ザッ..
......
ド
BADUM
ド
BADUM
ド
BADUM
UH... NO, I DIDN'T MEAN TO...

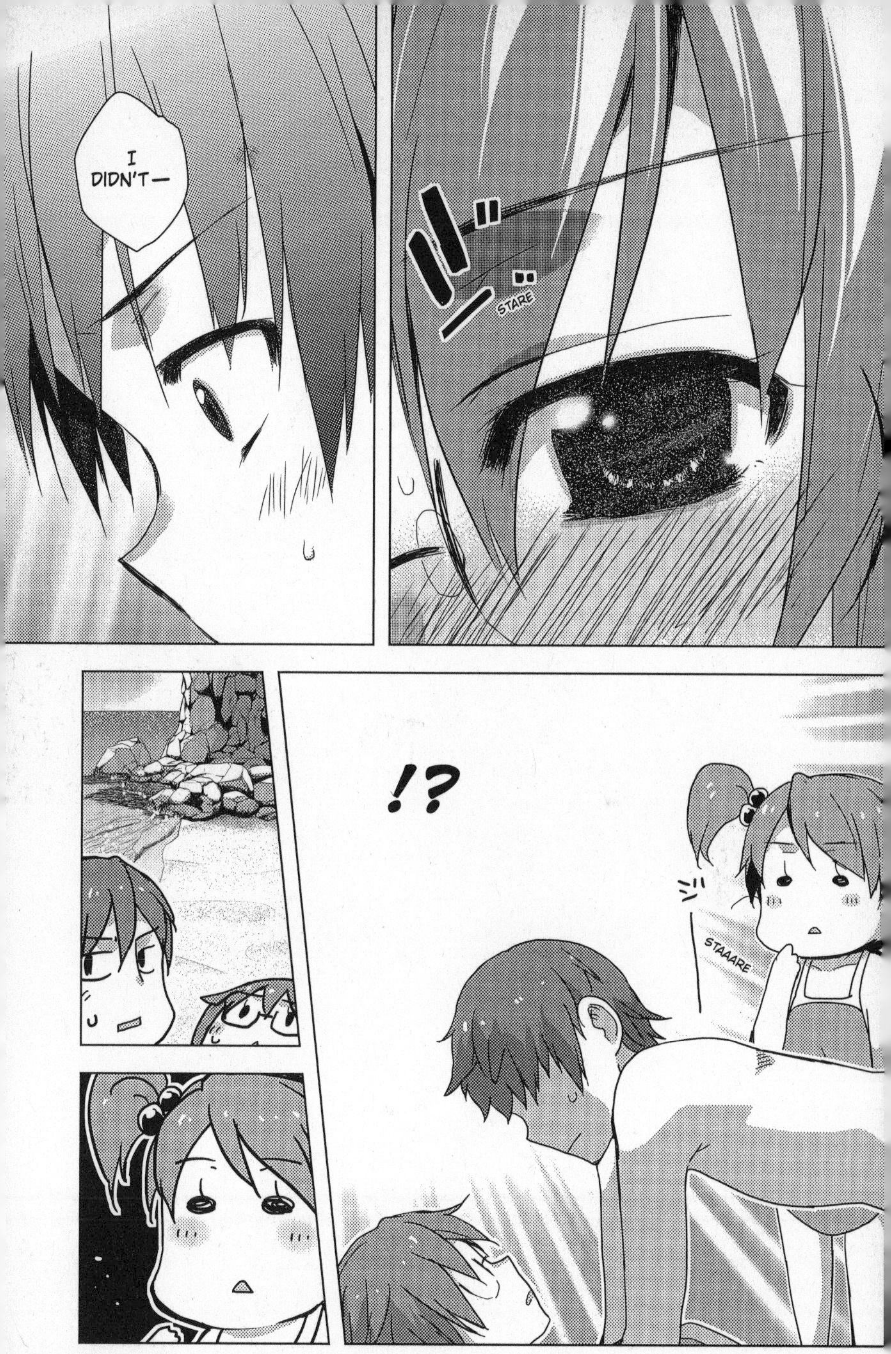
STARE
I DIDN'T—
!?
STAAARE

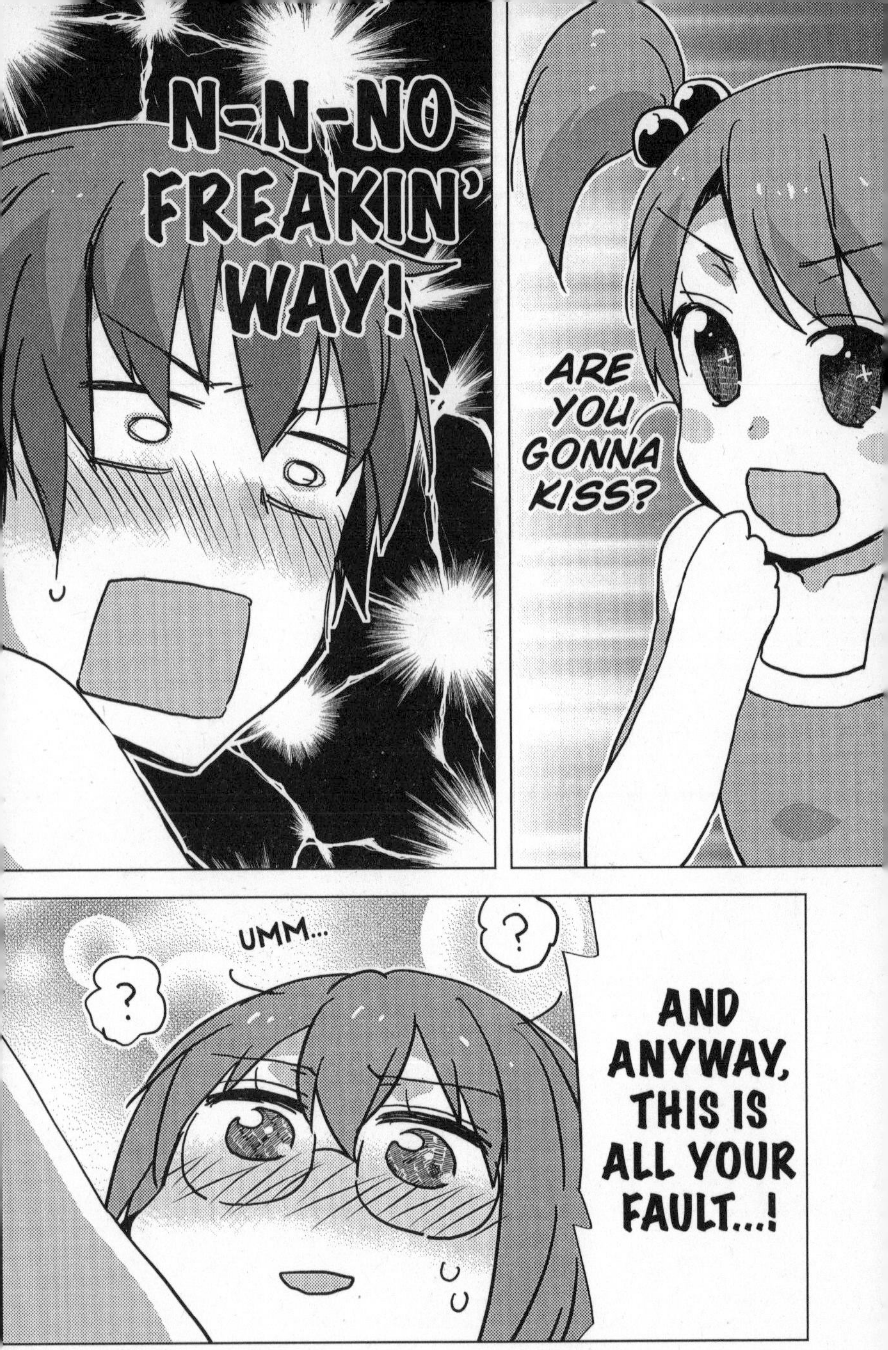
ARE YOU GONNA KISS?
N-N-NO FREAKIN' WAY!
?
UMM...
?
AND ANYWAY, THIS IS ALL YOUR FAULT...!

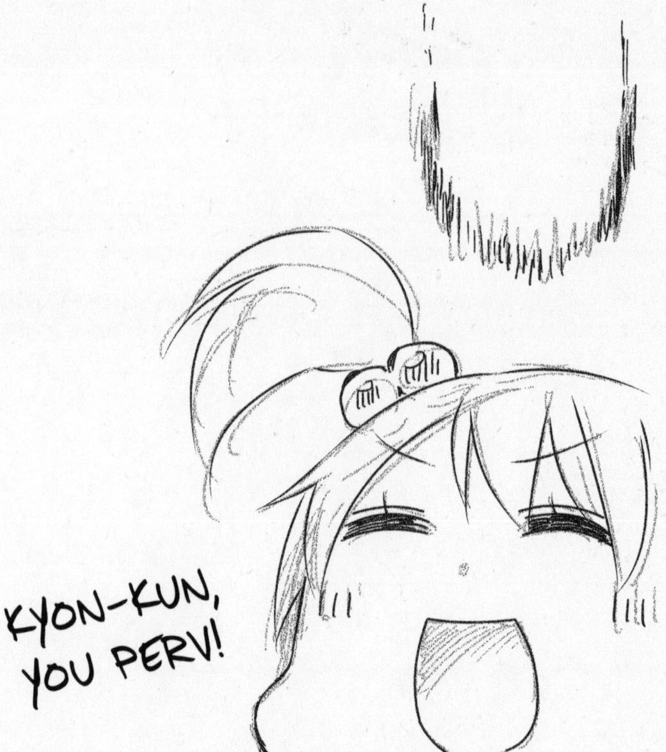
KYON-KUN, YOU PERV!

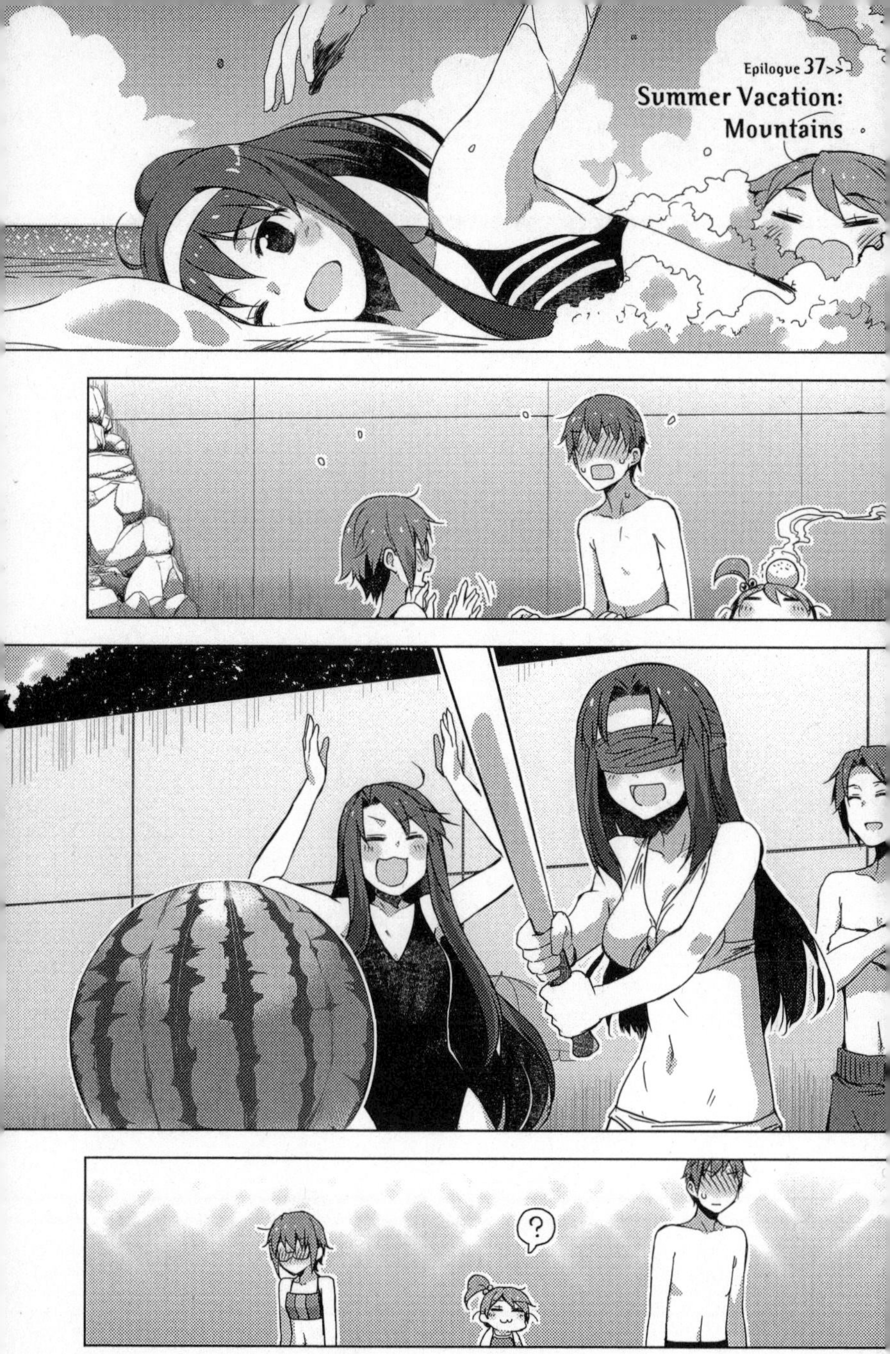
Epilogue 37>>
Summer Vacation: Mountains
?

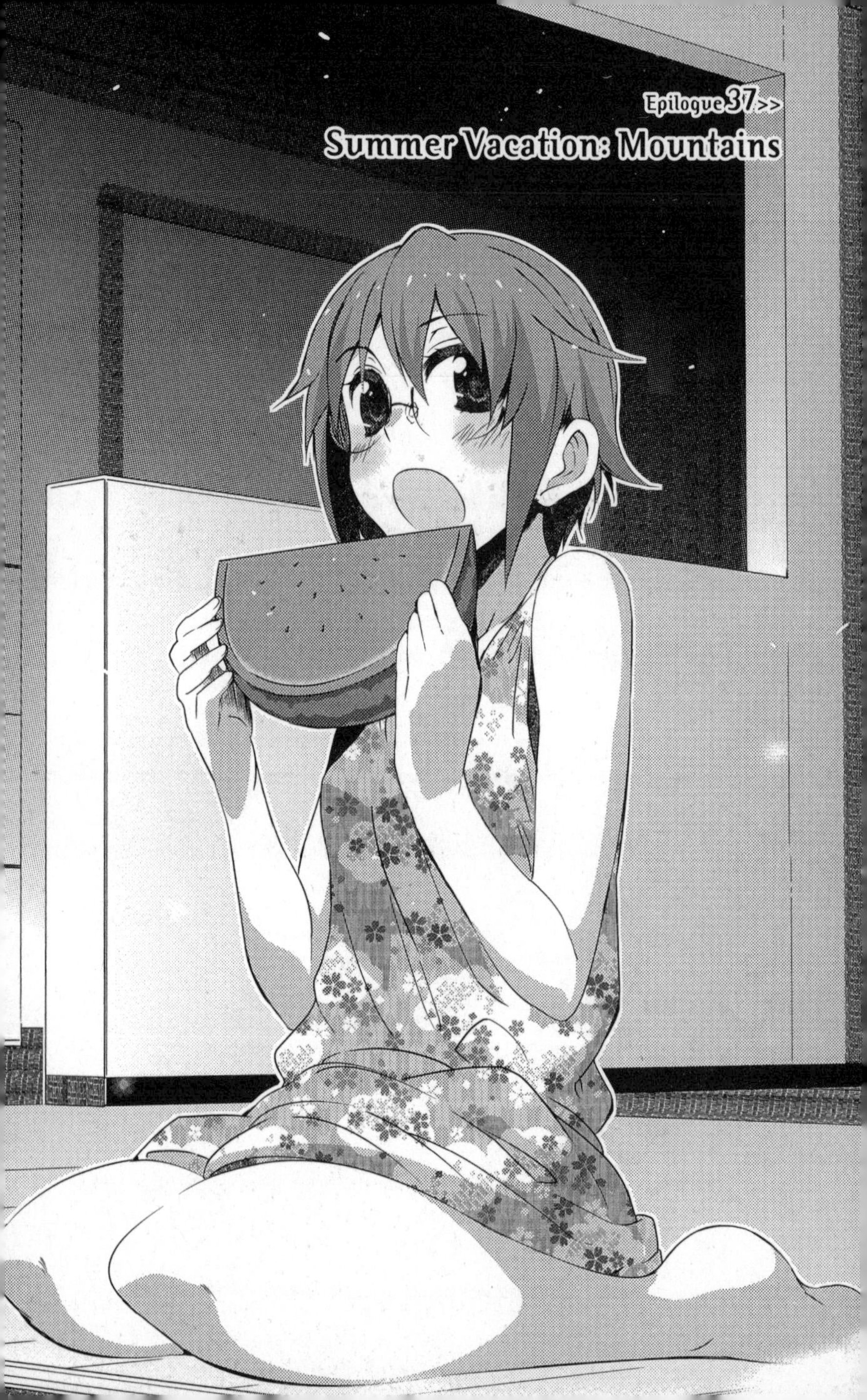
Epilogue 37>>
Summer Vacation: Mountains

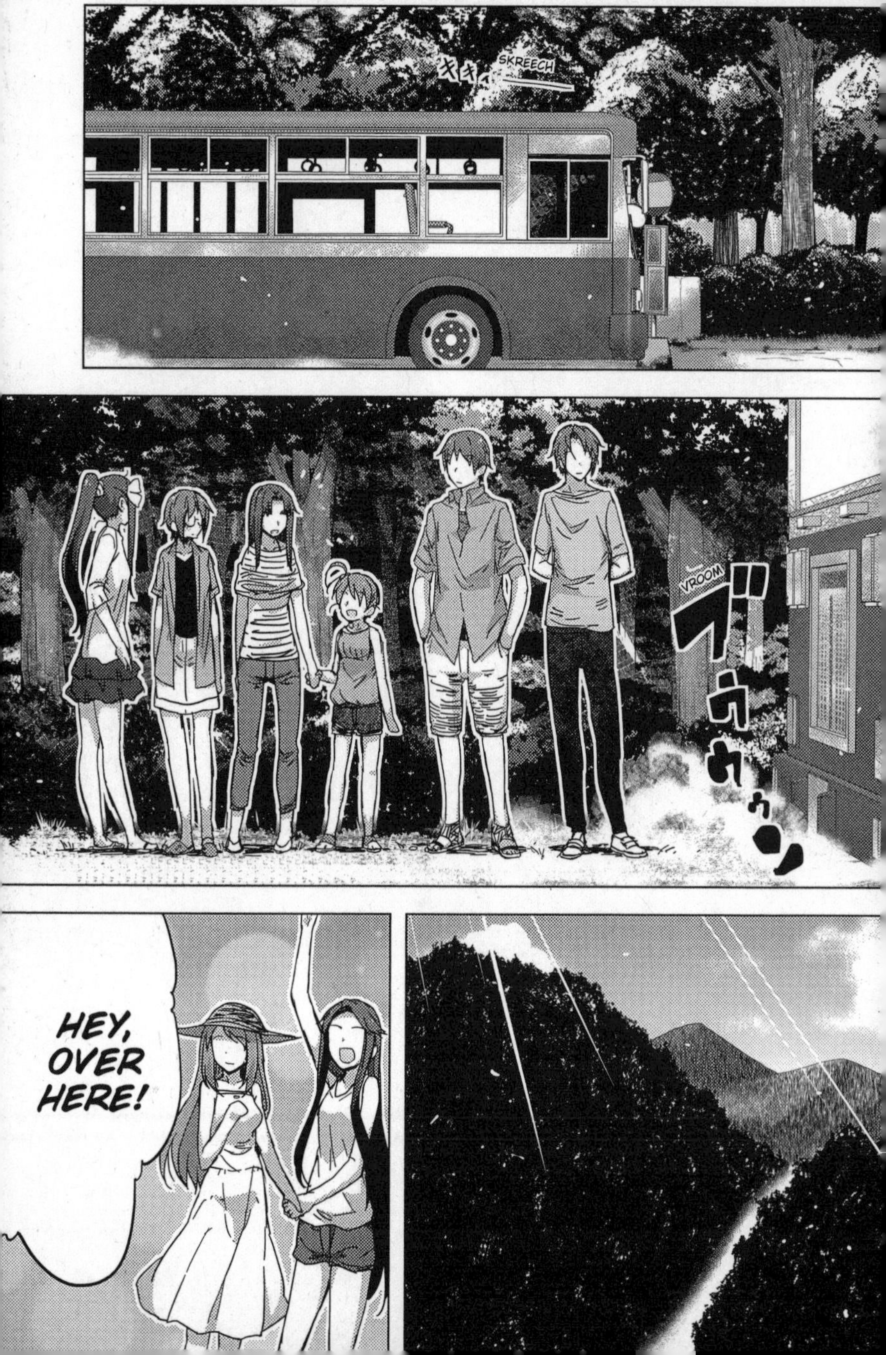
SKREECH
VROOM
HEY, OVER HERE!

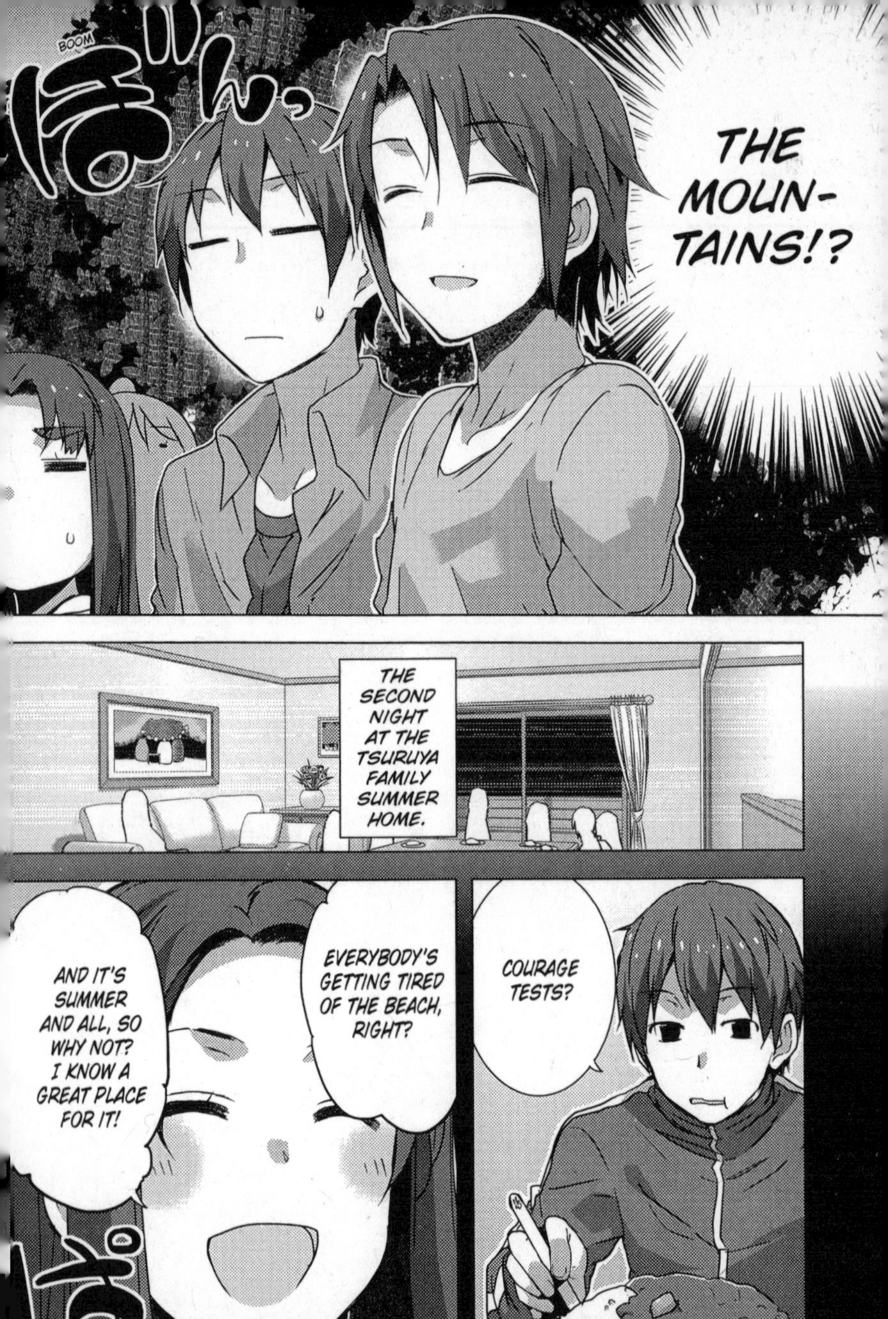

BOOM
THE MOUNTAINS!?
THE SECOND NIGHT AT THE TSURUYA FAMILY SUMMER HOME.
COURAGE TESTS?
EVERYBODY'S GETTING TIRED OF THE BEACH, RIGHT?
AND IT'S SUMMER AND ALL, SO WHY NOT? I KNOW A GREAT PLACE FOR IT!

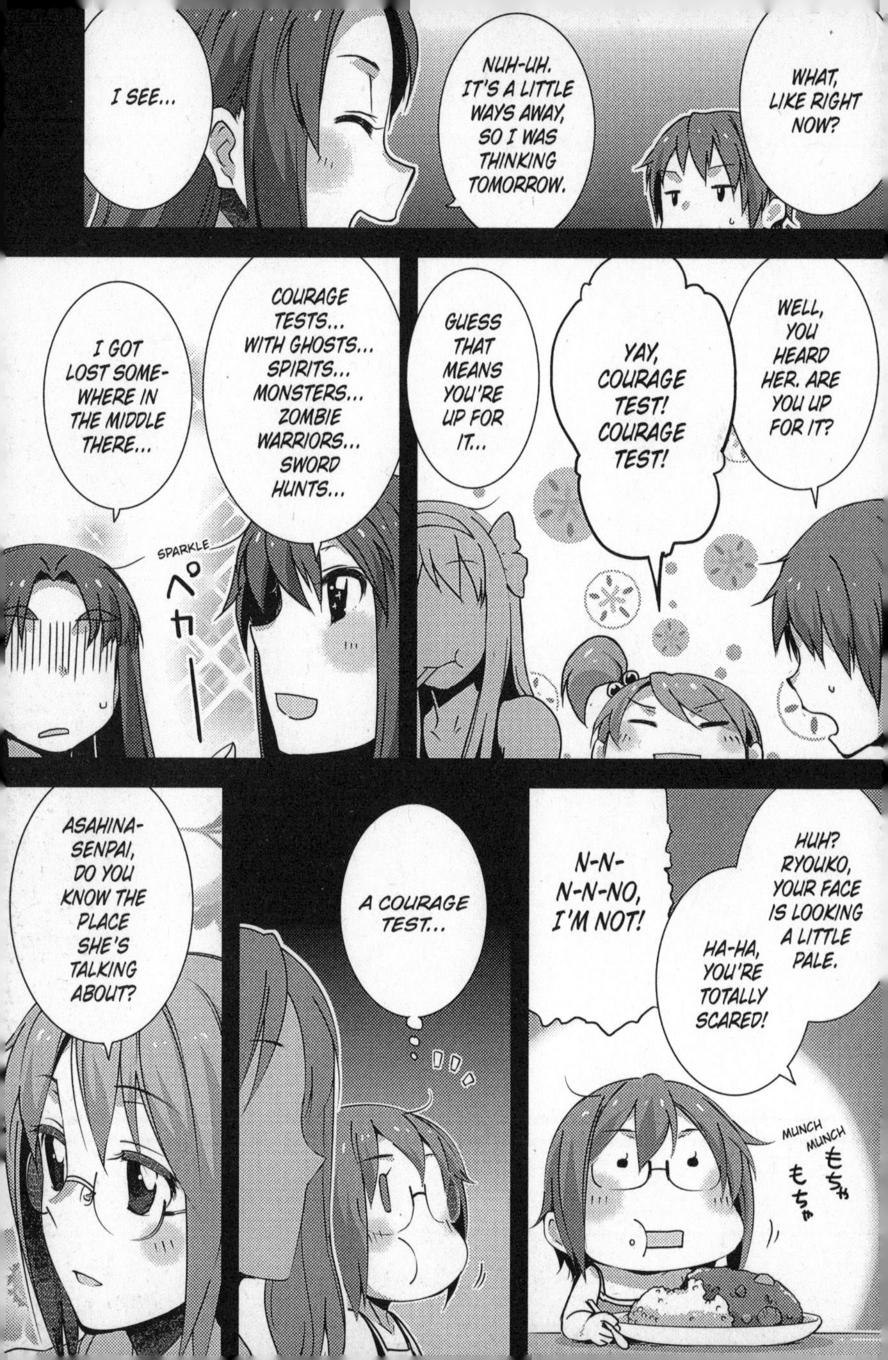
WHAT, LIKE RIGHT NOW?
NUH-UH. IT'S A LITTLE WAYS AWAY, SO I WAS THINKING TOMORROW.
I SEE...
WELL, YOU HEARD HER. ARE YOU UP FOR IT?
YAY, COURAGE TEST! COURAGE TEST!
GUESS THAT MEANS YOU'RE UP FOR IT...
COURAGE TESTS... WITH GHOSTS... SPIRITS... MONSTERS... ZOMBIE WARRIORS... SWORD HUNTS...
SPARKLE
ペカー
I GOT LOST SOME-WHERE IN THE MIDDLE THERE...
HUH? RYOUKO, YOUR FACE IS LOOKING A LITTLE PALE.
HA-HA, YOU'RE TOTALLY SCARED!
N-N-N-N-NO, I'M NOT!
MUNCH MUNCH
もちゃもちゃ
A COURAGE TEST...
ASAHINA-SENPAI, DO YOU KNOW THE PLACE SHE'S TALKING ABOUT?

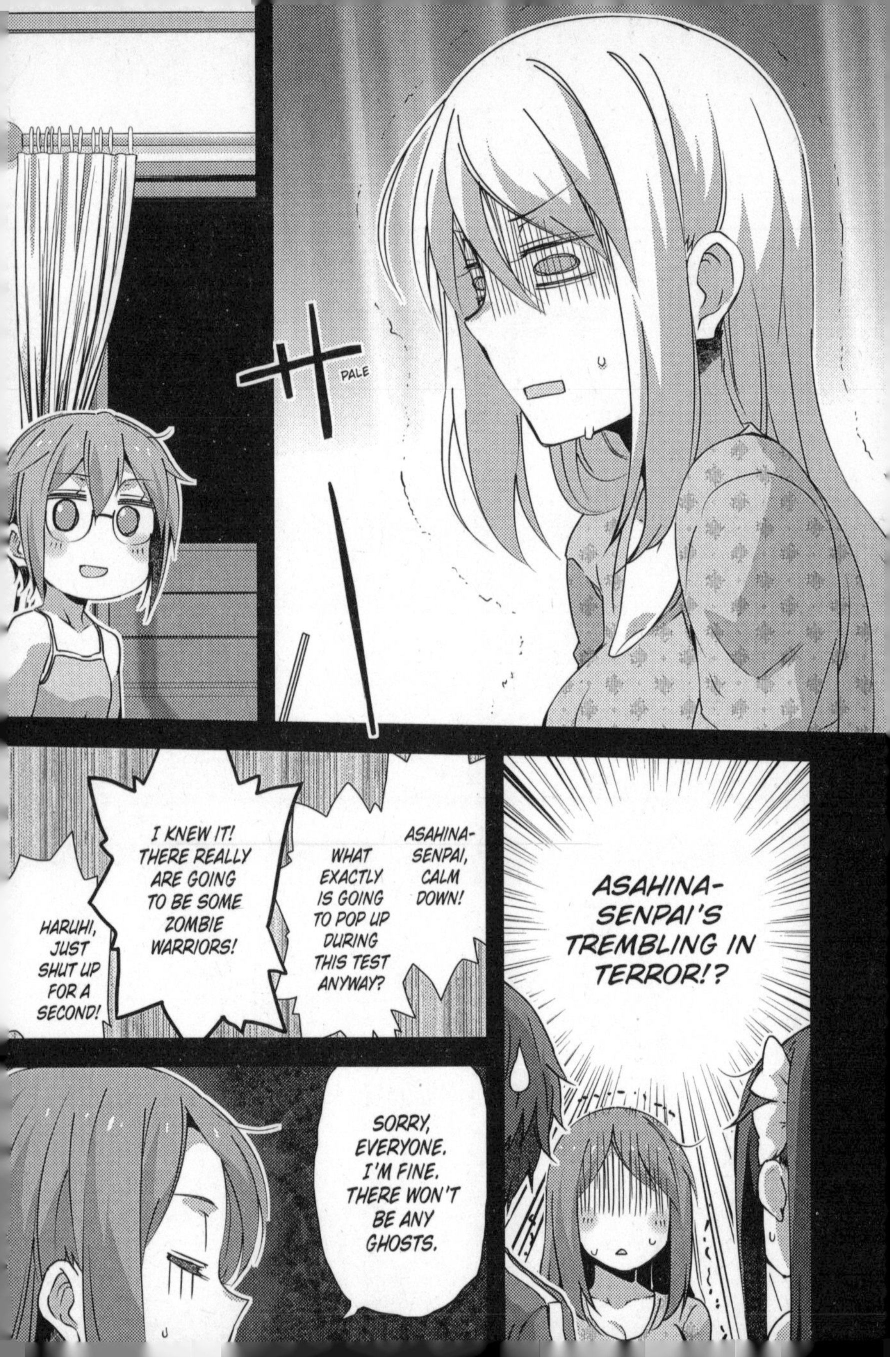
PALE
ASAHINA-SENPAI'S TREMBLING IN TERROR!?
ASAHINA-SENPAI, CALM DOWN!
WHAT EXACTLY IS GOING TO POP UP DURING THIS TEST ANYWAY?
I KNEW IT! THERE REALLY ARE GOING TO BE SOME ZOMBIE WARRIORS!
HARUHI, JUST SHUT UP FOR A SECOND!
SORRY, EVERYONE. I'M FINE. THERE WON'T BE ANY GHOSTS.

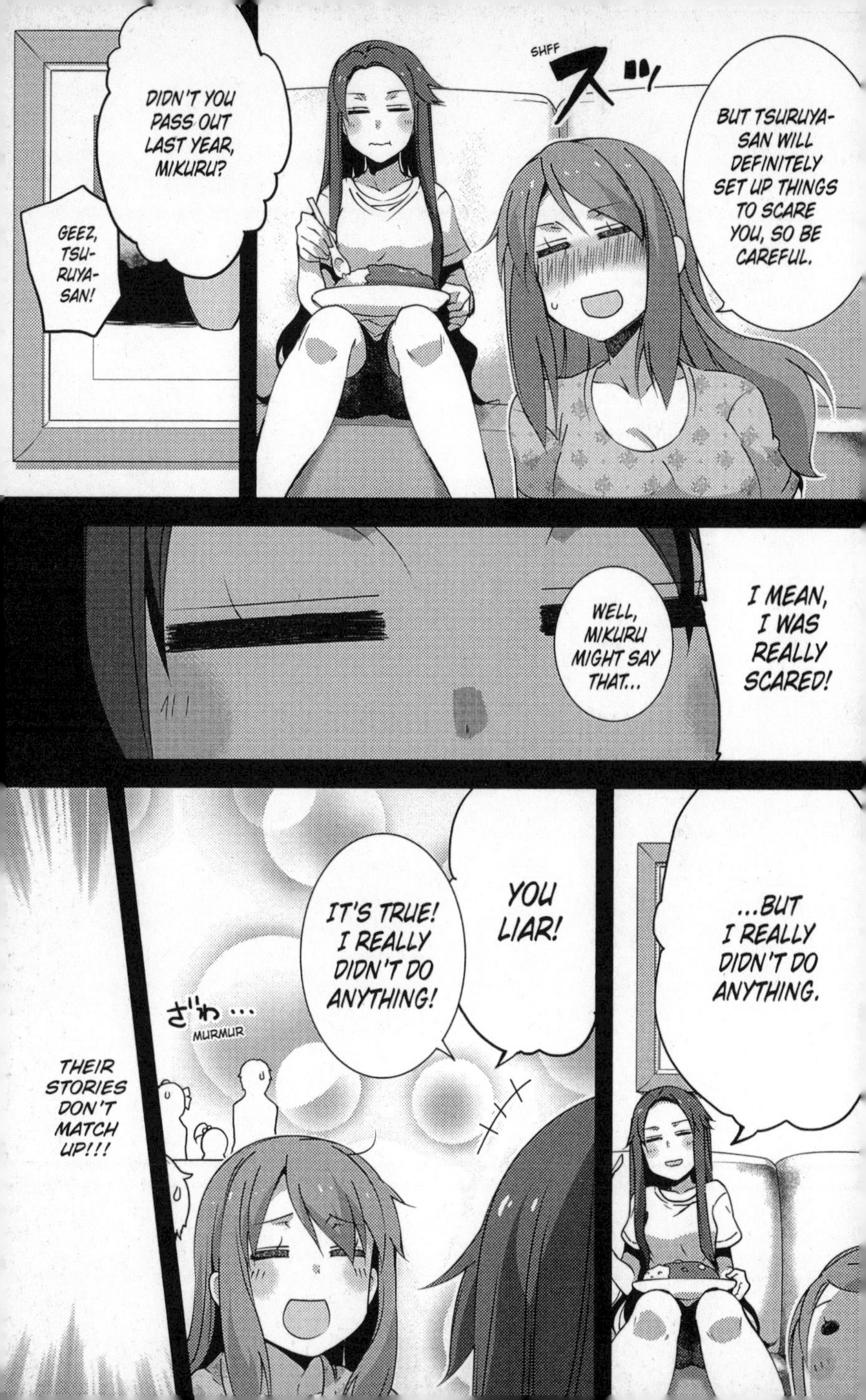
SHFF
BUT TSURUYA-SAN WILL DEFINITELY SET UP THINGS TO SCARE YOU, SO BE CAREFUL.
DIDN'T YOU PASS OUT LAST YEAR, MIKURU?
GEEZ, TSURUYA-SAN!
WELL, MIKURU MIGHT SAY THAT...
I MEAN, I WAS REALLY SCARED!
...BUT I REALLY DIDN'T DO ANYTHING.
YOU LIAR!
IT'S TRUE! I REALLY DIDN'T DO ANYTHING!
ざわ…
MURMUR
THEIR STORIES DON'T MATCH UP!!!

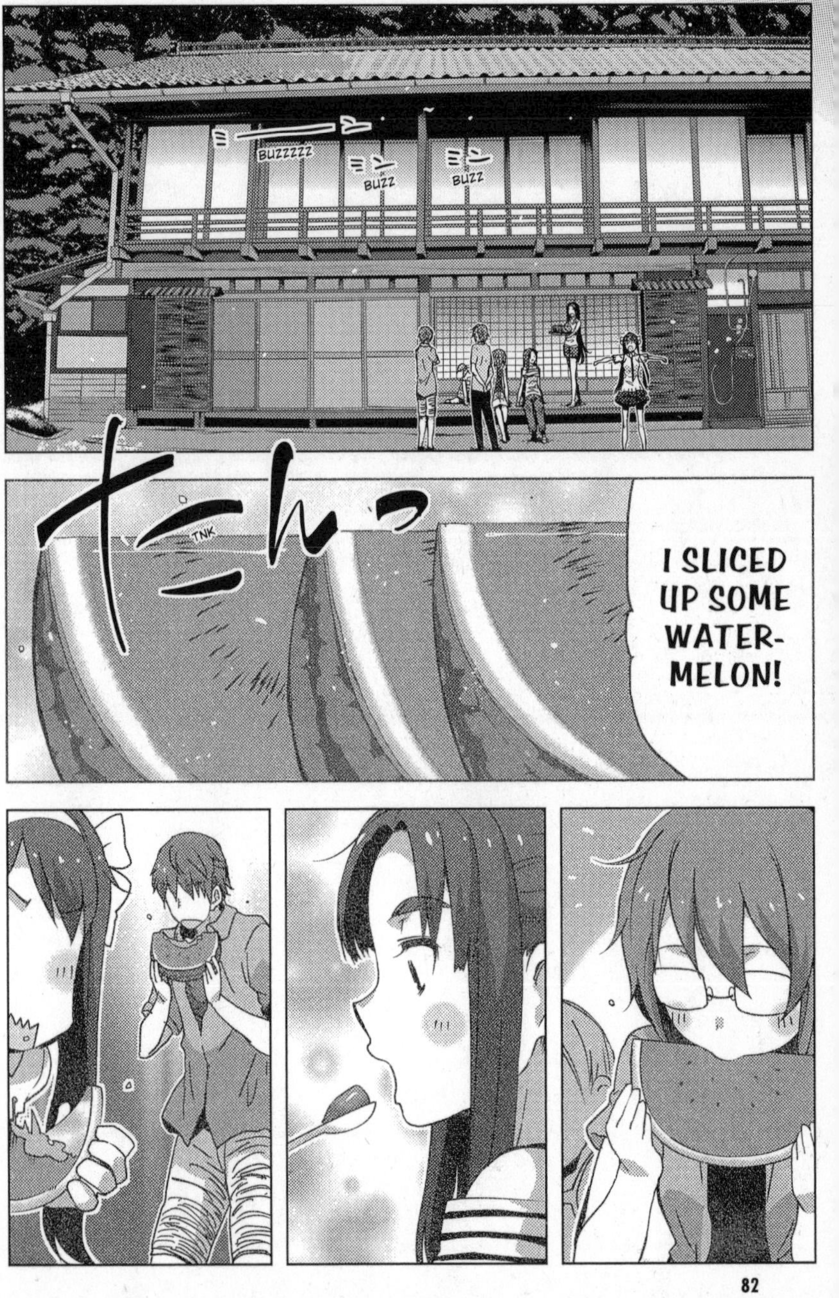
BUZZZZZ
BUZZ
BUZZ
TNK
I SLICED UP SOME WATER-MELON!

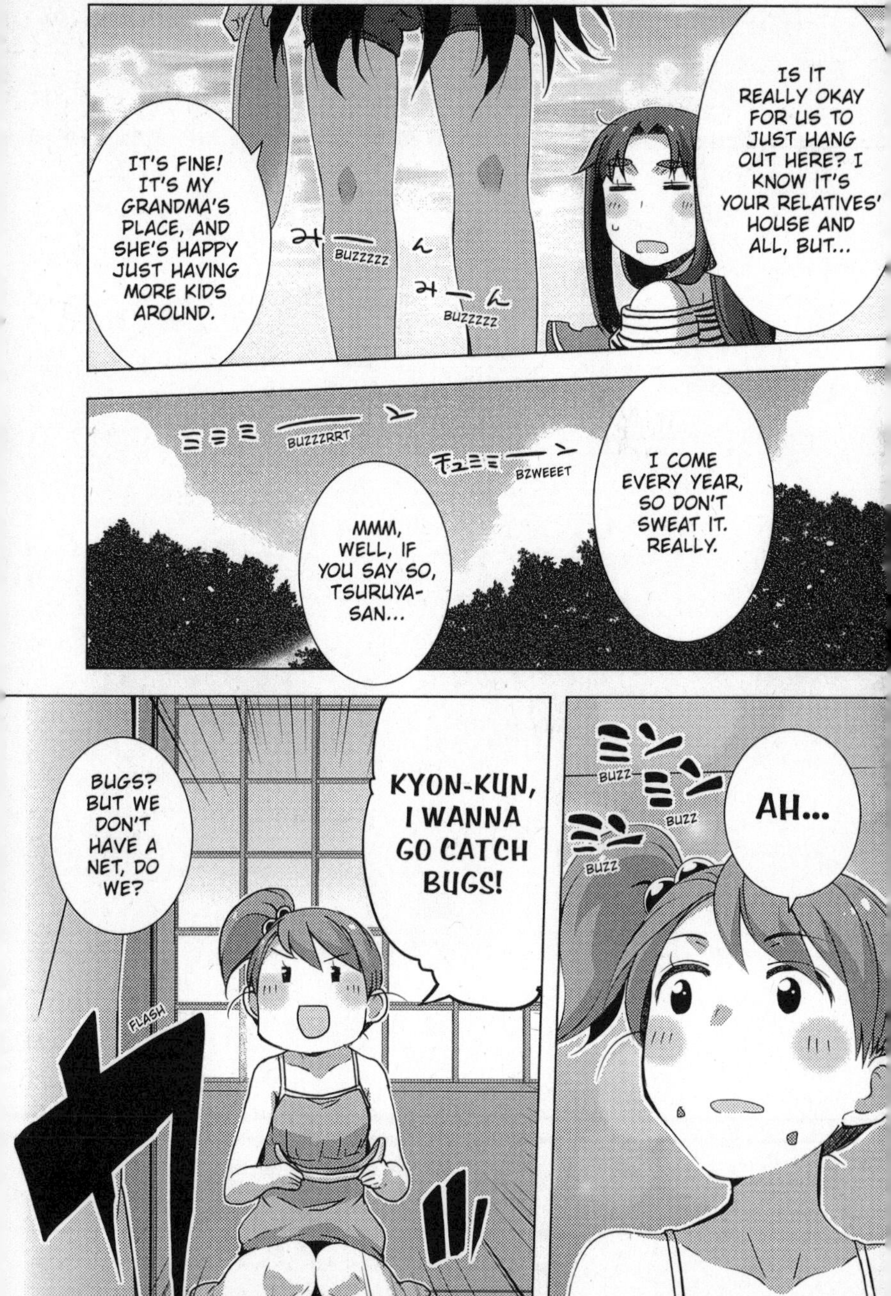
IS IT REALLY OKAY FOR US TO JUST HANG OUT HERE? I KNOW IT'S YOUR RELATIVES' HOUSE AND ALL, BUT...
みーん
BUZZZZZ
みーん
BUZZZZZ
IT'S FINE! IT'S MY GRANDMA'S PLACE, AND SHE'S HAPPY JUST HAVING MORE KIDS AROUND.
I COME EVERY YEAR, SO DON'T SWEAT IT. REALLY.
BUZZZRRRT
BZWEEET
MMM, WELL, IF YOU SAY SO, TSURUYA-SAN...
BUZZ
BUZZ
BUZZ
AH...
KYON-KUN, I WANNA GO CATCH BUGS!
BUGS? BUT WE DON'T HAVE A NET, DO WE?
FLASH

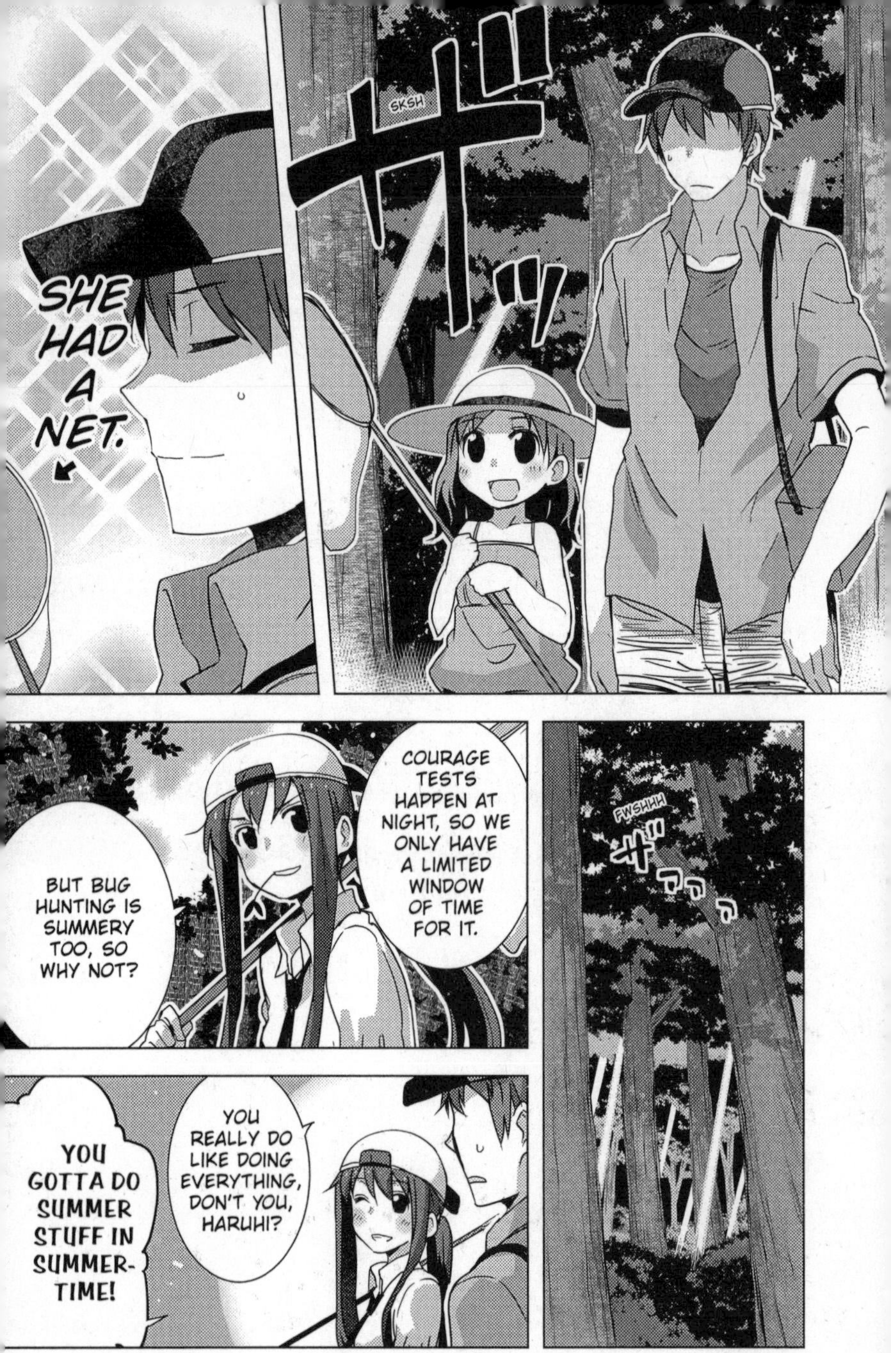
SKSH
SHE HAD A NET.
FWSHHH
COURAGE TESTS HAPPEN AT NIGHT, SO WE ONLY HAVE A LIMITED WINDOW OF TIME FOR IT.
BUT BUG HUNTING IS SUMMERY TOO, SO WHY NOT?
YOU REALLY DO LIKE DOING EVERYTHING, DON'T YOU, HARUHI?
YOU GOTTA DO SUMMER STUFF IN SUMMER-TIME!

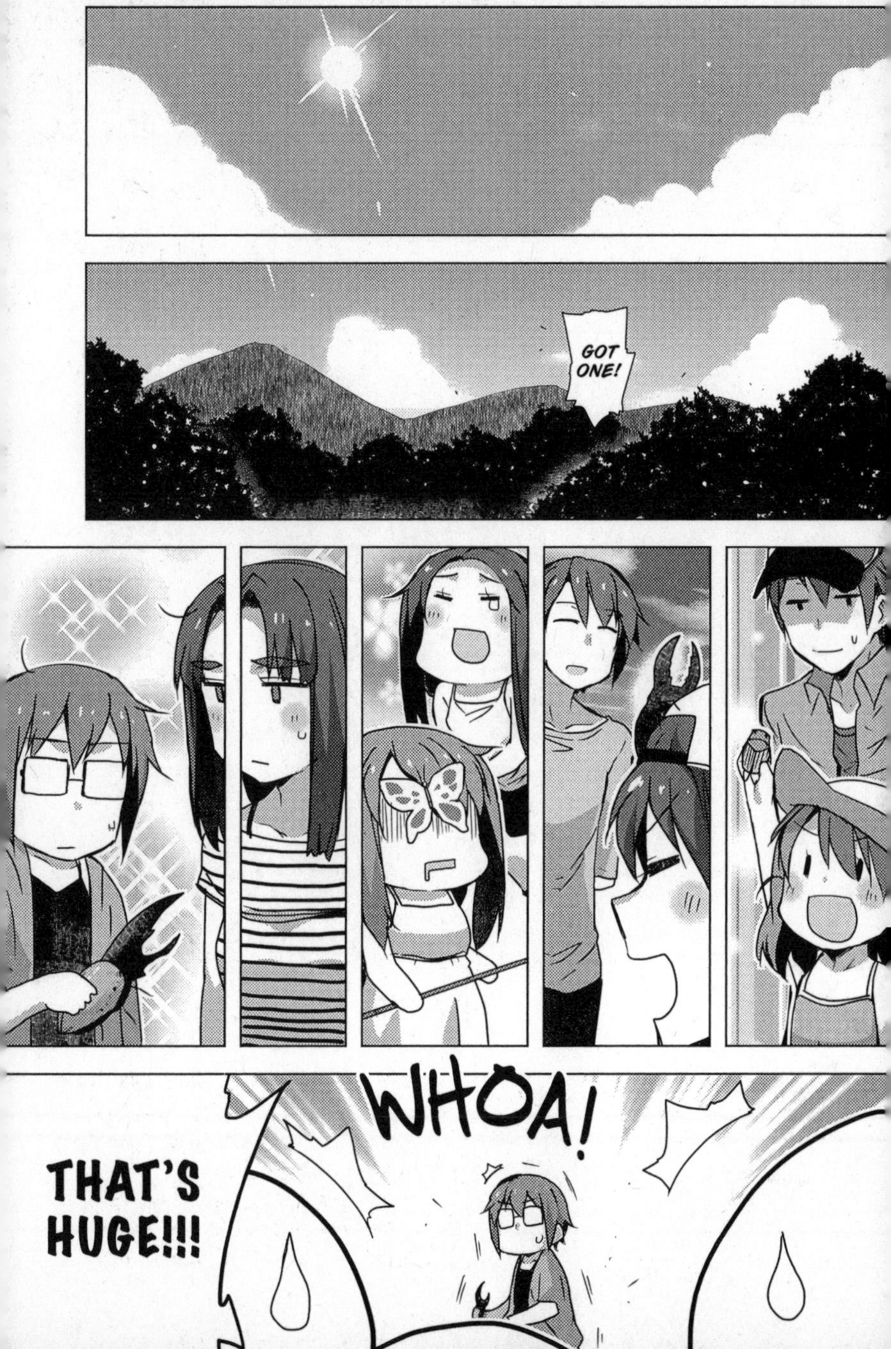
GOT ONE!
WHOA!
THAT'S HUGE!!!

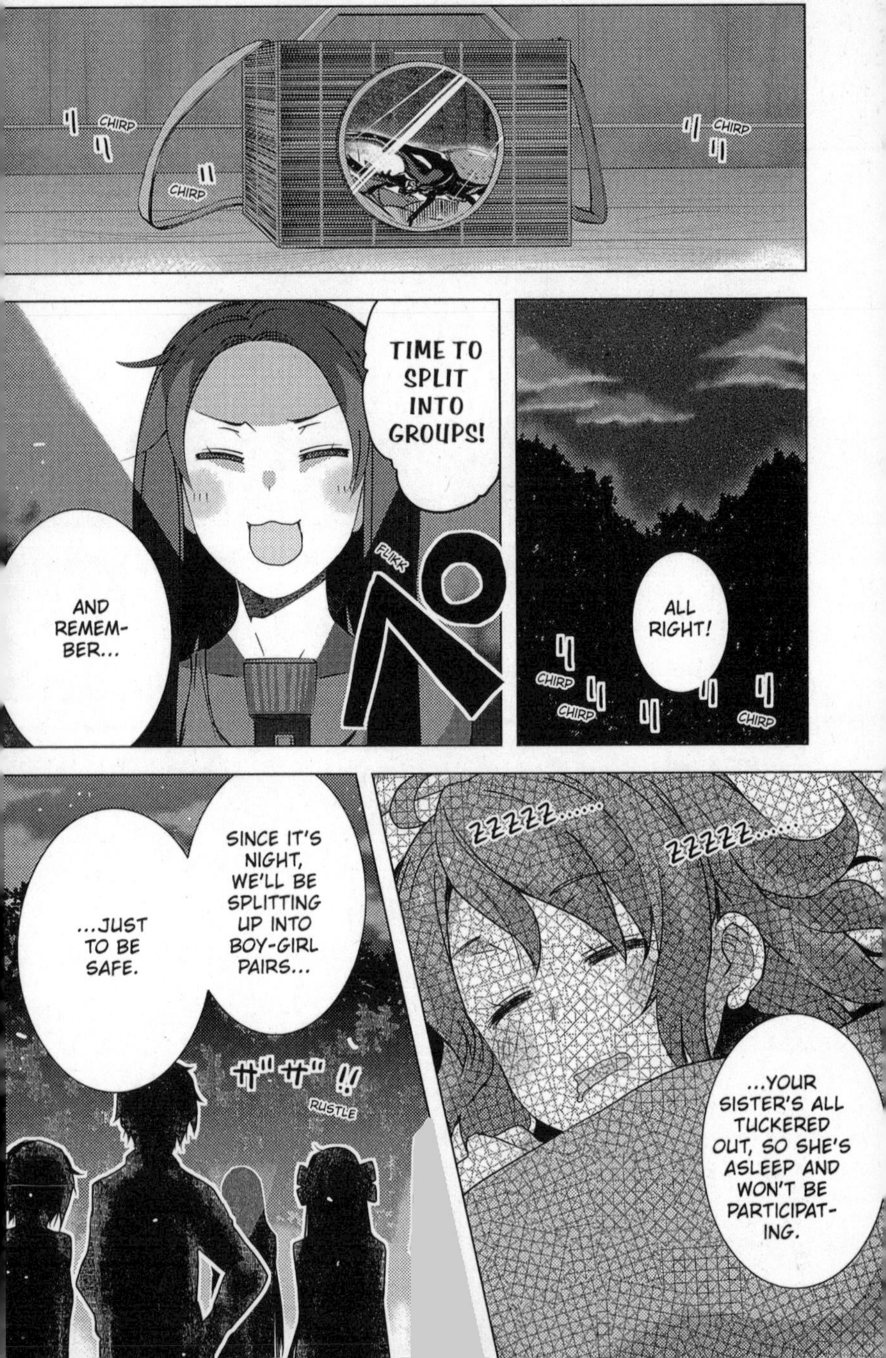
CHIRP
CHIRP
CHIRP
ALL RIGHT!
CHIRP
CHIRP
CHIRP
TIME TO SPLIT INTO GROUPS!
FLIKK
AND REMEMBER...
ZZZZZ......
ZZZZZ......
...YOUR SISTER'S ALL TUCKERED OUT, SO SHE'S ASLEEP AND WON'T BE PARTICIPATING.
SINCE IT'S NIGHT, WE'LL BE SPLITTING UP INTO BOY-GIRL PAIRS...
...JUST TO BE SAFE.
RUSTLE

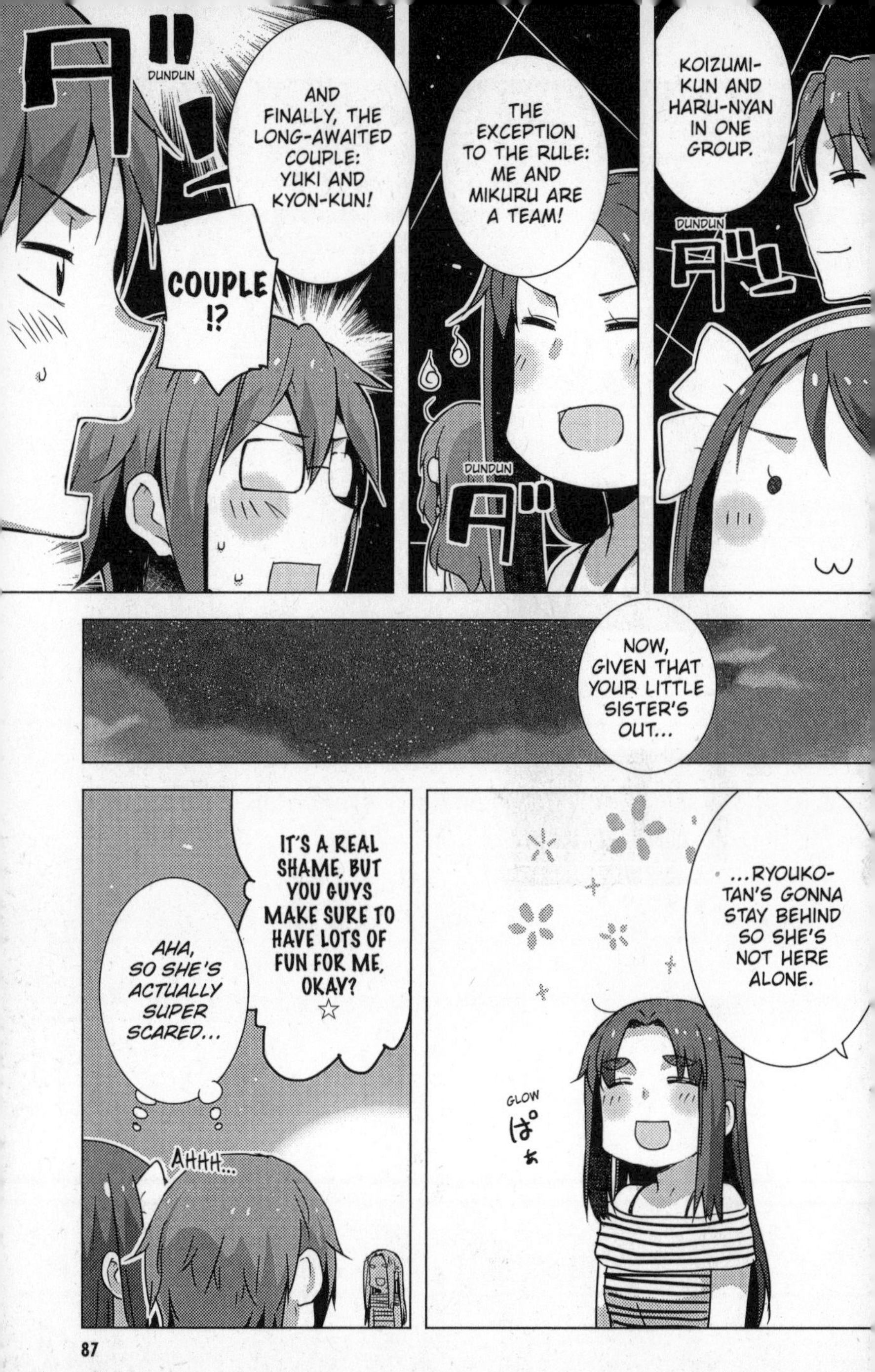
KOIZUMI-KUN AND HARU-NYAN IN ONE GROUP.
DUNDUN
THE EXCEPTION TO THE RULE: ME AND MIKURU ARE A TEAM!
DUNDUN
AND FINALLY, THE LONG-AWAITED COUPLE: YUKI AND KYON-KUN!
DUNDUN
COUPLE!?
NOW, GIVEN THAT YOUR LITTLE SISTER'S OUT...
...RYOUKO-TAN'S GONNA STAY BEHIND SO SHE'S NOT HERE ALONE.
GLOW
ぱぁ
IT'S A REAL SHAME, BUT YOU GUYS MAKE SURE TO HAVE LOTS OF FUN FOR ME, OKAY? ☆
AHA, SO SHE'S ACTUALLY SUPER SCARED...
AHHH...

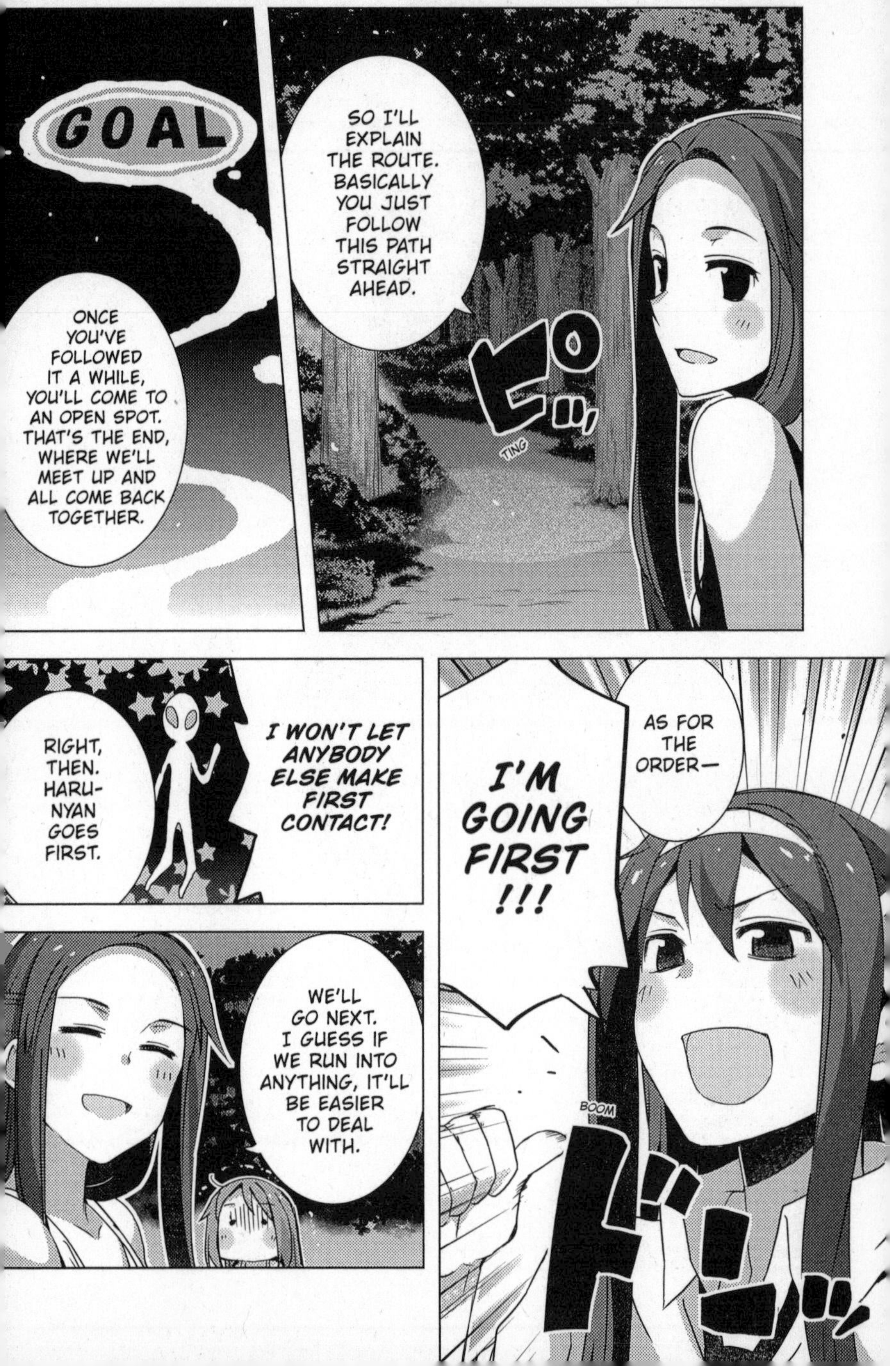
SO I'LL EXPLAIN THE ROUTE. BASICALLY YOU JUST FOLLOW THIS PATH STRAIGHT AHEAD.
TING
GOAL
ONCE YOU'VE FOLLOWED IT A WHILE, YOU'LL COME TO AN OPEN SPOT. THAT'S THE END, WHERE WE'LL MEET UP AND ALL COME BACK TOGETHER.
AS FOR THE ORDER—
I'M GOING FIRST!!!
BOOM
RIGHT, THEN. HARU-NYAN GOES FIRST.
I WON'T LET ANYBODY ELSE MAKE FIRST CONTACT!
WE'LL GO NEXT. I GUESS IF WE RUN INTO ANYTHING, IT'LL BE EASIER TO DEAL WITH.

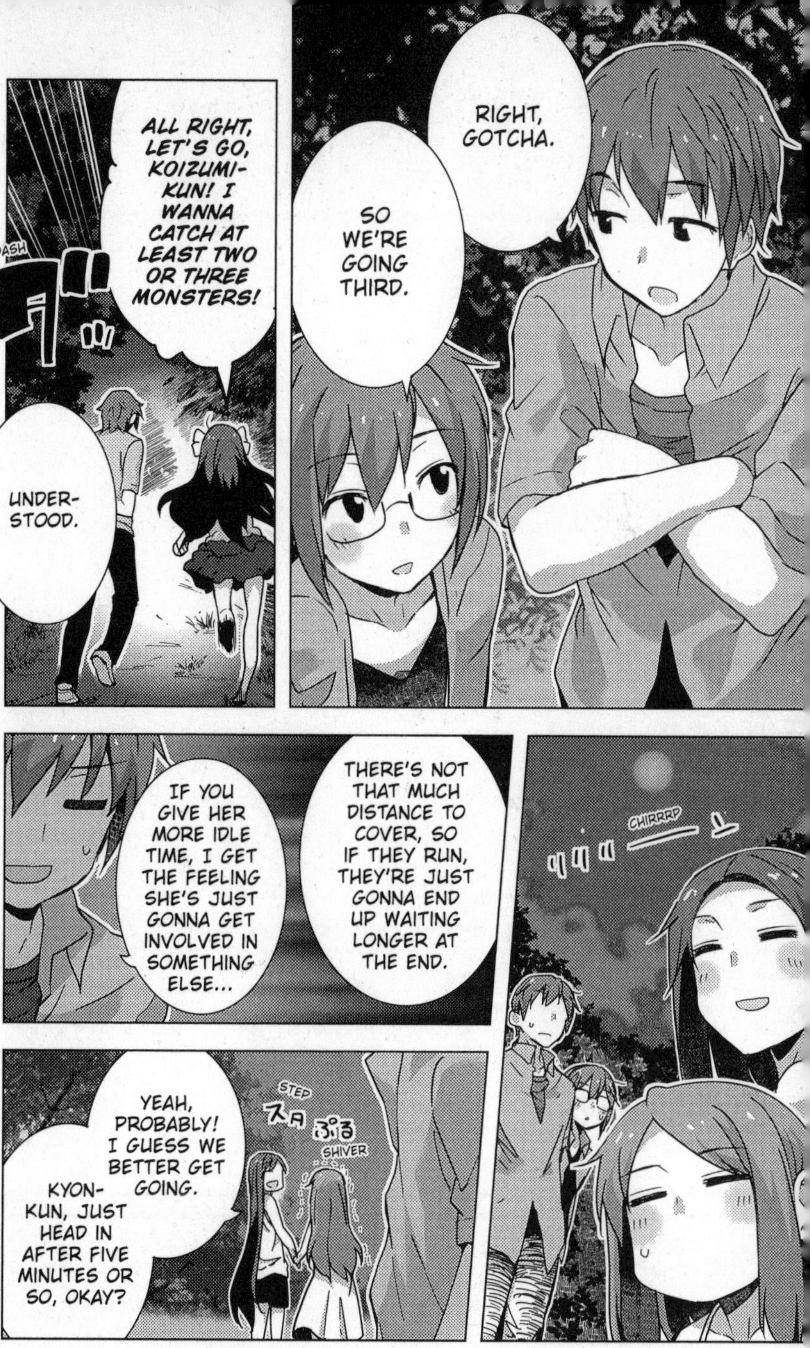
RIGHT, GOTCHA.
SO WE'RE GOING THIRD.
ALL RIGHT, LET'S GO, KOIZUMI-KUN! I WANNA CATCH AT LEAST TWO OR THREE MONSTERS!
DASH
UNDER-STOOD.
CHIRRRP
THERE'S NOT THAT MUCH DISTANCE TO COVER, SO IF THEY RUN, THEY'RE JUST GONNA END UP WAITING LONGER AT THE END.
IF YOU GIVE HER MORE IDLE TIME, I GET THE FEELING SHE'S JUST GONNA GET INVOLVED IN SOMETHING ELSE...
YEAH, PROBABLY! I GUESS WE BETTER GET GOING. KYON-KUN, JUST HEAD IN AFTER FIVE MINUTES OR SO, OKAY?
STEP
SHIVER

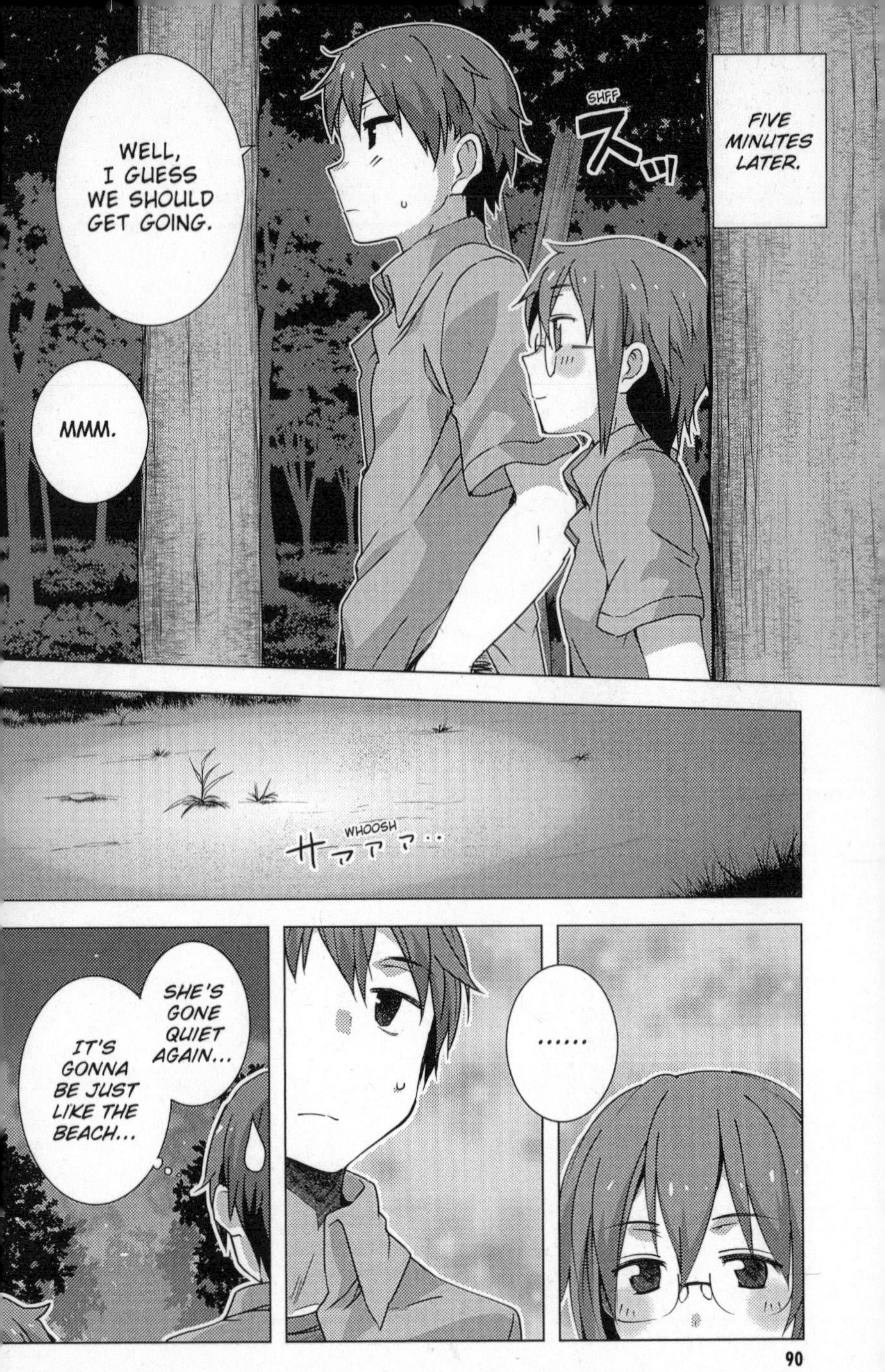
FIVE MINUTES LATER.
SHFF
スッ
WELL, I GUESS WE SHOULD GET GOING.
MMM.
WHOOSH
サァァァ‥
......
SHE'S GONE QUIET AGAIN...
IT'S GONNA BE JUST LIKE THE BEACH...

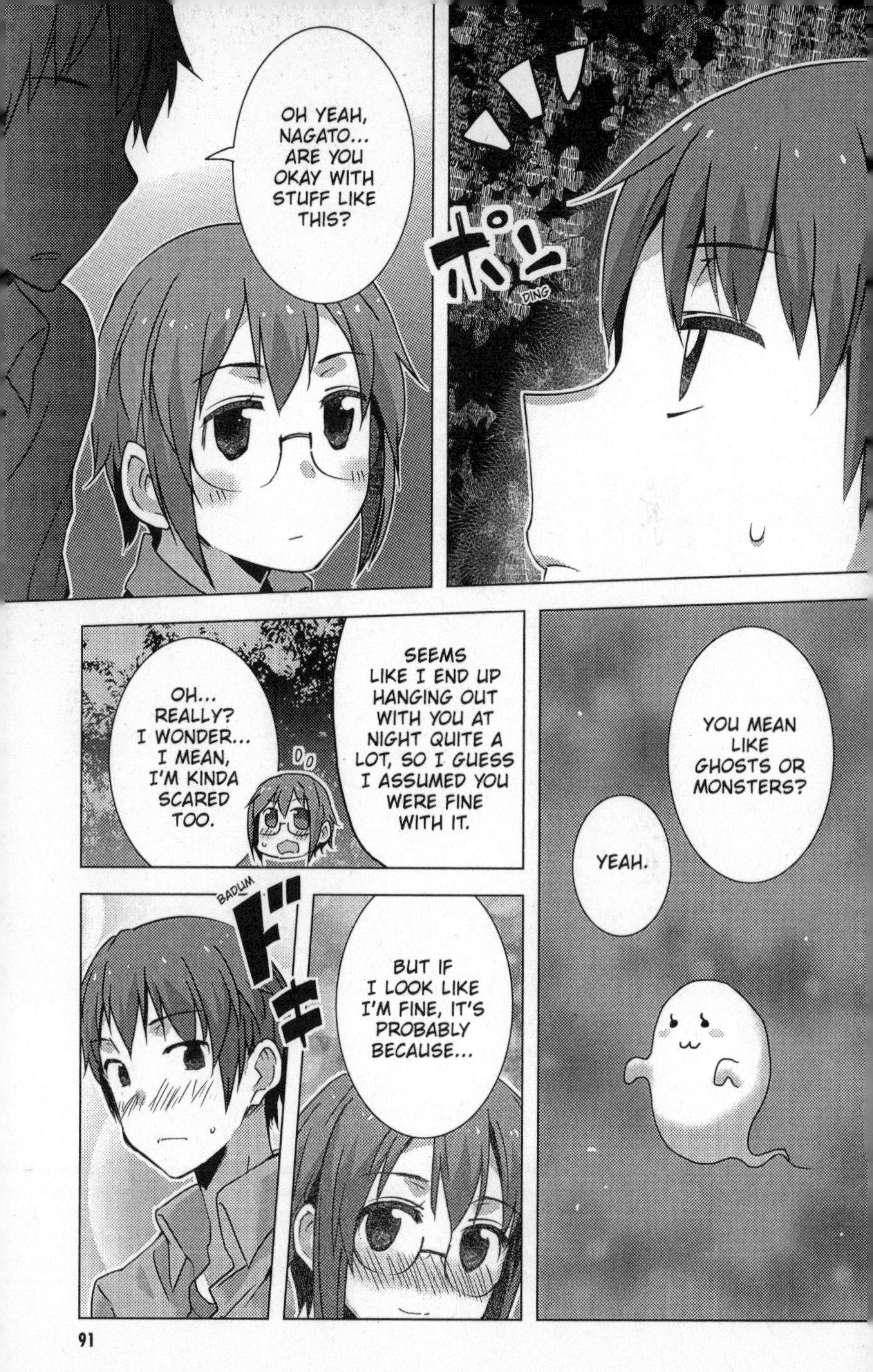
DING
OH YEAH, NAGATO... ARE YOU OKAY WITH STUFF LIKE THIS?
YOU MEAN LIKE GHOSTS OR MONSTERS?
YEAH.
SEEMS LIKE I END UP HANGING OUT WITH YOU AT NIGHT QUITE A LOT, SO I GUESS I ASSUMED YOU WERE FINE WITH IT.
OH... REALLY? I WONDER... I MEAN, I'M KINDA SCARED TOO.
BUT IF I LOOK LIKE I'M FINE, IT'S PROBABLY BECAUSE...
BADUM

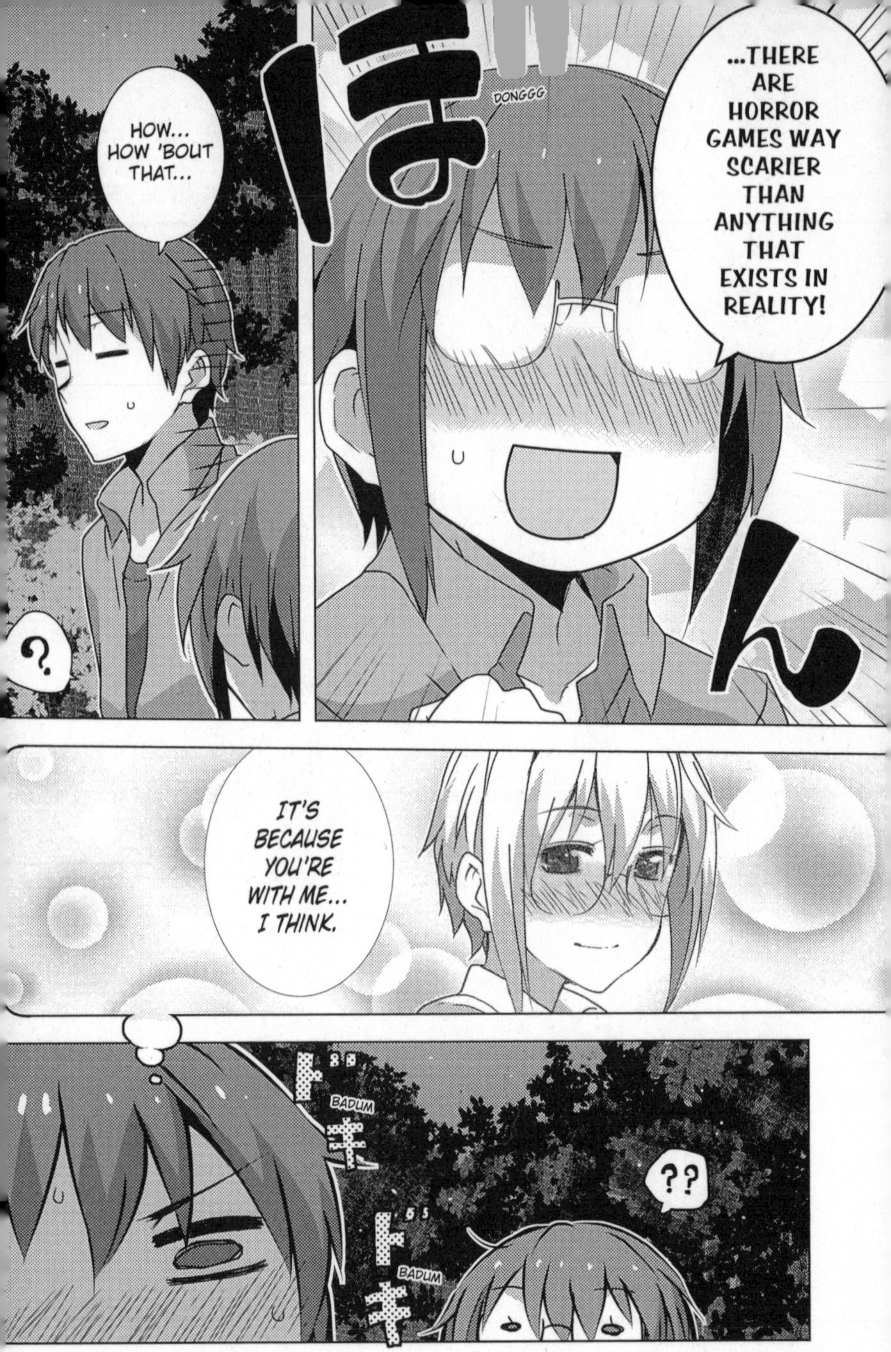
DONGGG
...THERE ARE HORROR GAMES WAY SCARIER THAN ANYTHING THAT EXISTS IN REALITY!
HOW... HOW 'BOUT THAT...
?
IT'S BECAUSE YOU'RE WITH ME... I THINK.
BADUM
BADUM
??

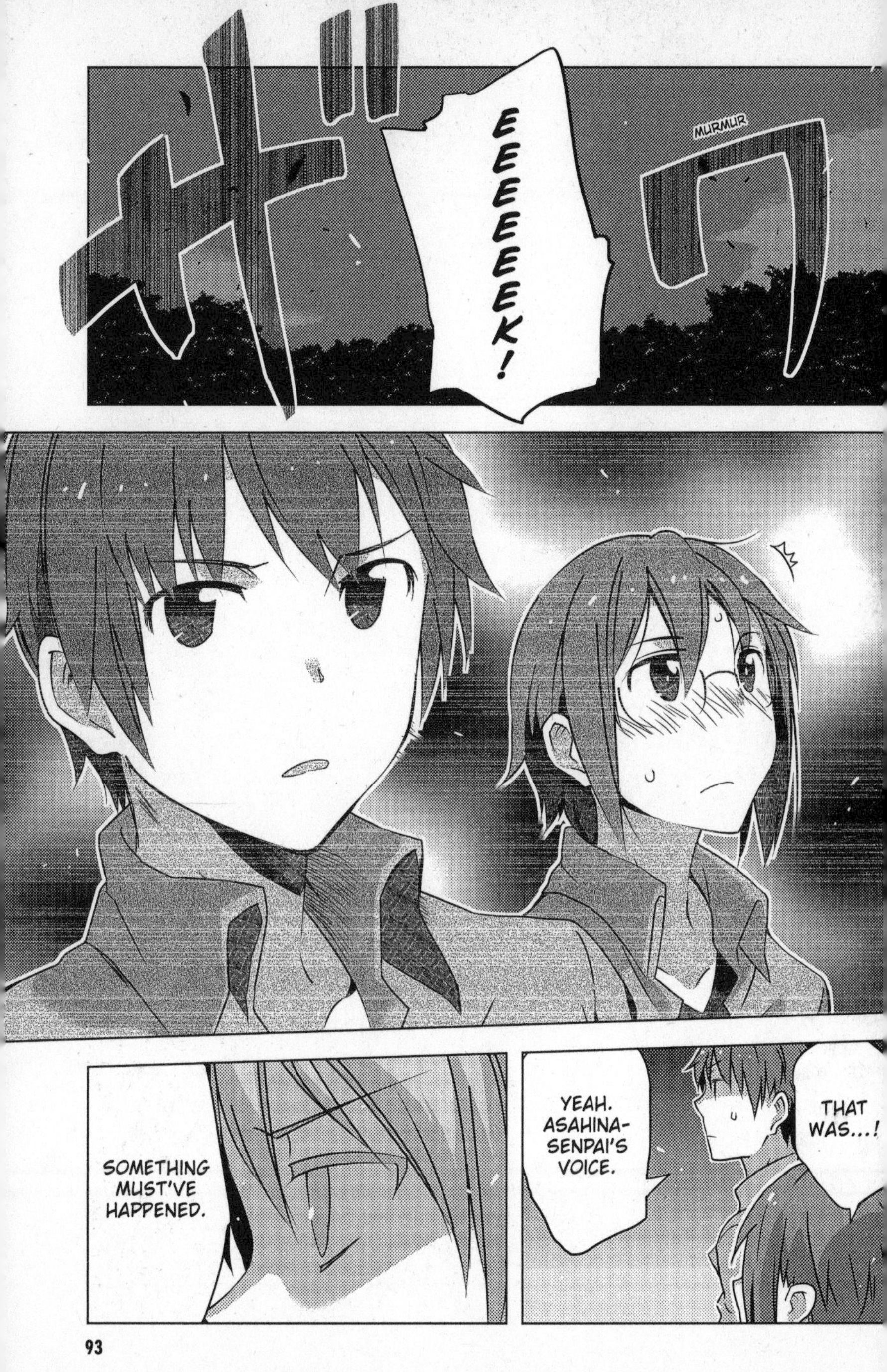
EEEEEEEK!
MURMUR
THAT WAS...!
YEAH. ASAHINA-SENPAI'S VOICE.
SOMETHING MUST'VE HAPPENED.

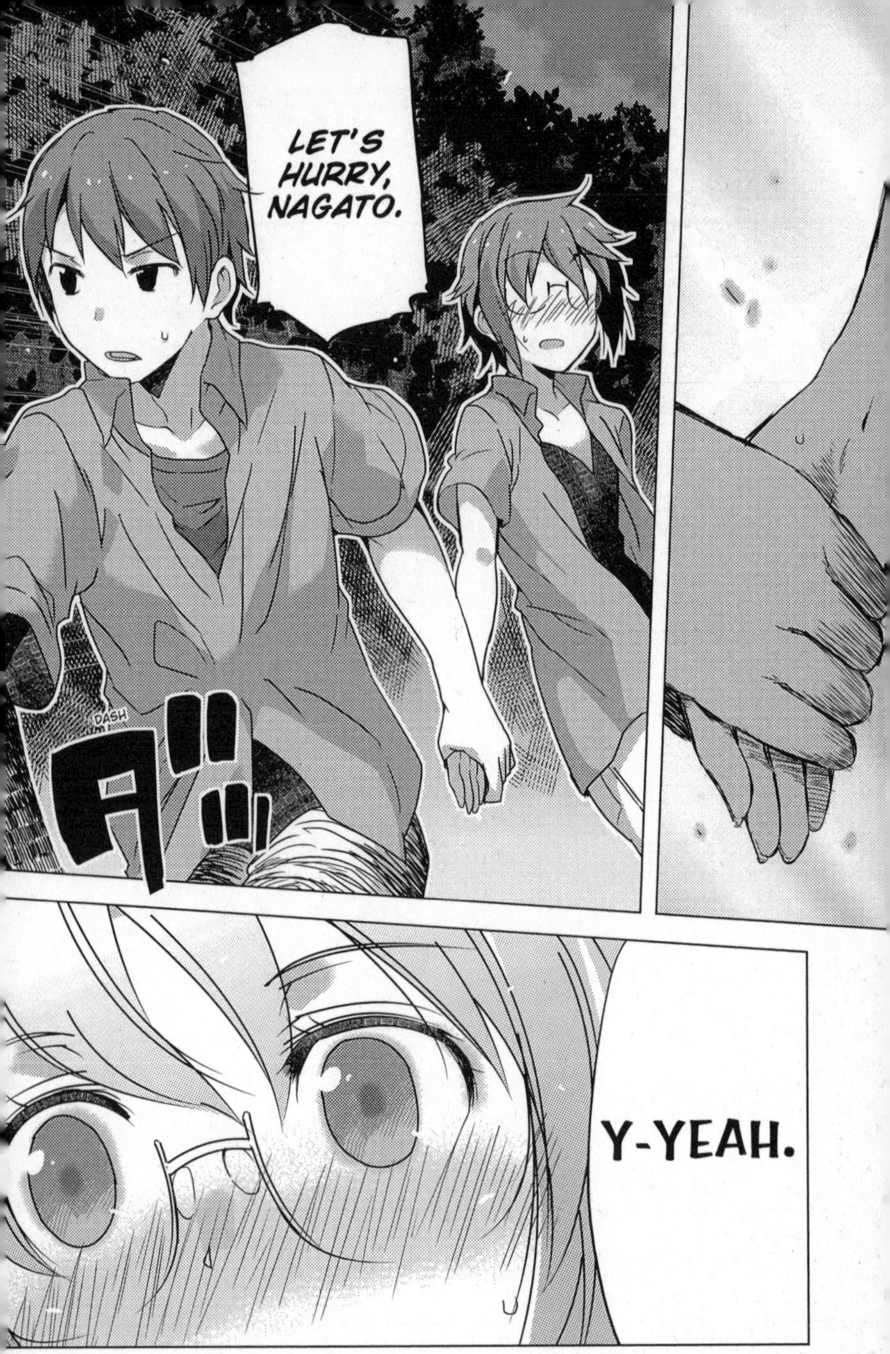
LET'S HURRY, NAGATO.
DASH
タ゛ッ
Y-YEAH.

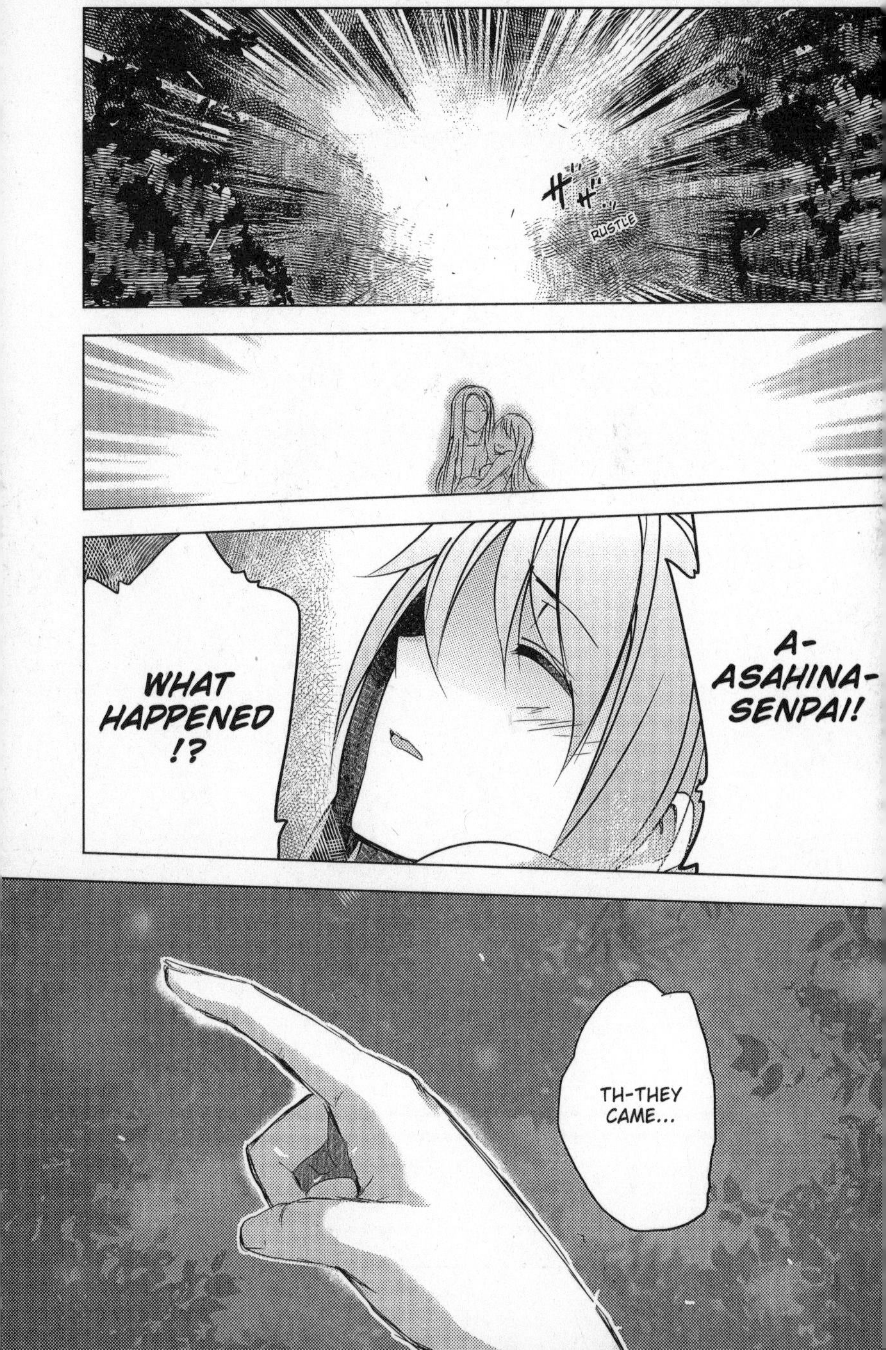
RUSTLE
A-ASAHINA-SENPAI!
WHAT HAPPENED!?
TH-THEY CAME...

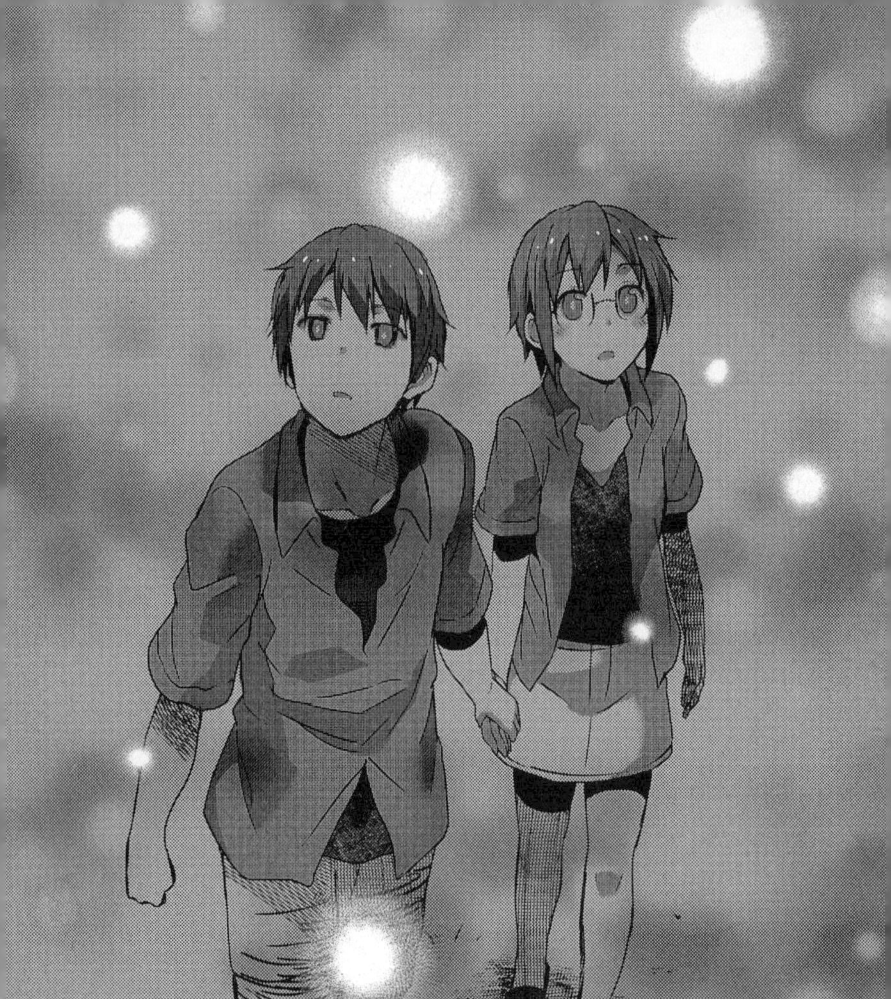

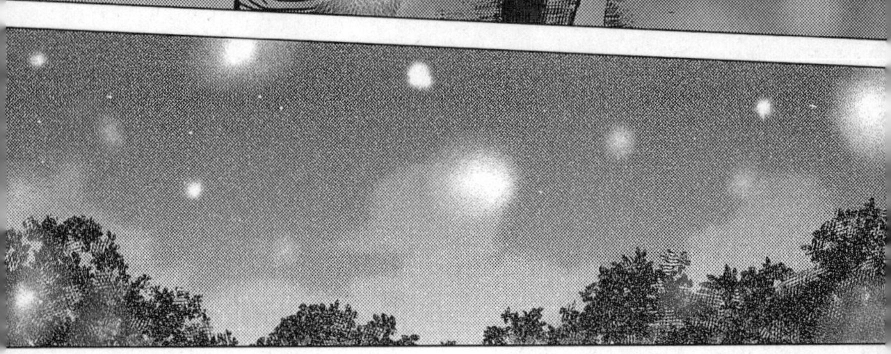

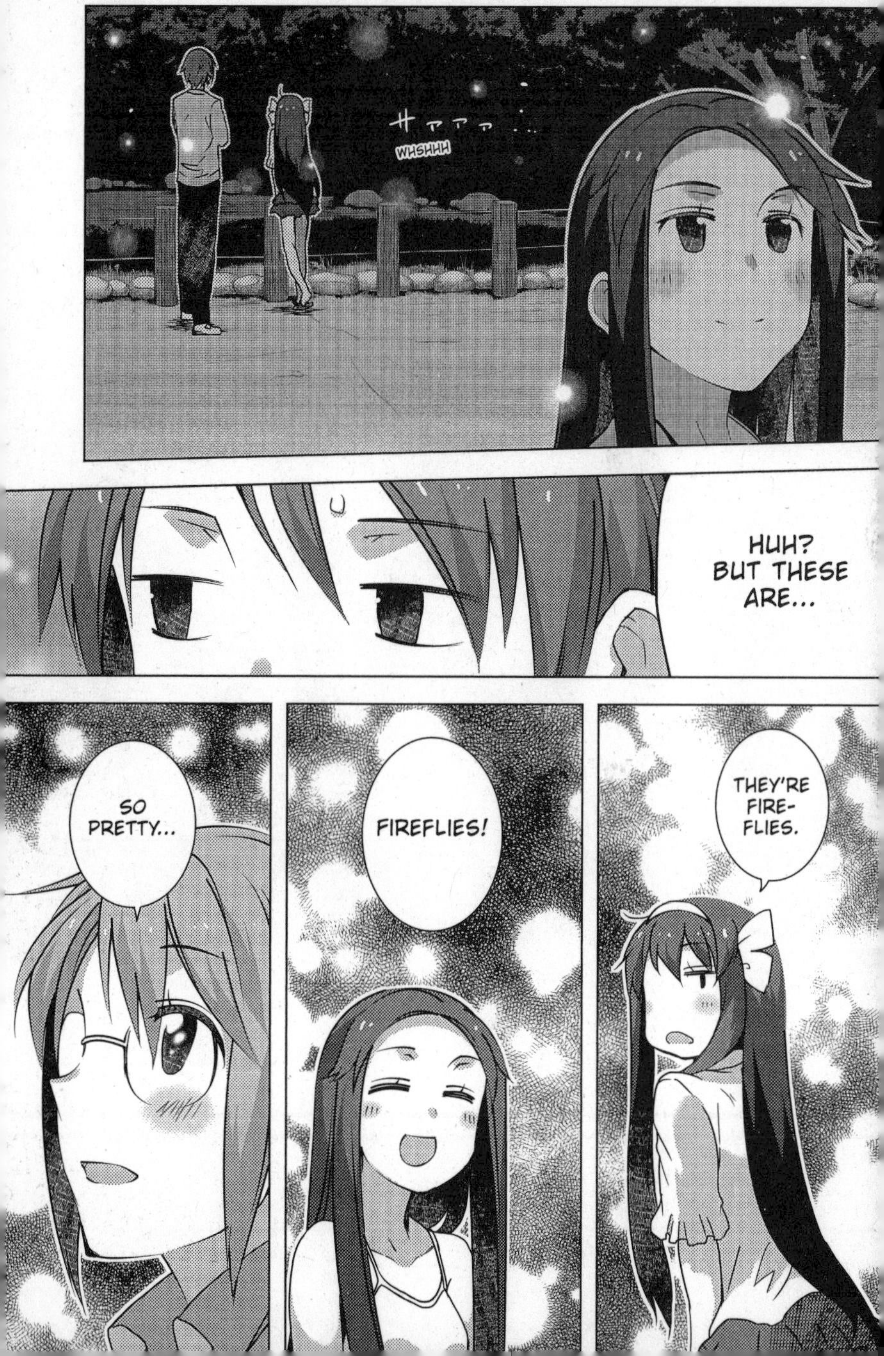
サァァァ…
WHSHHH
HUH? BUT THESE ARE...
THEY'RE FIRE-FLIES.
FIREFLIES!
SO PRETTY...

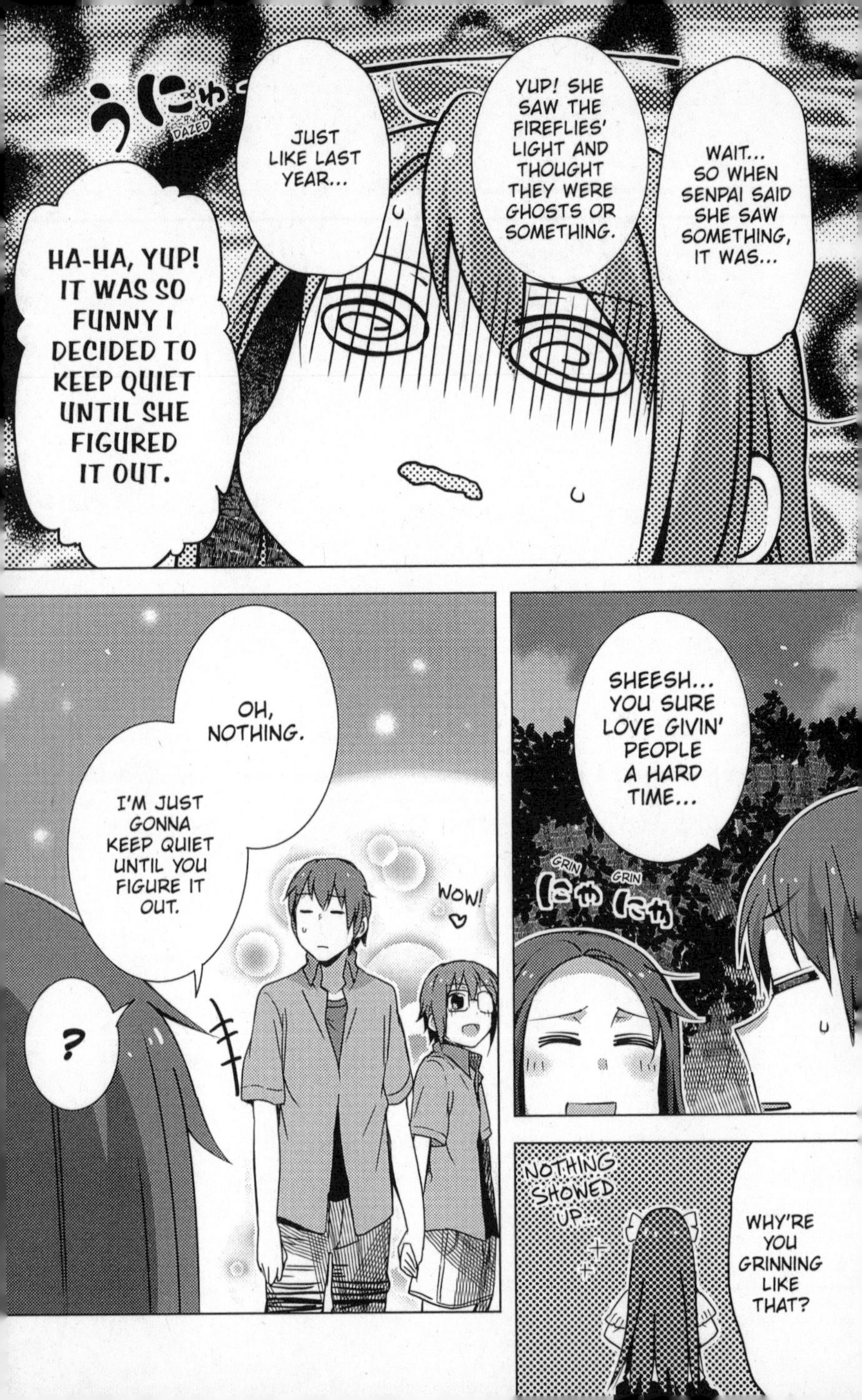
WAIT... SO WHEN SENPAI SAID SHE SAW SOMETHING, IT WAS...
YUP! SHE SAW THE FIREFLIES' LIGHT AND THOUGHT THEY WERE GHOSTS OR SOMETHING.
JUST LIKE LAST YEAR...
DAZED
HA-HA, YUP! IT WAS SO FUNNY I DECIDED TO KEEP QUIET UNTIL SHE FIGURED IT OUT.
SHEESH... YOU SURE LOVE GIVIN' PEOPLE A HARD TIME...
GRIN GRIN
NOTHING SHOWED UP...
WHY'RE YOU GRINNING LIKE THAT?
OH, NOTHING.
I'M JUST GONNA KEEP QUIET UNTIL YOU FIGURE IT OUT.
WOW!
?

Epilogue 38>> Summer Vacation: Festival

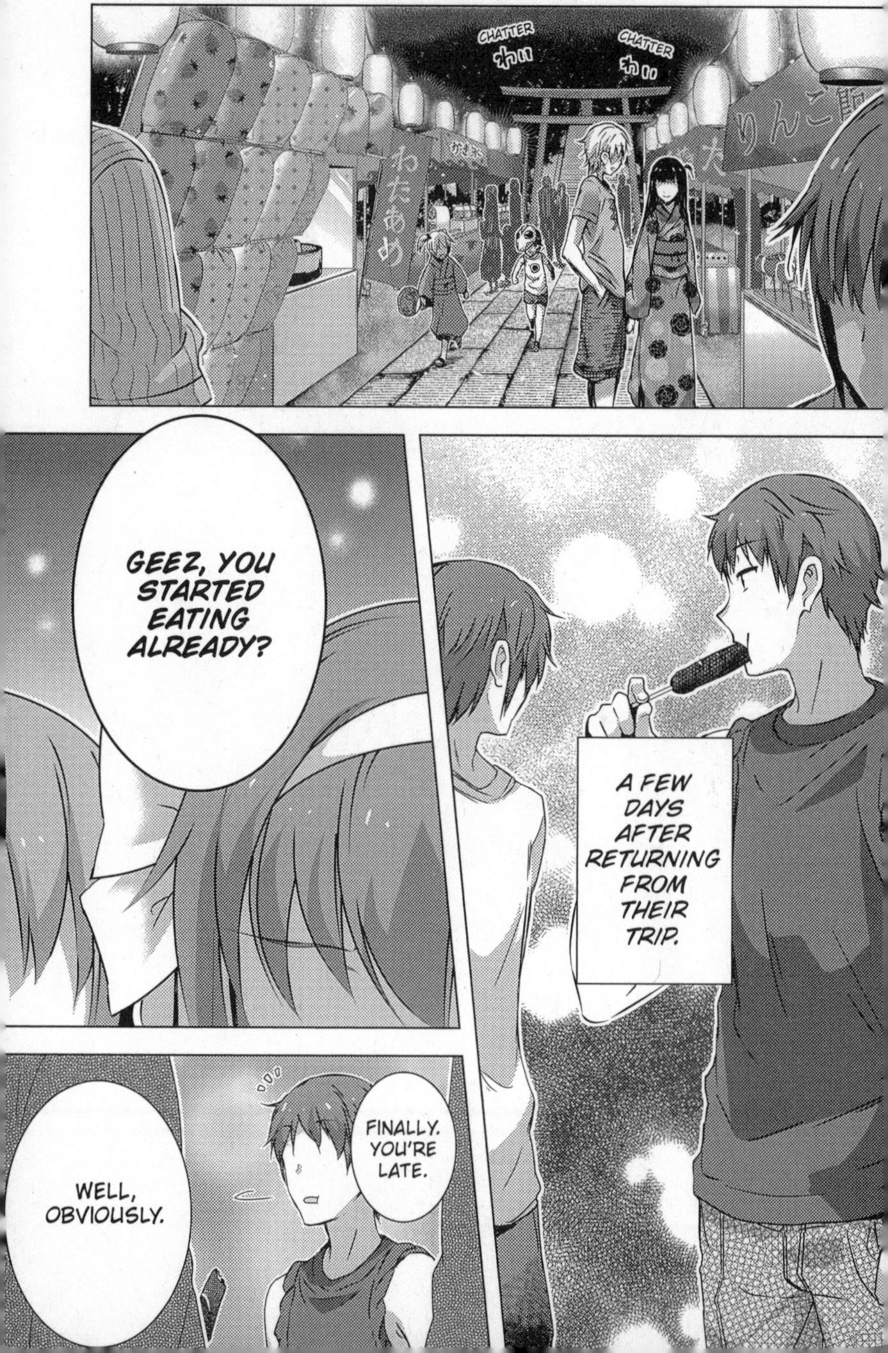
CHATTER
わい
CHATTER
わい
わたあめ
A FEW DAYS AFTER RETURNING FROM THEIR TRIP.
GEEZ, YOU STARTED EATING ALREADY?
FINALLY. YOU'RE LATE.
WELL, OBVIOUSLY.

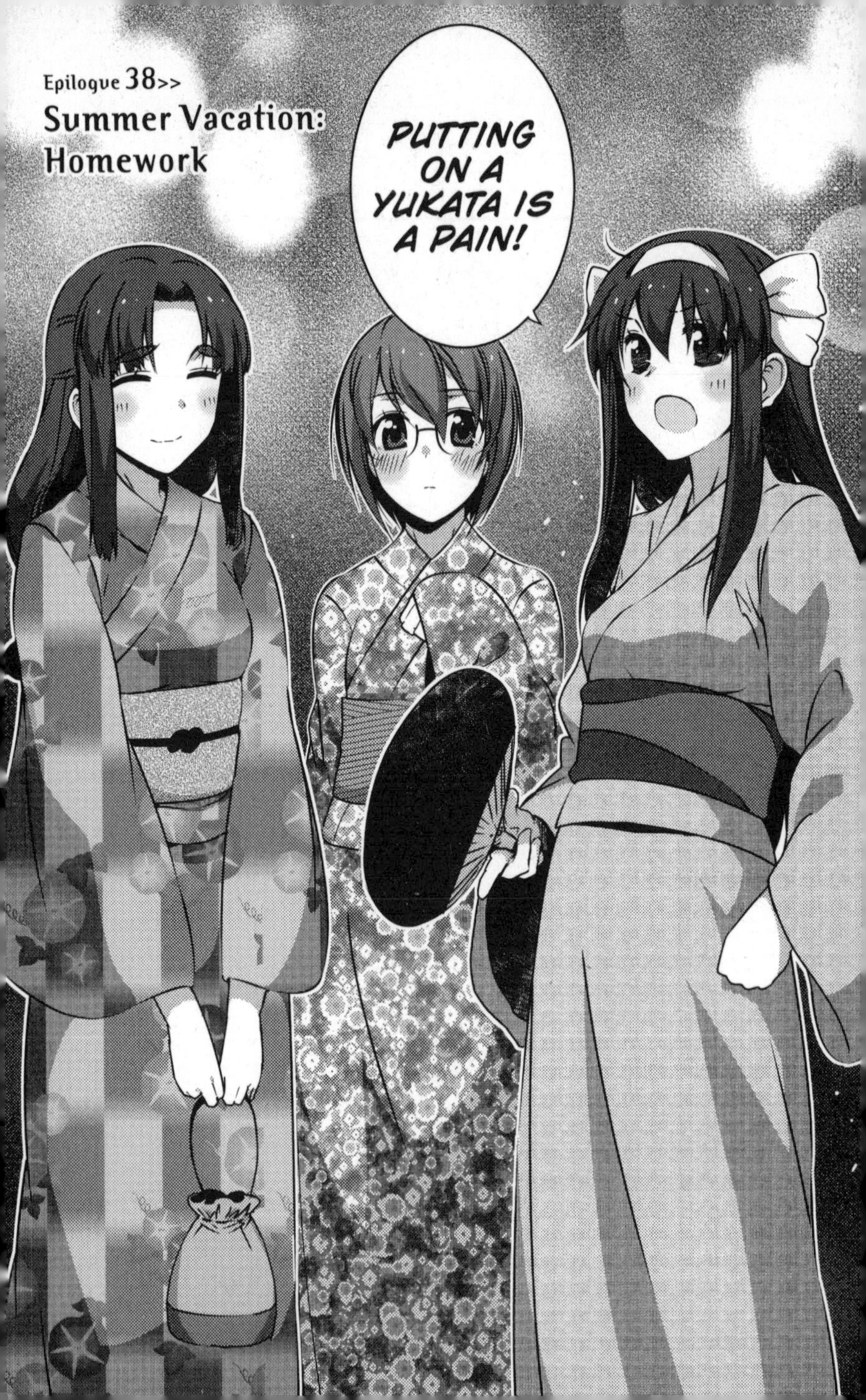
Epilogue 38>>
Summer Vacation: Homework
PUTTING ON A YUKATA IS A PAIN!

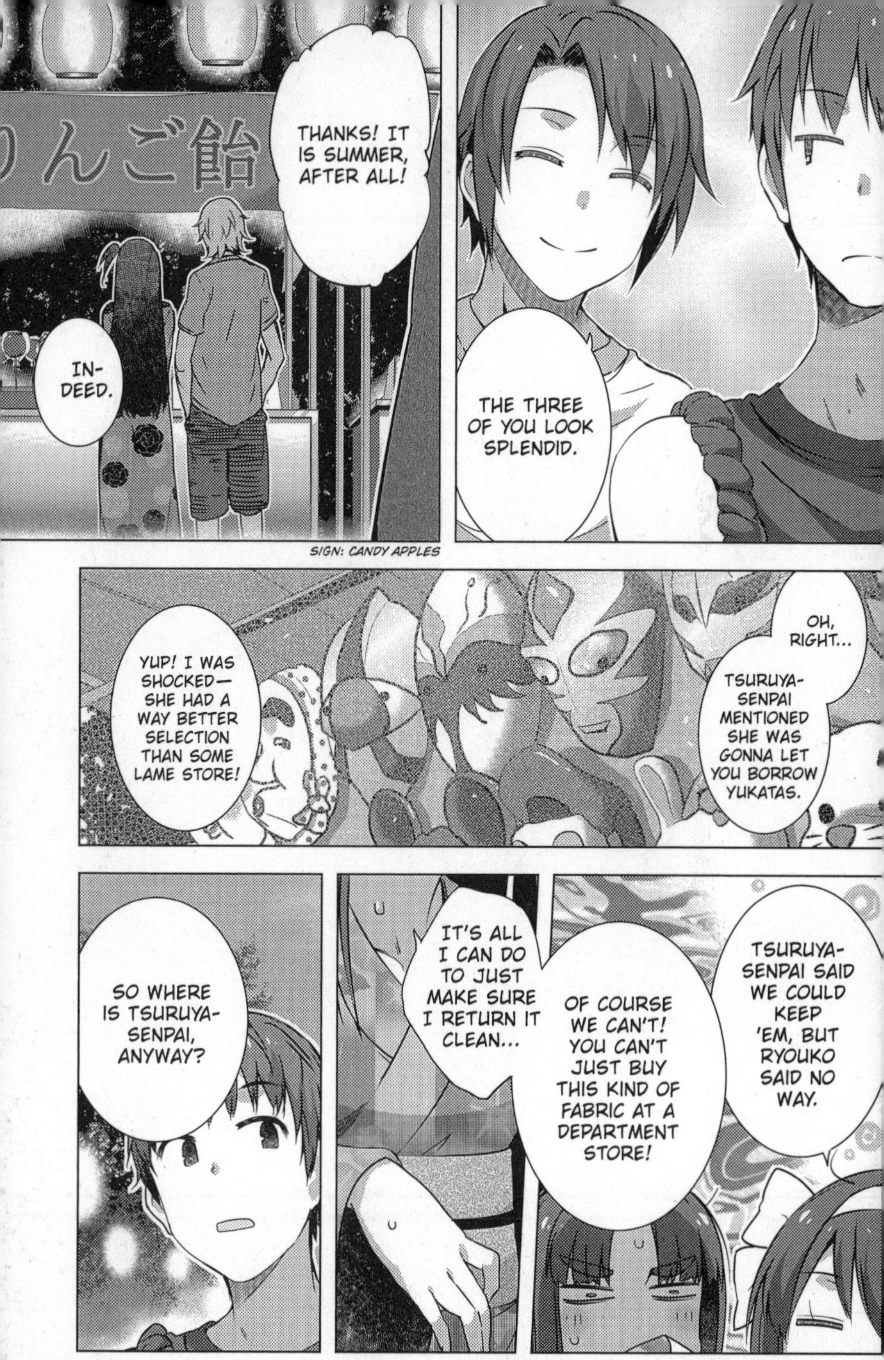
THE THREE OF YOU LOOK SPLENDID.
THANKS! IT IS SUMMER, AFTER ALL!
IN-DEED.
OH, RIGHT...
TSURUYA-SENPAI MENTIONED SHE WAS GONNA LET YOU BORROW YUKATAS.
YUP! I WAS SHOCKED—SHE HAD A WAY BETTER SELECTION THAN SOME LAME STORE!
TSURUYA-SENPAI SAID WE COULD KEEP 'EM, BUT RYOUKO SAID NO WAY.
OF COURSE WE CAN'T! YOU CAN'T JUST BUY THIS KIND OF FABRIC AT A DEPARTMENT STORE!
IT'S ALL I CAN DO TO JUST MAKE SURE I RETURN IT CLEAN...
SO WHERE IS TSURUYA-SENPAI, ANYWAY?

SIGN: CANDY APPLES

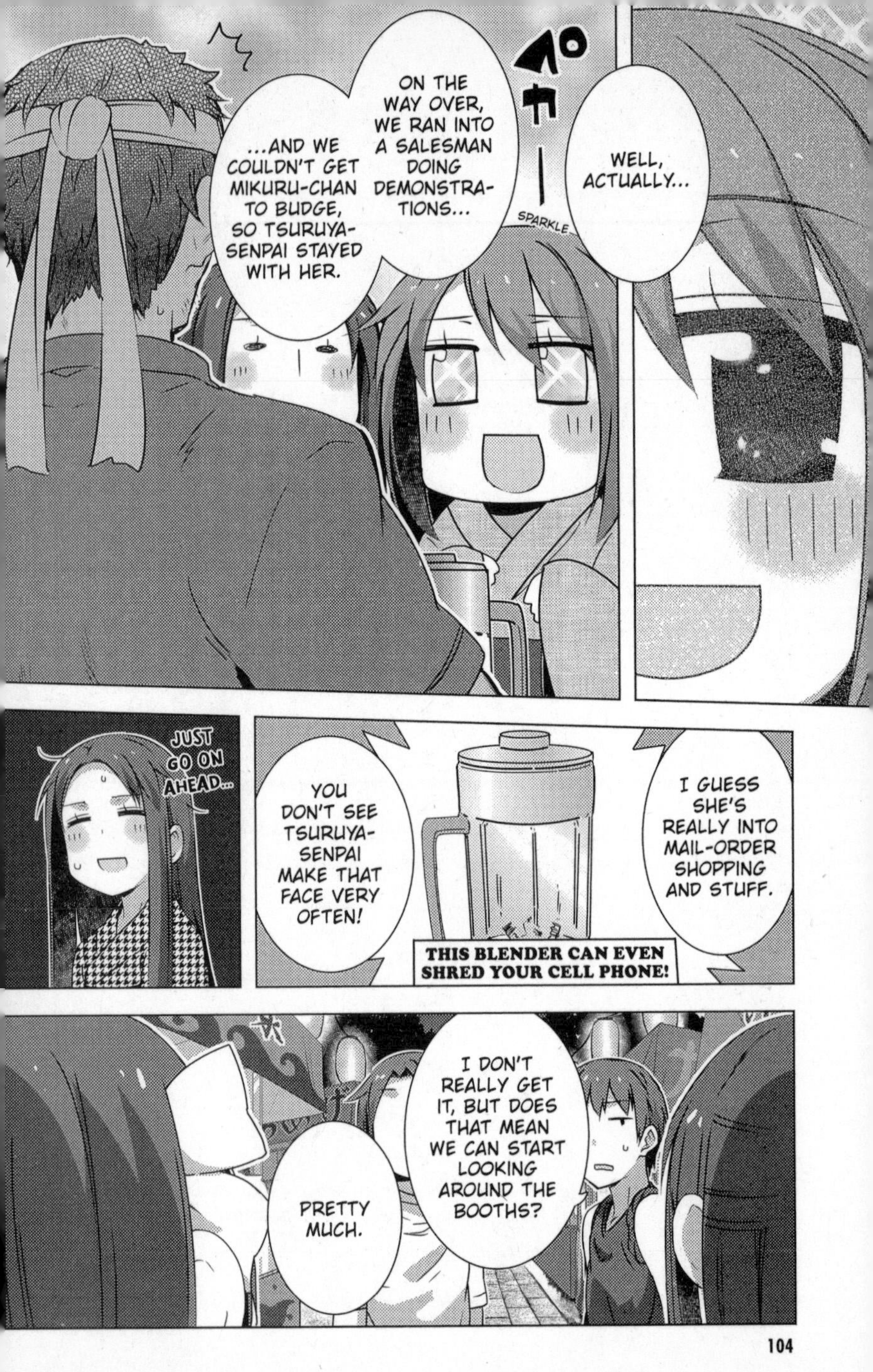
WELL, ACTUALLY...
ペカー
SPARKLE
ON THE WAY OVER, WE RAN INTO A SALESMAN DOING DEMONSTRATIONS...
...AND WE COULDN'T GET MIKURU-CHAN TO BUDGE, SO TSURUYA-SENPAI STAYED WITH HER.
I GUESS SHE'S REALLY INTO MAIL-ORDER SHOPPING AND STUFF.
YOU DON'T SEE TSURUYA-SENPAI MAKE THAT FACE VERY OFTEN!
THIS BLENDER CAN EVEN SHRED YOUR CELL PHONE!
JUST GO ON AHEAD...
I DON'T REALLY GET IT, BUT DOES THAT MEAN WE CAN START LOOKING AROUND THE BOOTHS?
PRETTY MUCH.

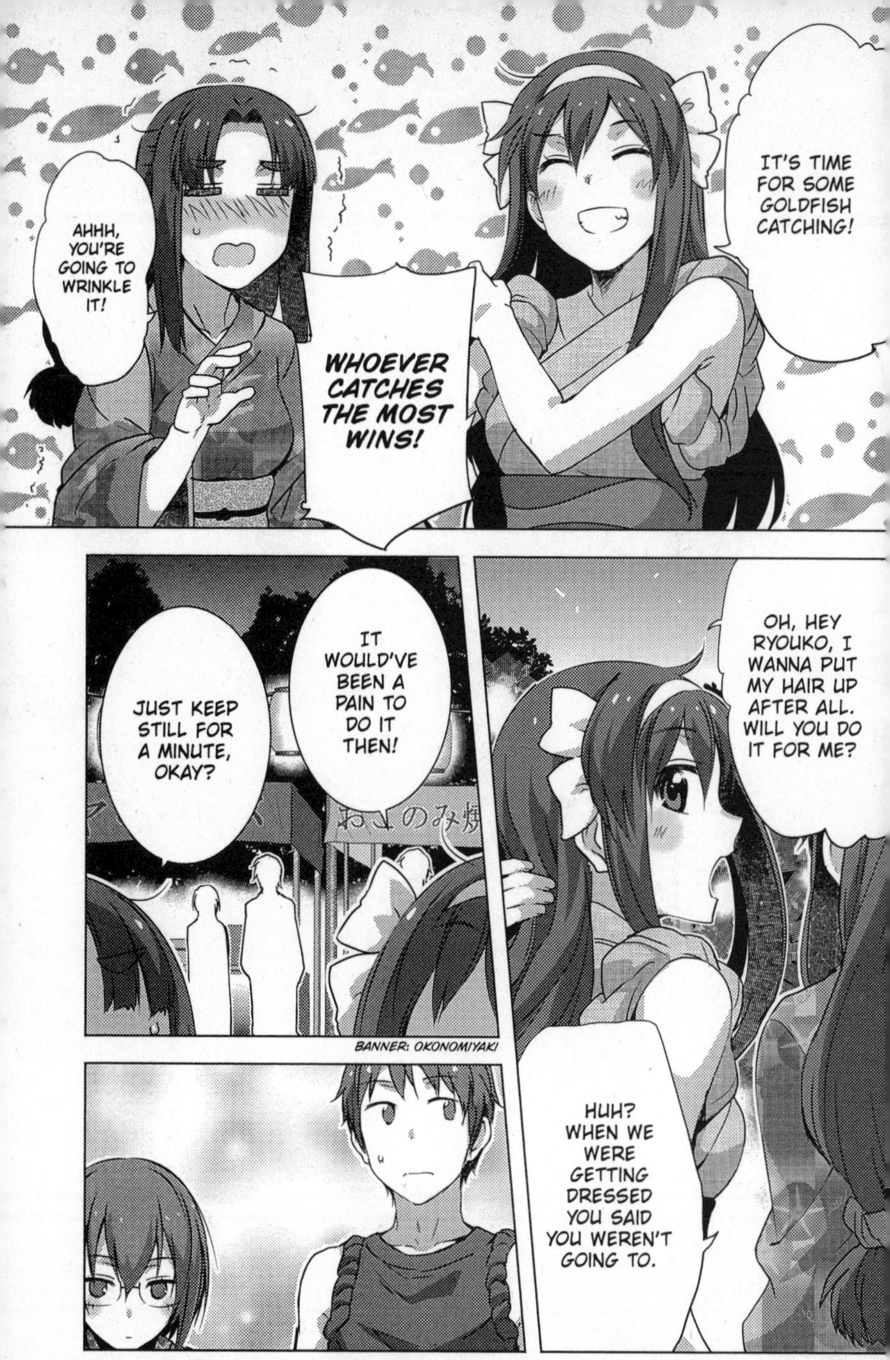
IT'S TIME FOR SOME GOLDFISH CATCHING!
WHOEVER CATCHES THE MOST WINS!
AHHH, YOU'RE GOING TO WRINKLE IT!
OH, HEY RYOUKO, I WANNA PUT MY HAIR UP AFTER ALL. WILL YOU DO IT FOR ME?
HUH? WHEN WE WERE GETTING DRESSED YOU SAID YOU WEREN'T GOING TO.
IT WOULD'VE BEEN A PAIN TO DO IT THEN!
JUST KEEP STILL FOR A MINUTE, OKAY?
BANNER: OKONOMIYAKI

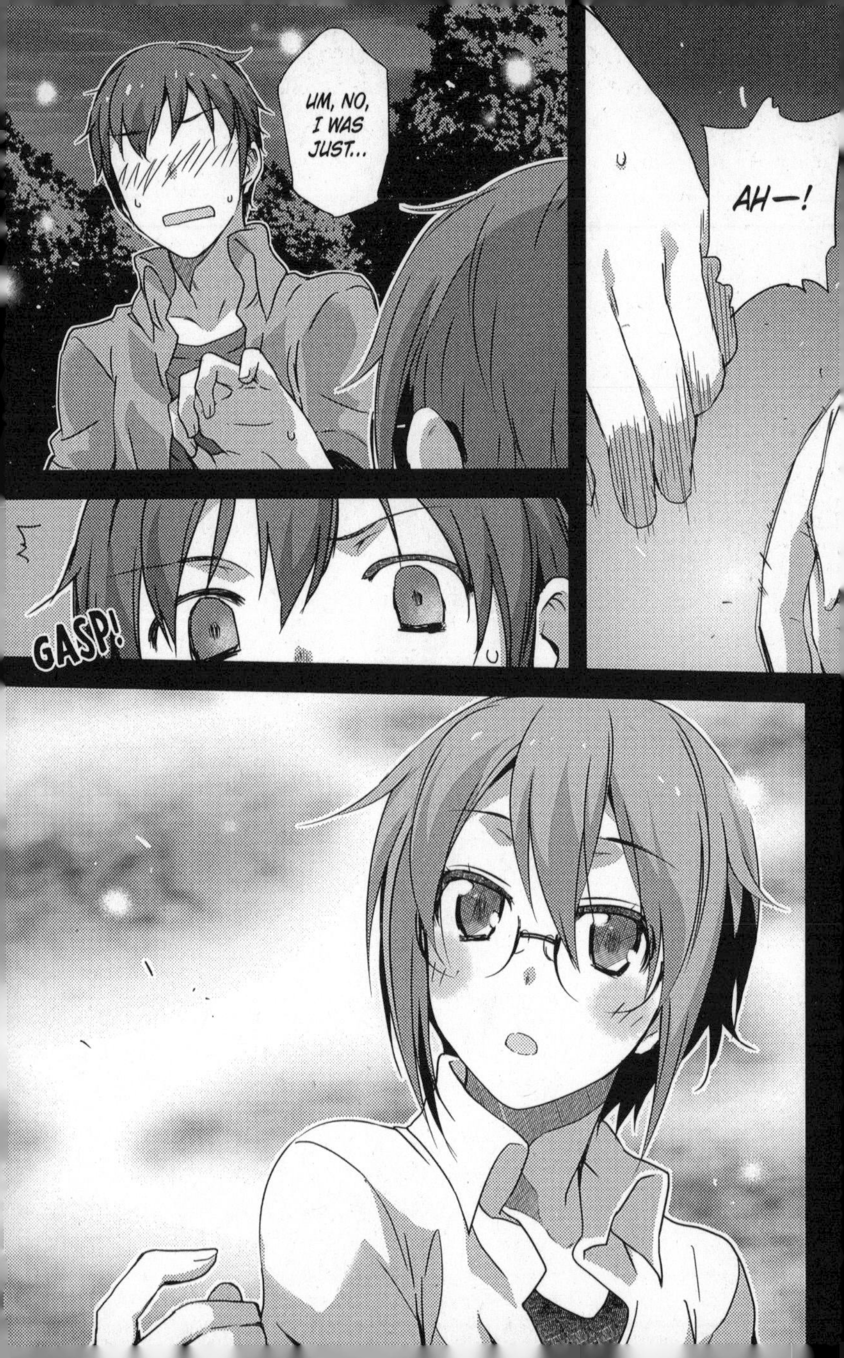
AH—!
UM, NO, I WAS JUST...
GASP!

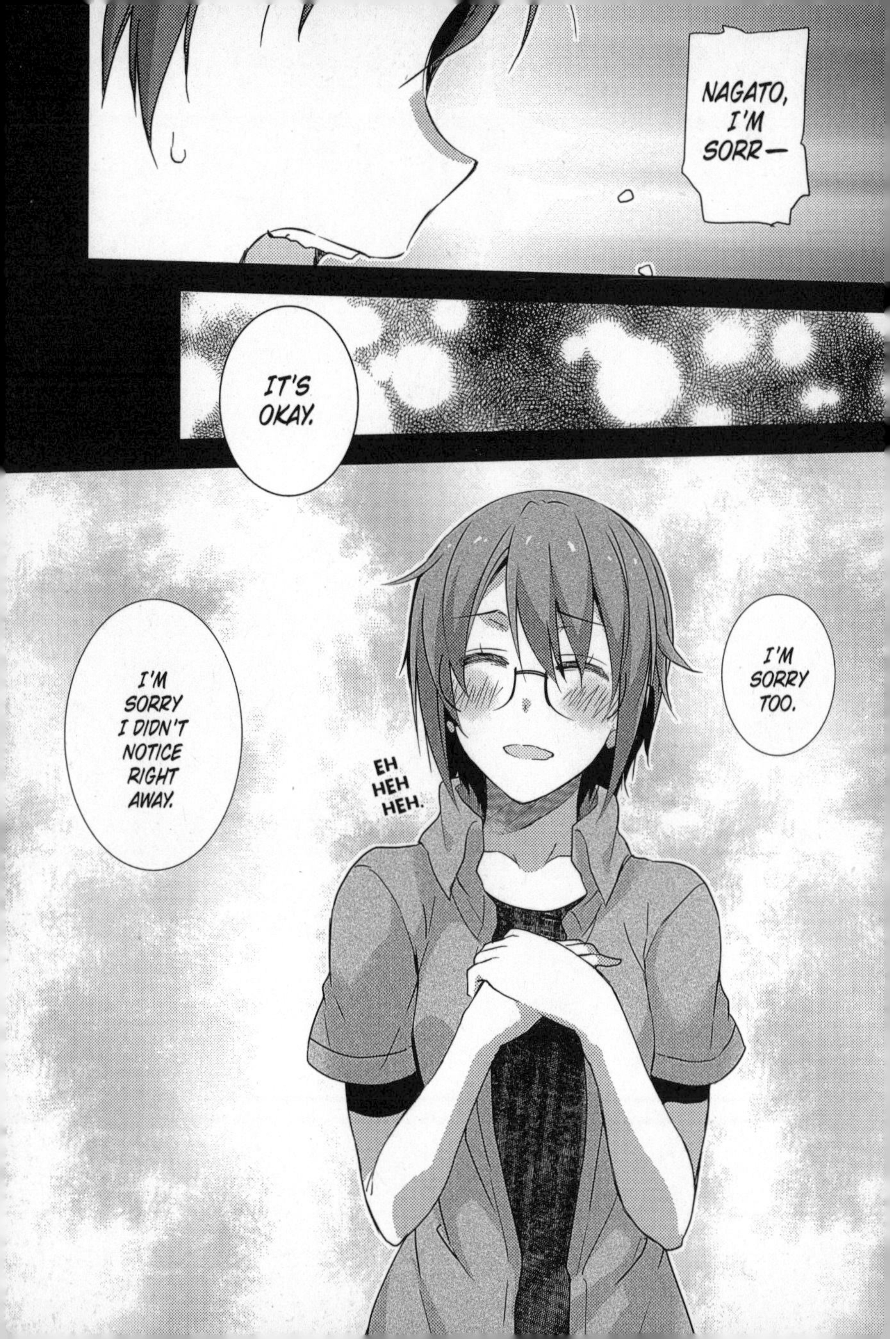
NAGATO, I'M SORR—
IT'S OKAY.
I'M SORRY TOO.
EH HEH HEH.
I'M SORRY I DIDN'T NOTICE RIGHT AWAY.

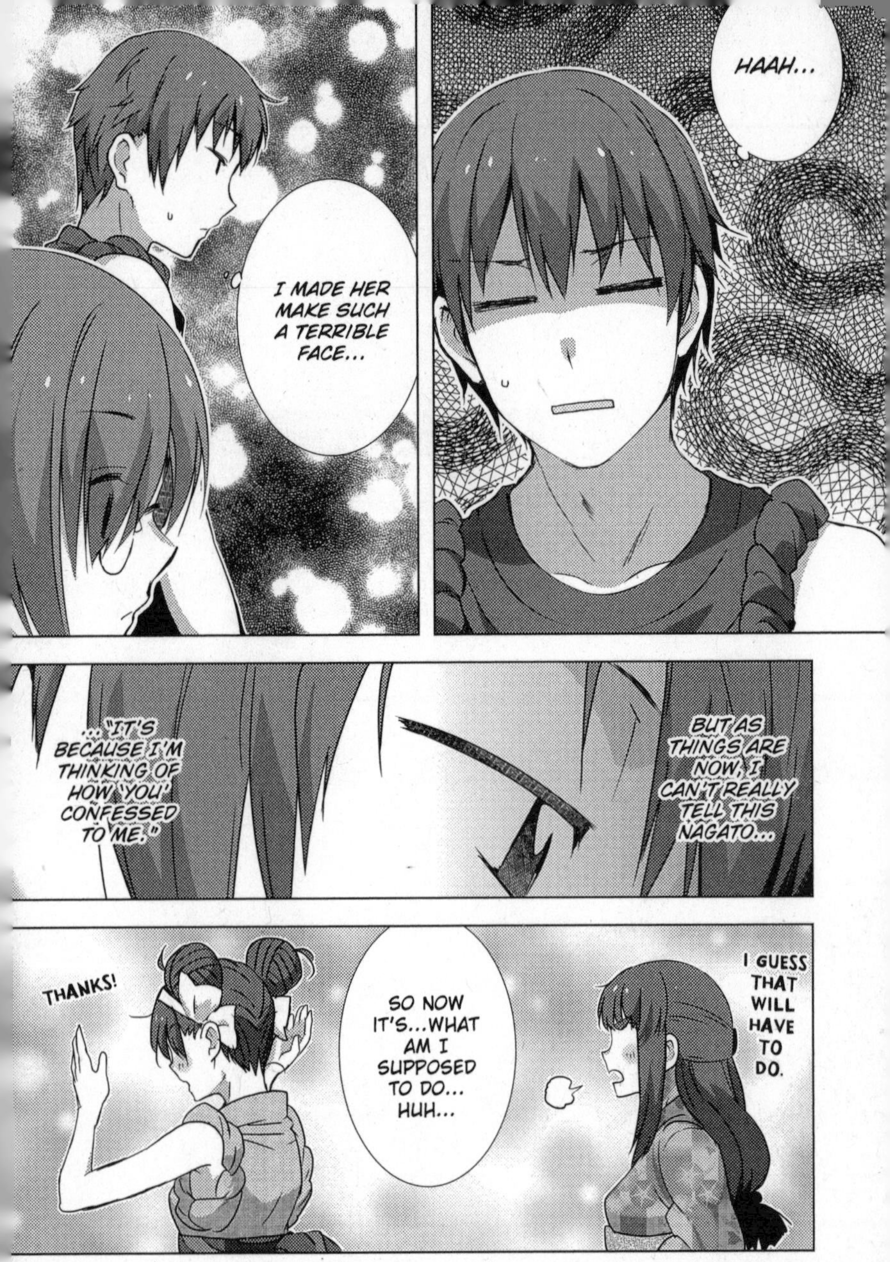
HAAH...
I MADE HER MAKE SUCH A TERRIBLE FACE...
BUT AS THINGS ARE NOW, I CAN'T REALLY TELL THIS NAGATO...
..."IT'S BECAUSE I'M THINKING OF HOW 'YOU' CONFESSED TO ME."
I GUESS THAT WILL HAVE TO DO.
SO NOW IT'S...WHAT AM I SUPPOSED TO DO... HUH...
THANKS!

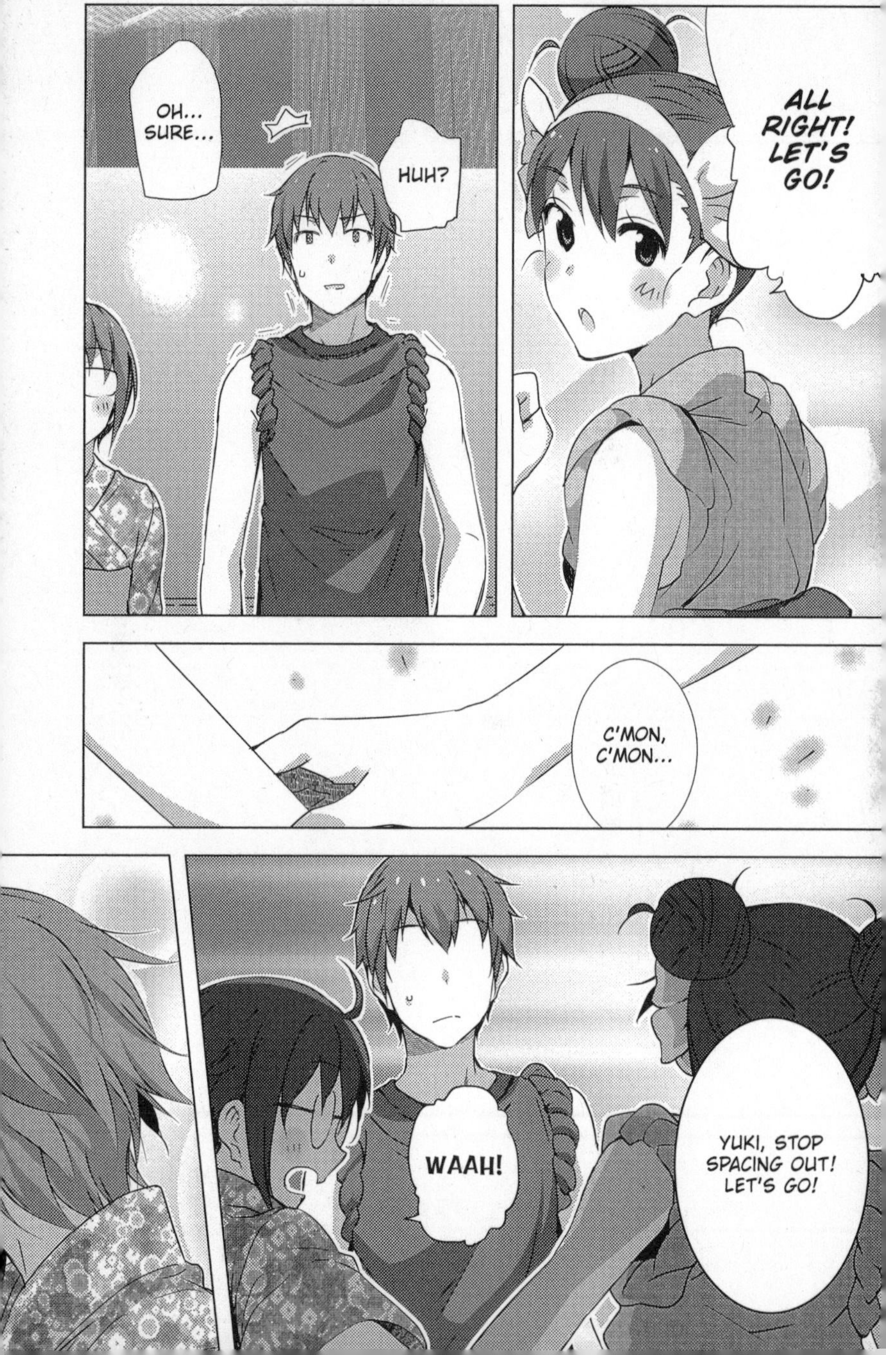
ALL RIGHT! LET'S GO!
HUH?
OH... SURE...
C'MON, C'MON...
YUKI, STOP SPACING OUT! LET'S GO!
WAAH!

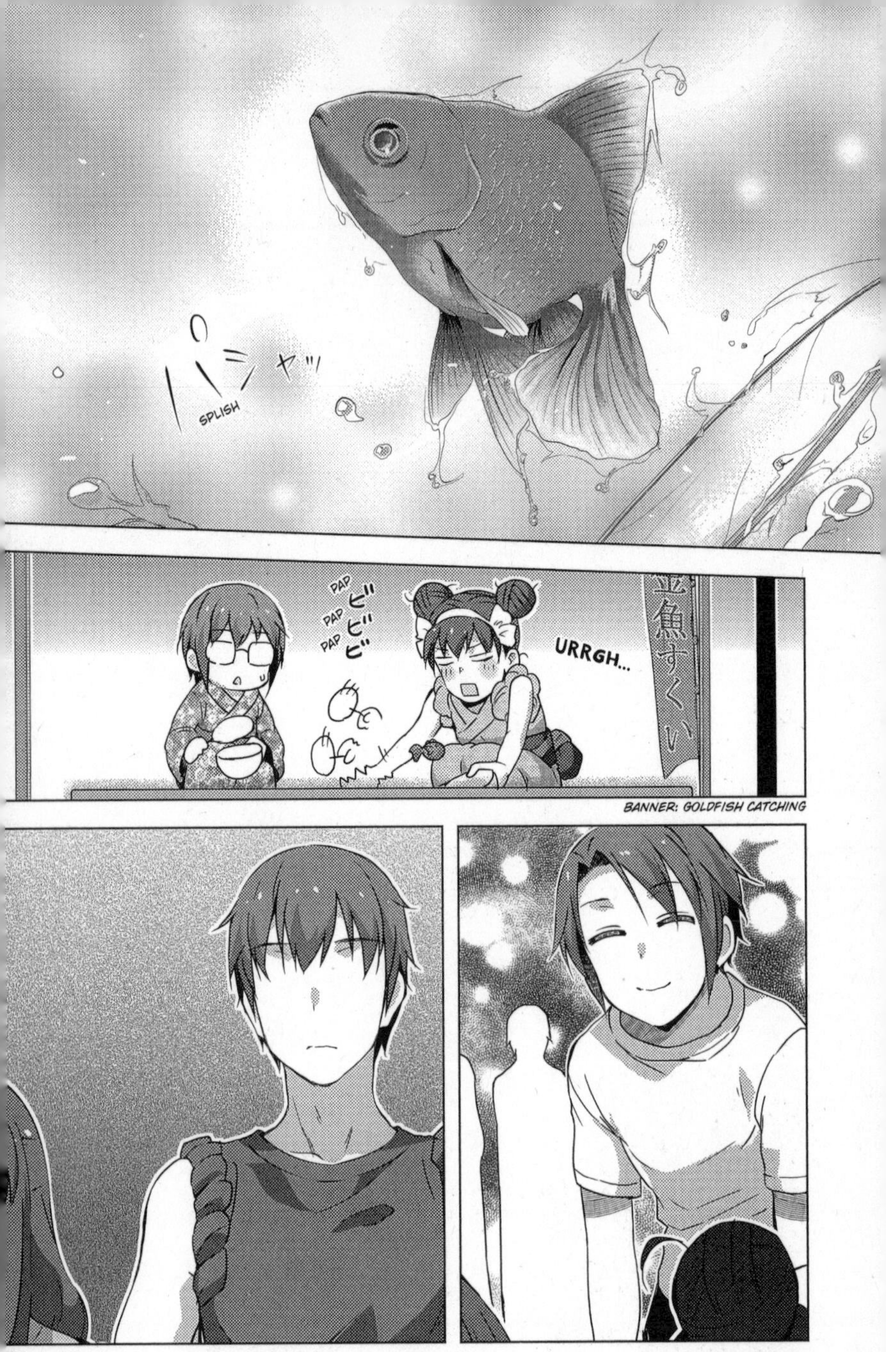
パシャッ
SPLISH
ビビビ
PAP PAP PAP
URRGH...
金魚すくい
BANNER: GOLDFISH CATCHING

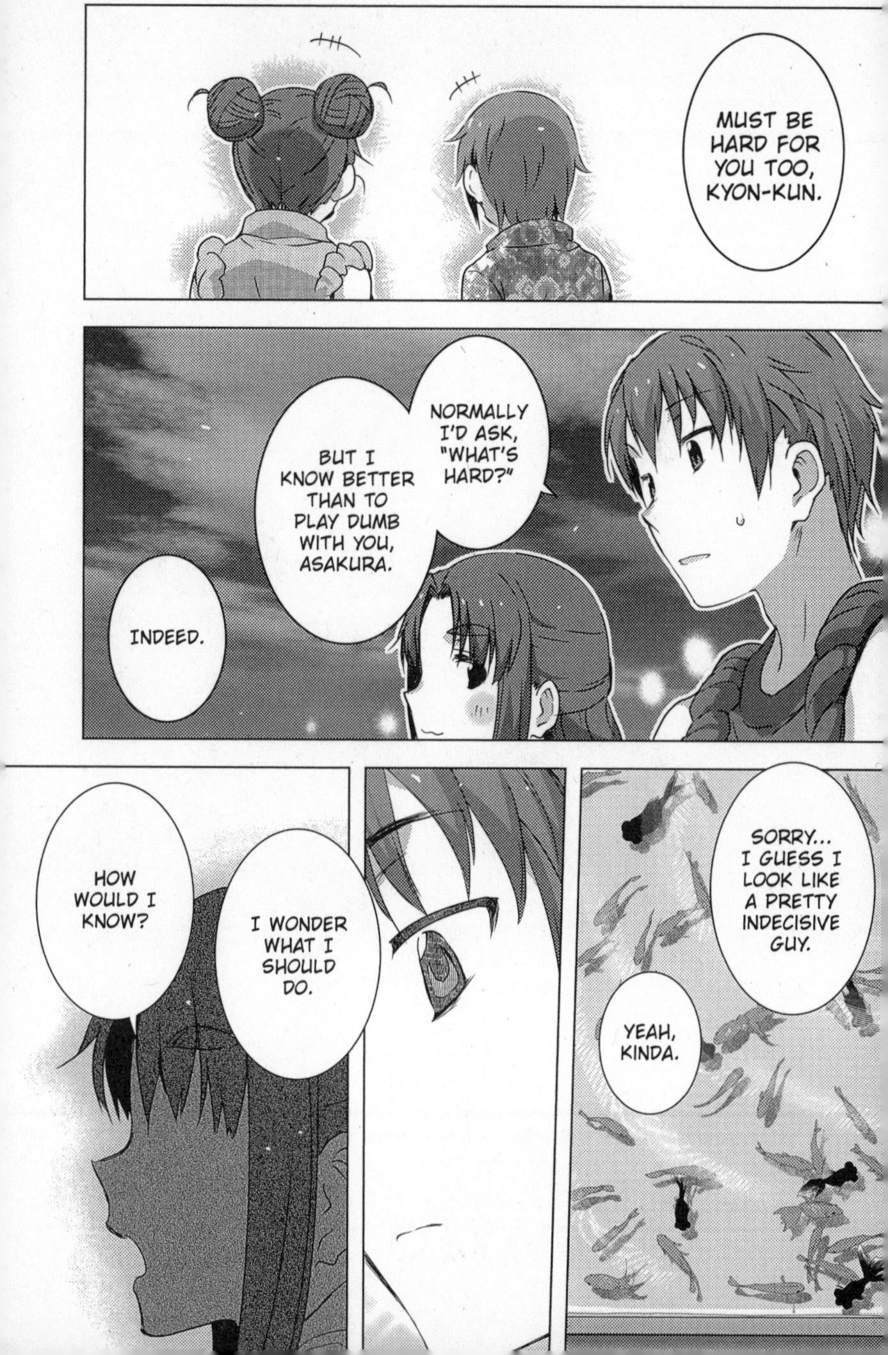
MUST BE HARD FOR YOU TOO, KYON-KUN.
NORMALLY I'D ASK, "WHAT'S HARD?"
BUT I KNOW BETTER THAN TO PLAY DUMB WITH YOU, ASAKURA.
INDEED.
SORRY... I GUESS I LOOK LIKE A PRETTY INDECISIVE GUY.
YEAH, KINDA.
I WONDER WHAT I SHOULD DO.
HOW WOULD I KNOW?

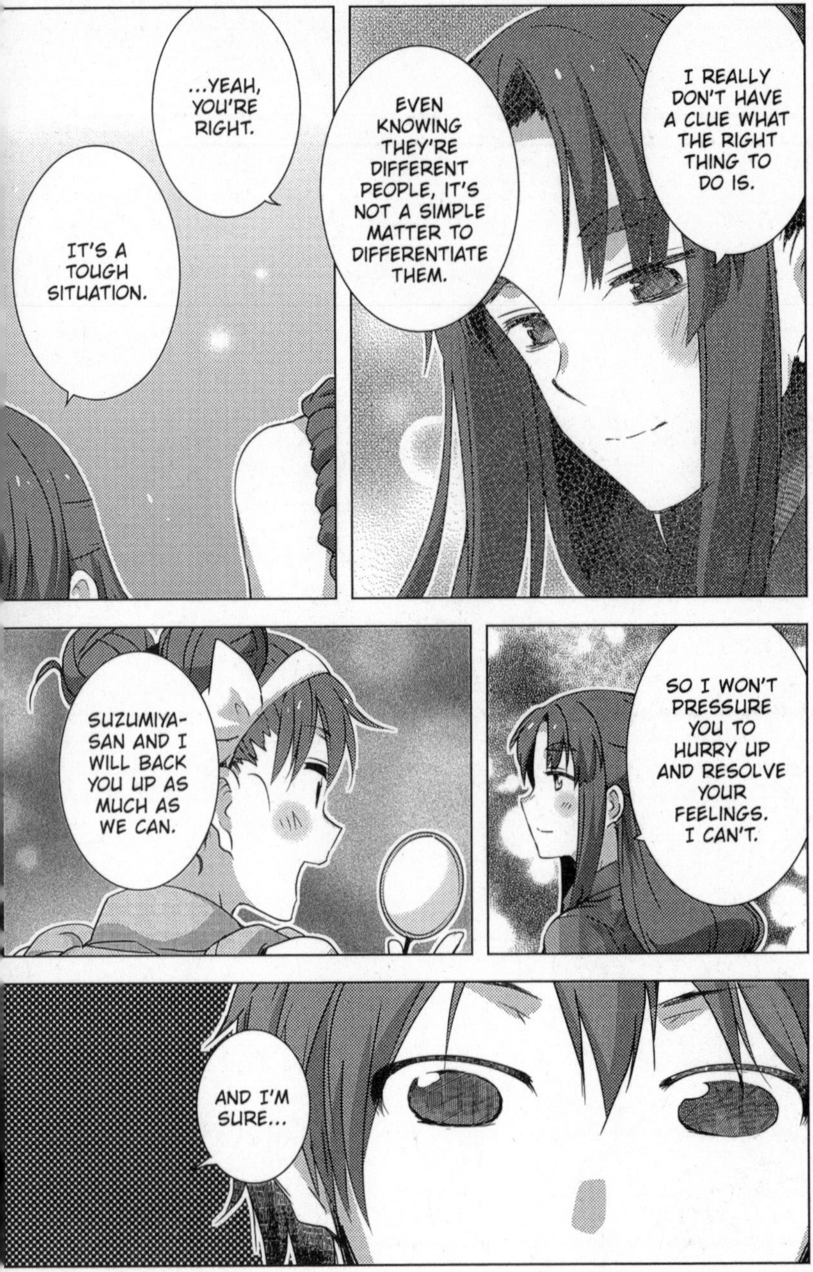
I REALLY DON'T HAVE A CLUE WHAT THE RIGHT THING TO DO IS.
EVEN KNOWING THEY'RE DIFFERENT PEOPLE, IT'S NOT A SIMPLE MATTER TO DIFFERENTIATE THEM.
...YEAH, YOU'RE RIGHT.
IT'S A TOUGH SITUATION.
SO I WON'T PRESSURE YOU TO HURRY UP AND RESOLVE YOUR FEELINGS. I CAN'T.
SUZUMIYA-SAN AND I WILL BACK YOU UP AS MUCH AS WE CAN.
AND I'M SURE...

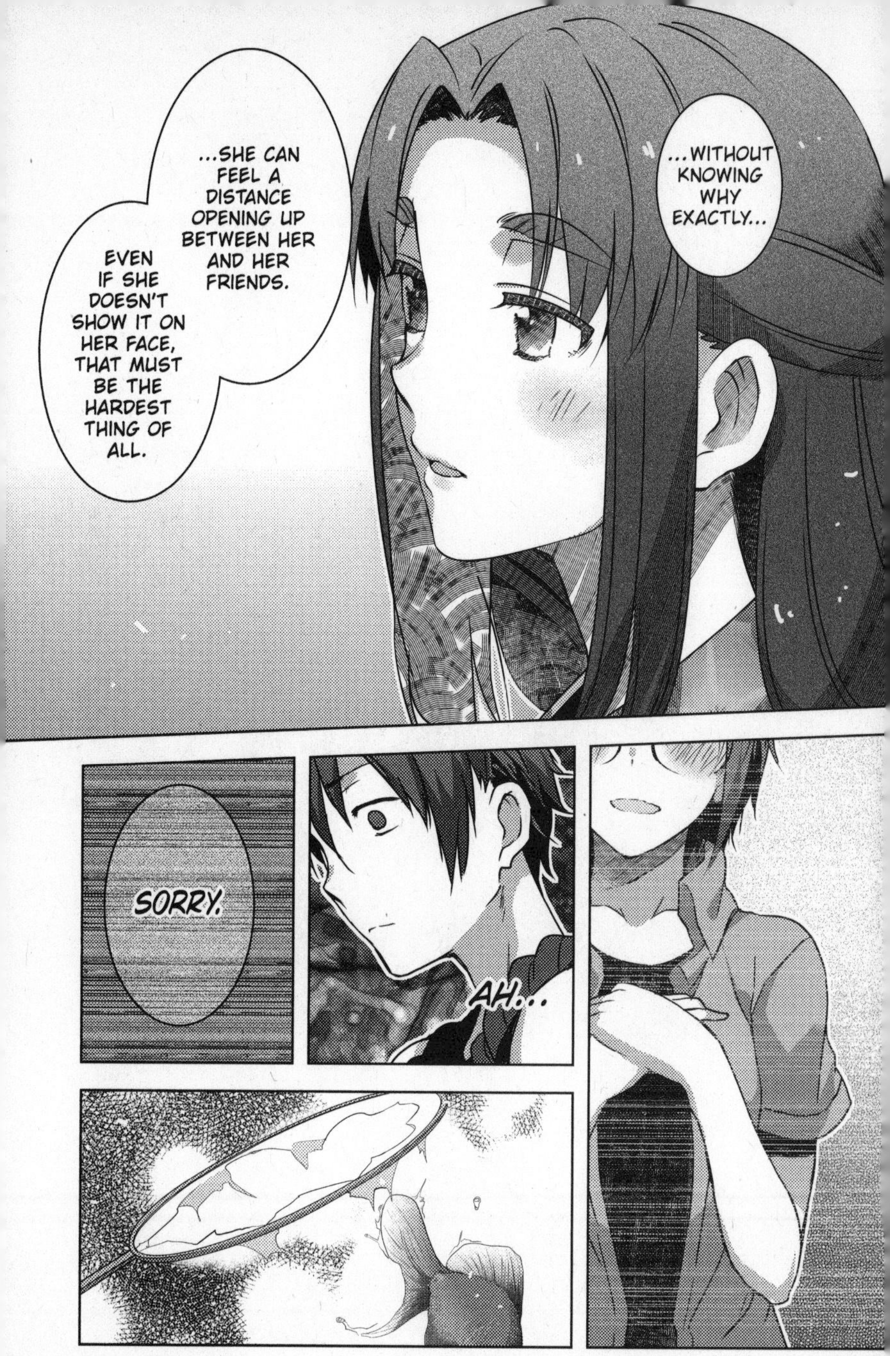
...WITHOUT KNOWING WHY EXACTLY...
...SHE CAN FEEL A DISTANCE OPENING UP BETWEEN HER AND HER FRIENDS.
EVEN IF SHE DOESN'T SHOW IT ON HER FACE, THAT MUST BE THE HARDEST THING OF ALL.
AH...
SORRY.

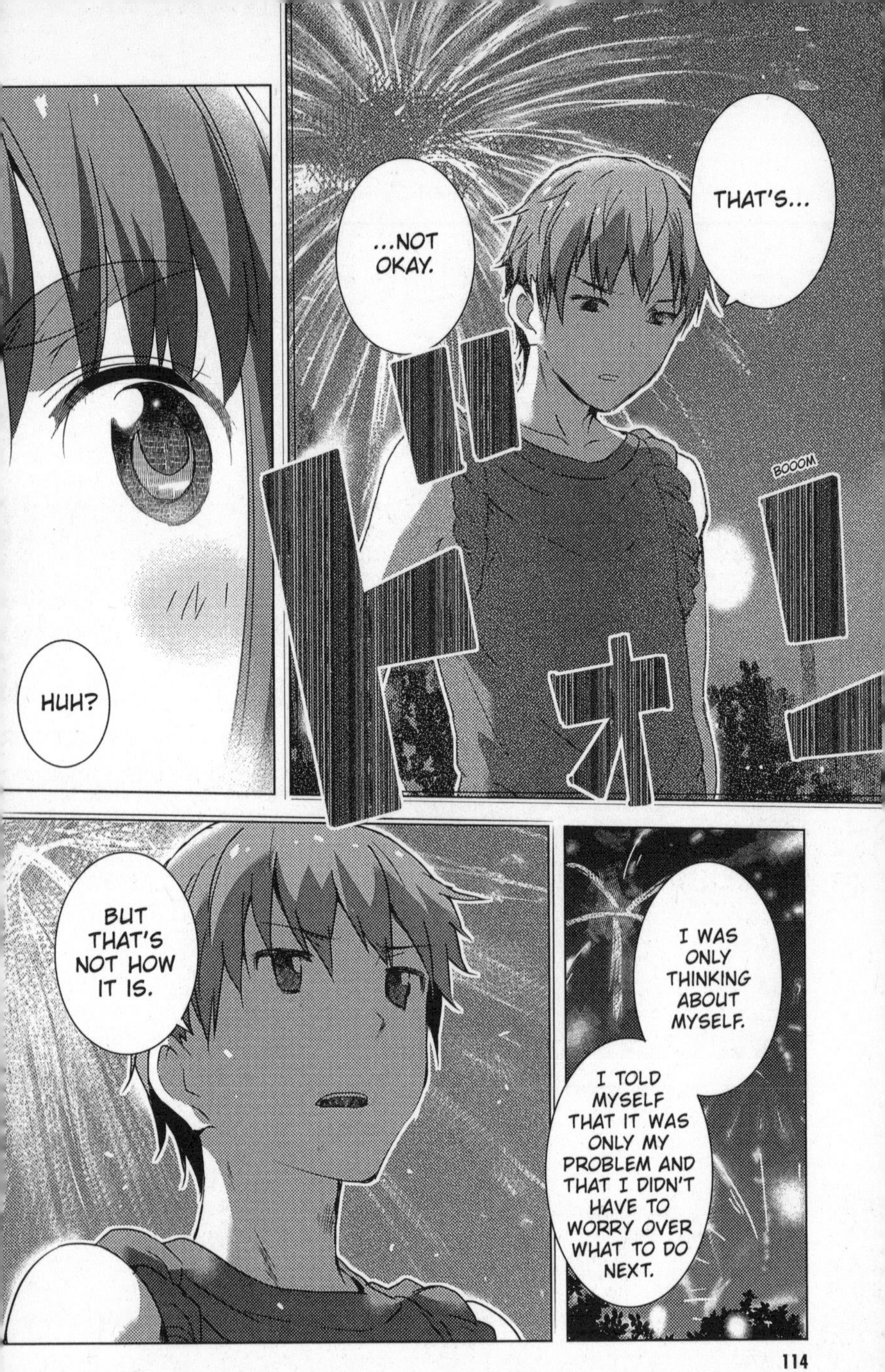
THAT'S...
...NOT OKAY.
BOOOM
HUH?
I WAS ONLY THINKING ABOUT MYSELF.
I TOLD MYSELF THAT IT WAS ONLY MY PROBLEM AND THAT I DIDN'T HAVE TO WORRY OVER WHAT TO DO NEXT.
BUT THAT'S NOT HOW IT IS.

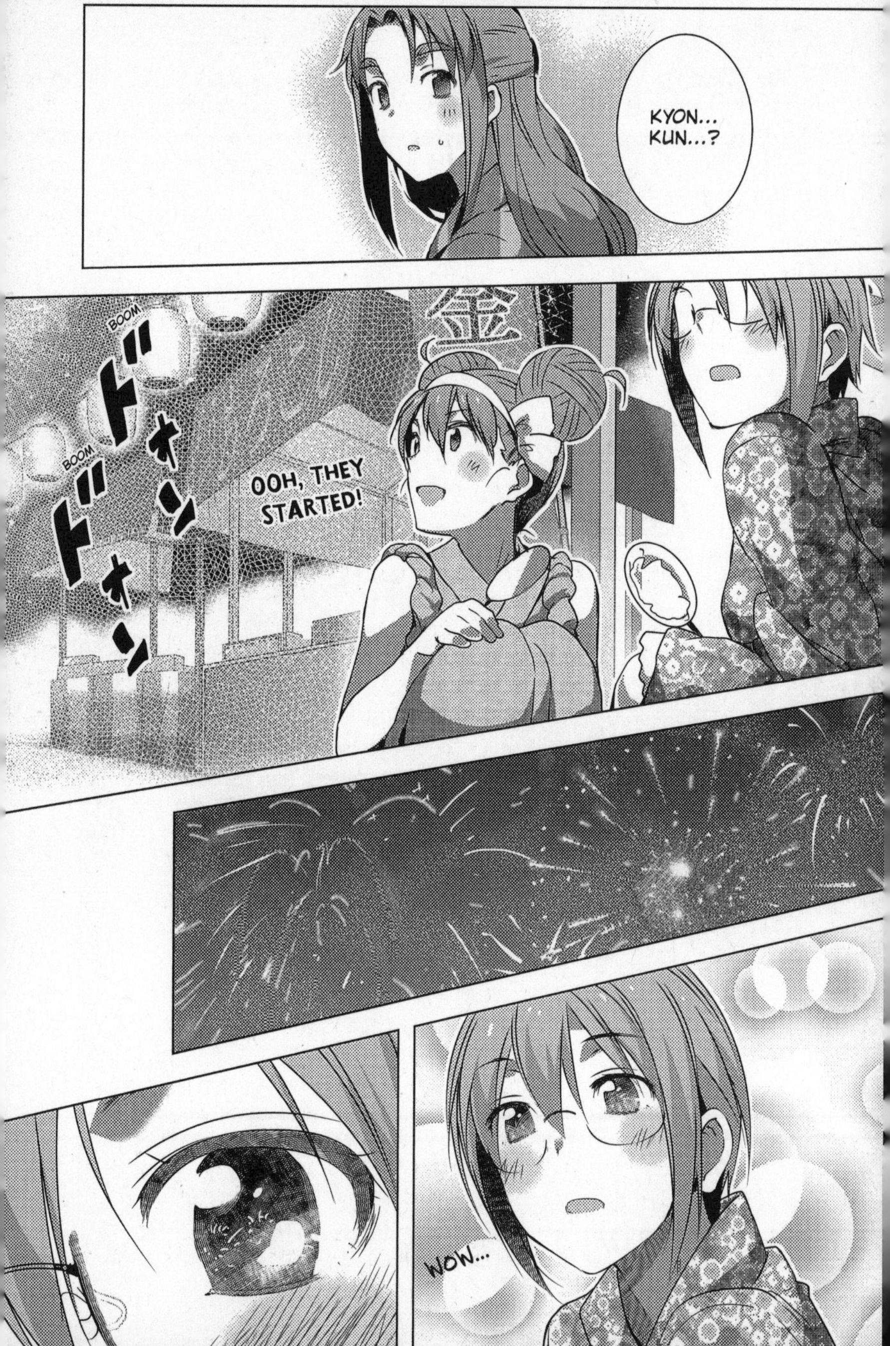
KYON... KUN...?
OOH, THEY STARTED!
ドォン
BOOM
ドォン
BOOM
NOW...

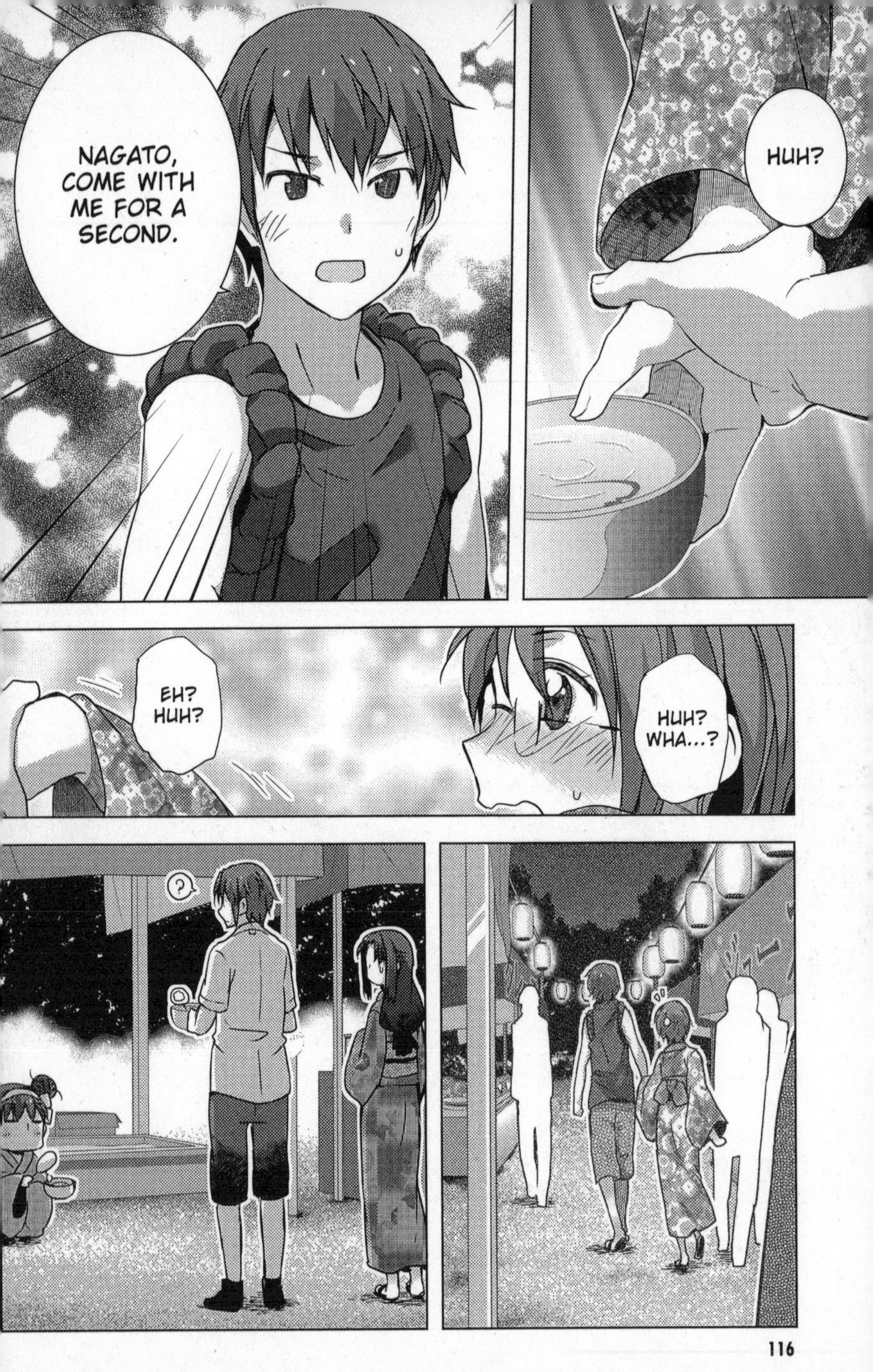
HUH?
NAGATO, COME WITH ME FOR A SECOND.
HUH? WHA...?
EH? HUH?

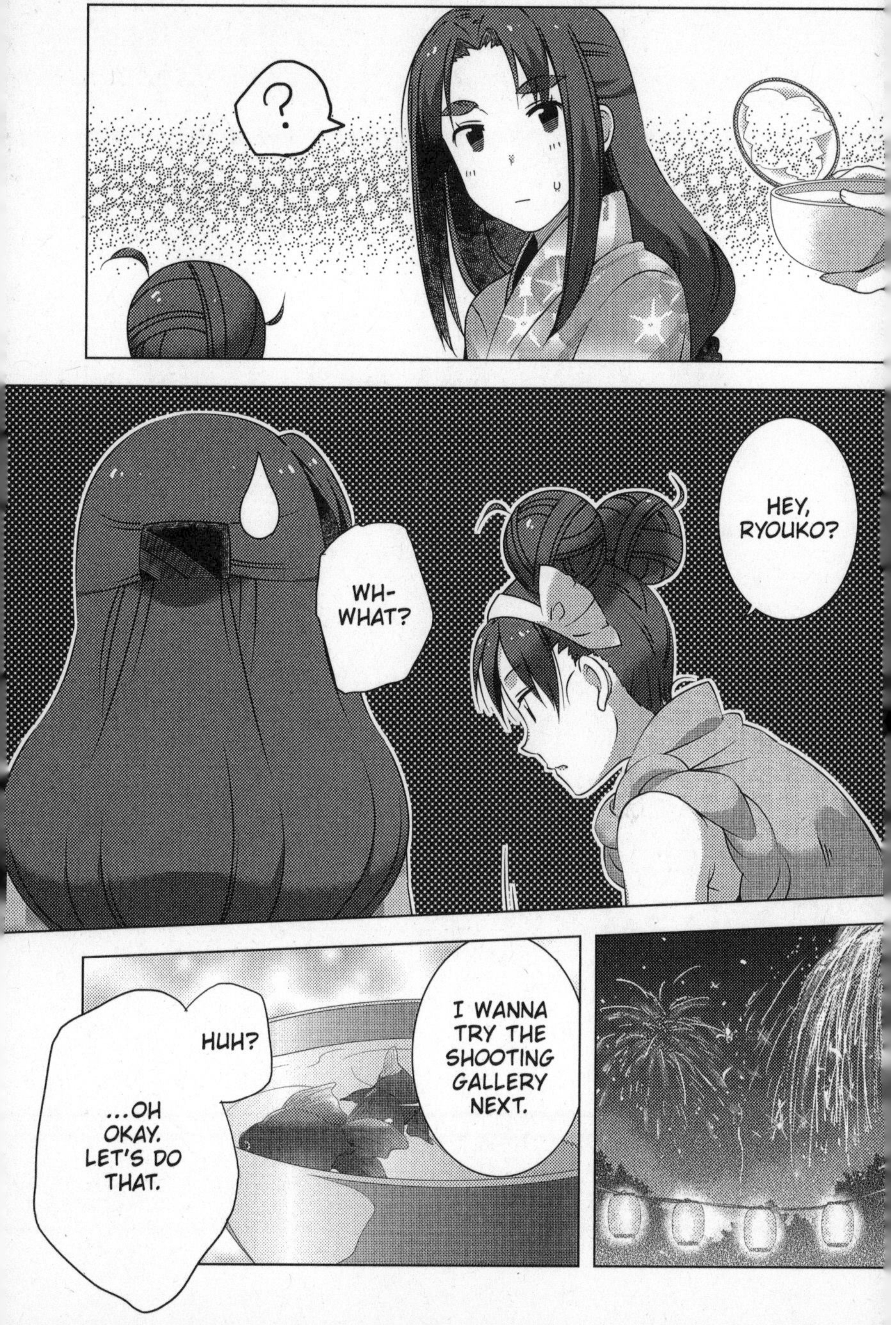
?
HEY, RYOUKO?
WH- WHAT?
I WANNA TRY THE SHOOTING GALLERY NEXT.
HUH?
...OH OKAY. LET'S DO THAT.

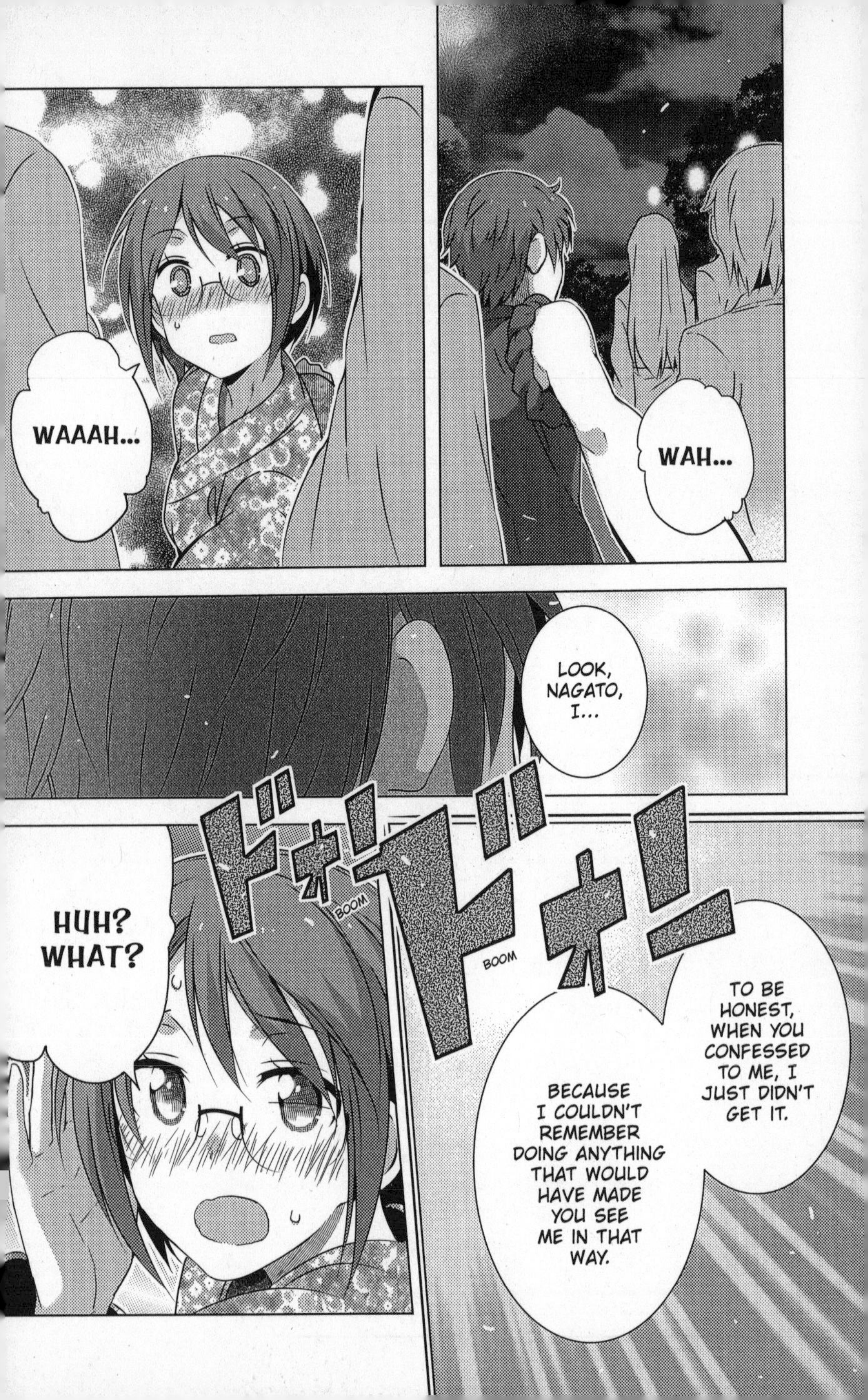
WAH...
WAAAH...
LOOK, NAGATO, I...
ドォ! BOOM
ドォ! BOOM
TO BE HONEST, WHEN YOU CONFESSED TO ME, I JUST DIDN'T GET IT.
BECAUSE I COULDN'T REMEMBER DOING ANYTHING THAT WOULD HAVE MADE YOU SEE ME IN THAT WAY.
HUH? WHAT?

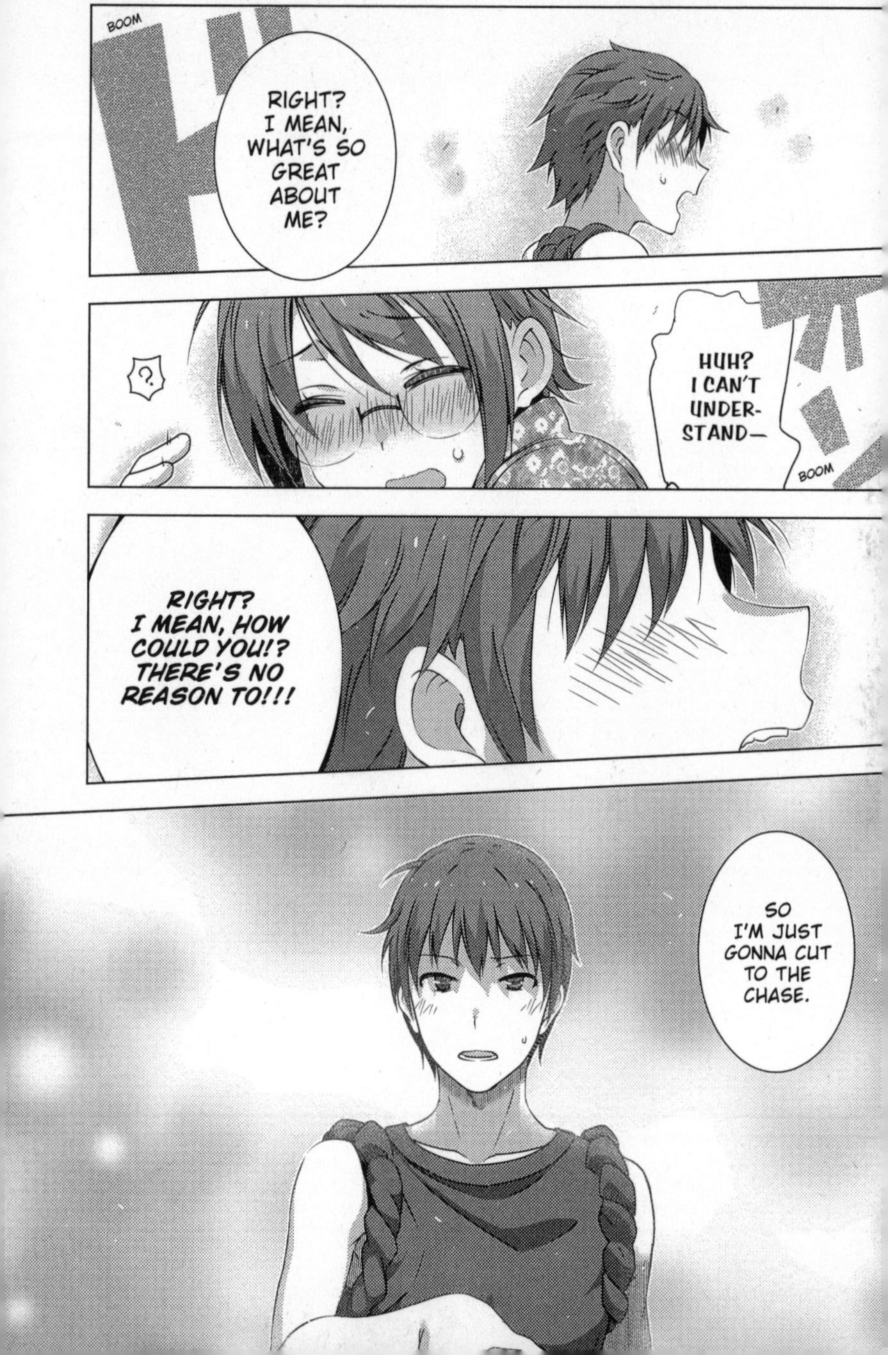
BOOM
RIGHT? I MEAN, WHAT'S SO GREAT ABOUT ME?
HUH? I CAN'T UNDER-STAND—
BOOM
RIGHT? I MEAN, HOW COULD YOU!? THERE'S NO REASON TO!!!
SO I'M JUST GONNA CUT TO THE CHASE.

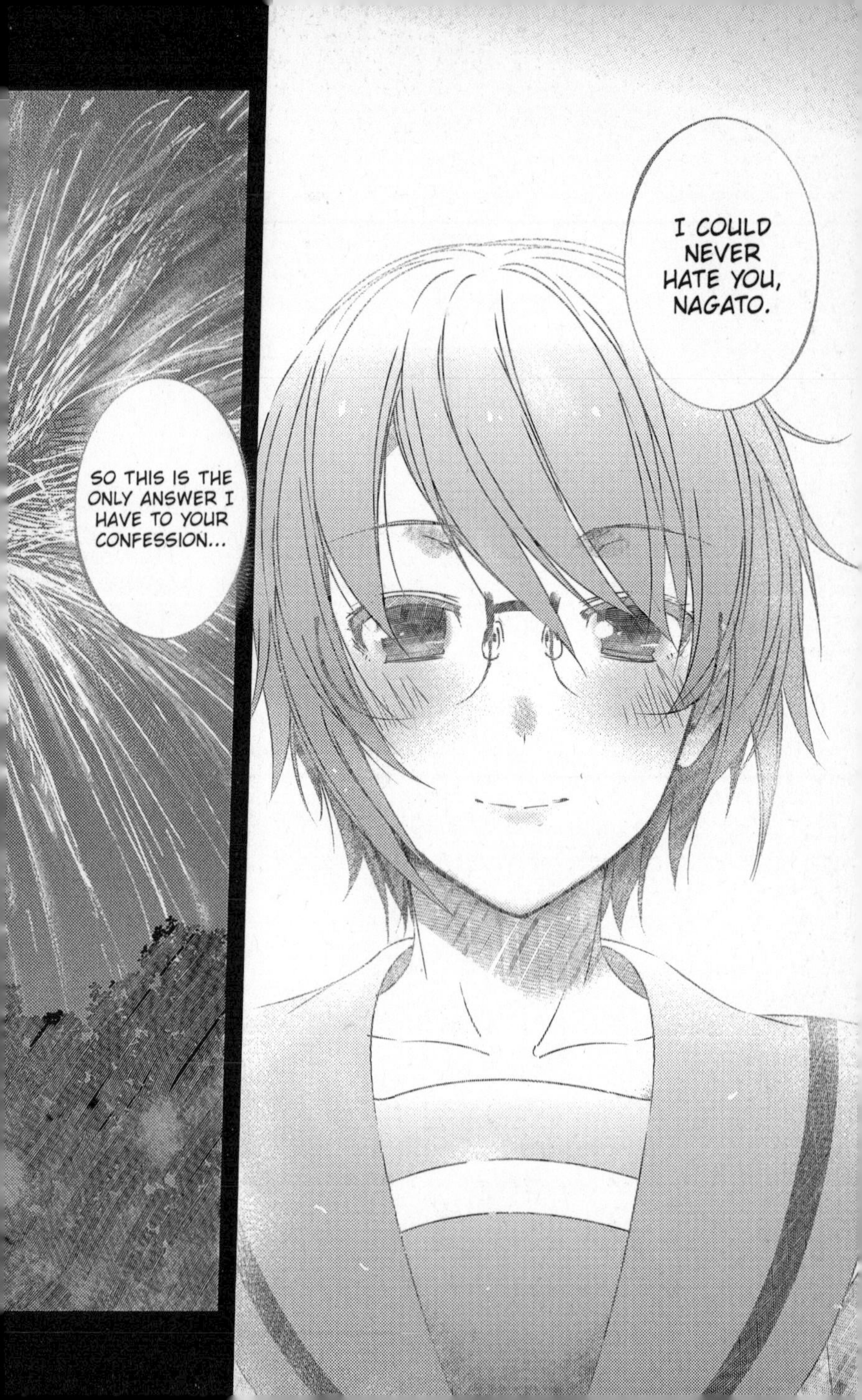
I COULD NEVER HATE YOU, NAGATO.
SO THIS IS THE ONLY ANSWER I HAVE TO YOUR CONFESSION...

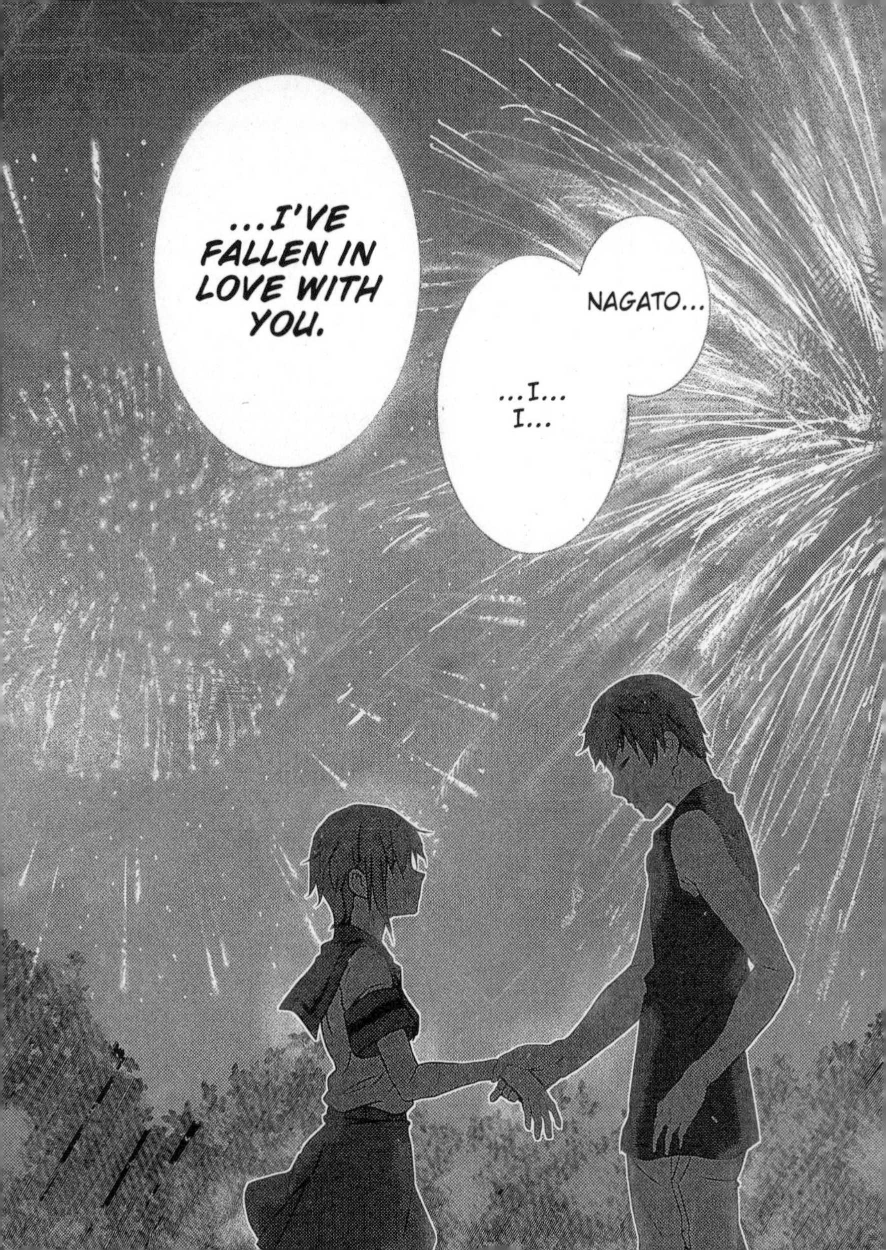
NAGATO...
...I... I...
...I'VE FALLEN IN LOVE WITH YOU.

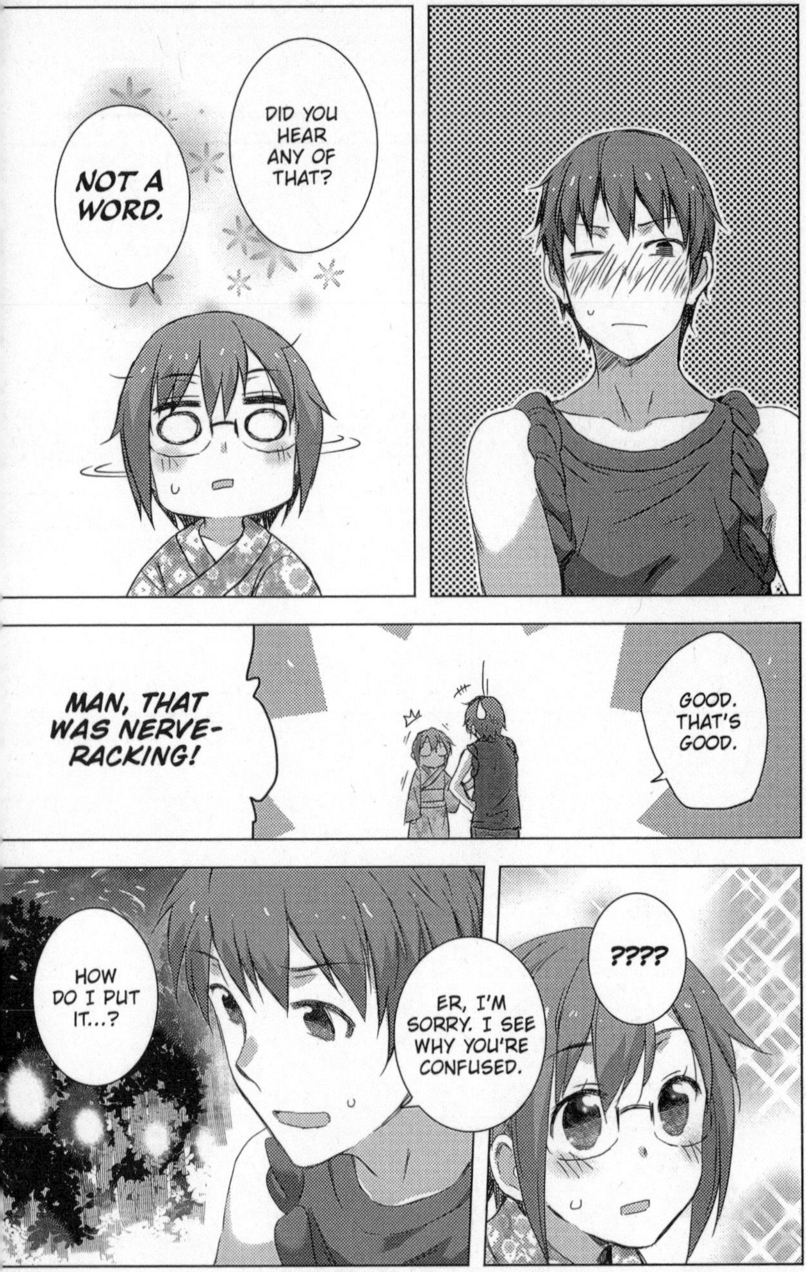
DID YOU HEAR ANY OF THAT?
NOT A WORD.
GOOD. THAT'S GOOD.
MAN, THAT WAS NERVE-RACKING!
????
ER, I'M SORRY. I SEE WHY YOU'RE CONFUSED.
HOW DO I PUT IT...?

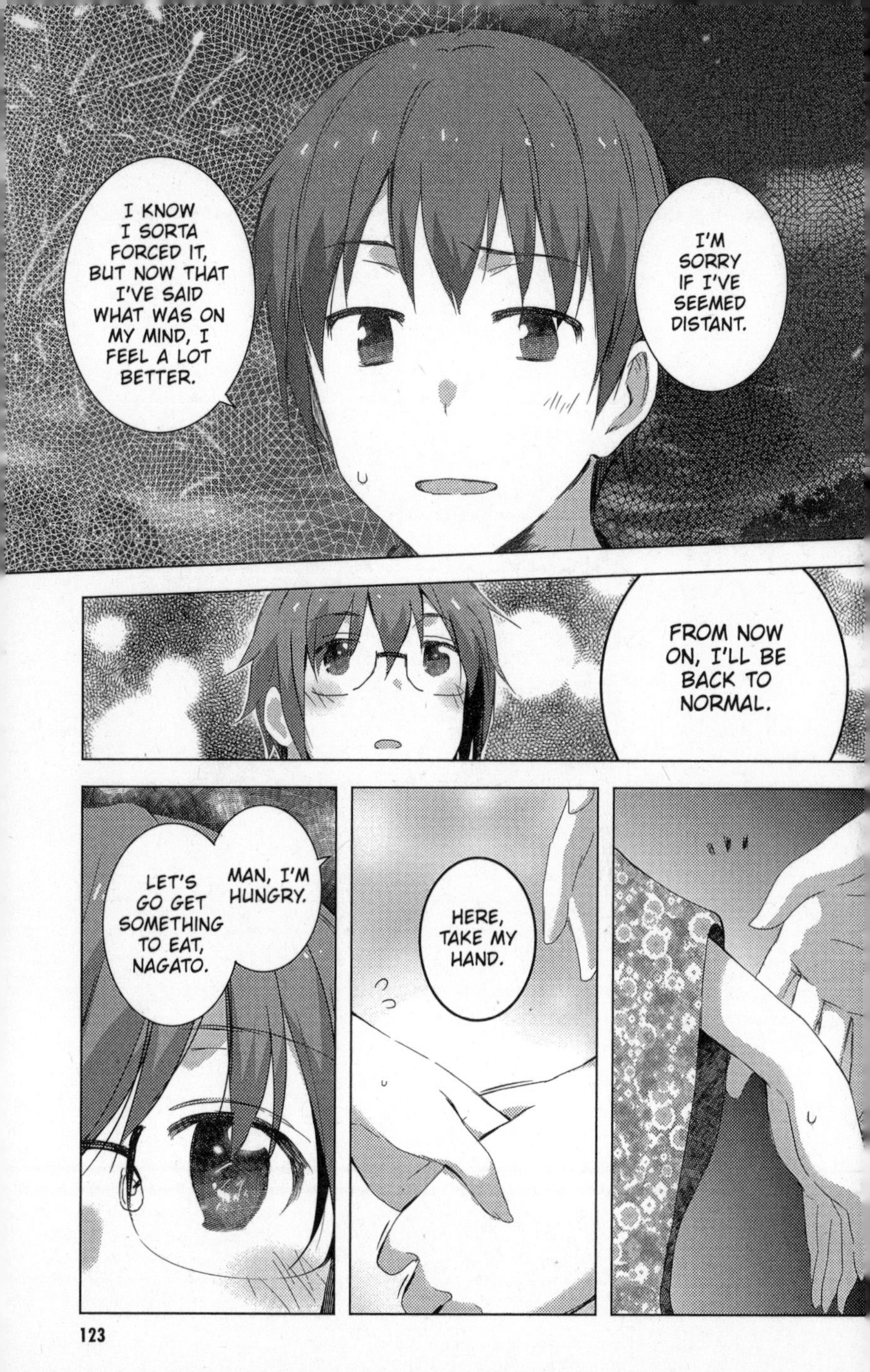
I'M SORRY IF I'VE SEEMED DISTANT.
I KNOW I SORTA FORCED IT, BUT NOW THAT I'VE SAID WHAT WAS ON MY MIND, I FEEL A LOT BETTER.
FROM NOW ON, I'LL BE BACK TO NORMAL.
HERE, TAKE MY HAND.
MAN, I'M HUNGRY.
LET'S GO GET SOMETHING TO EAT, NAGATO.

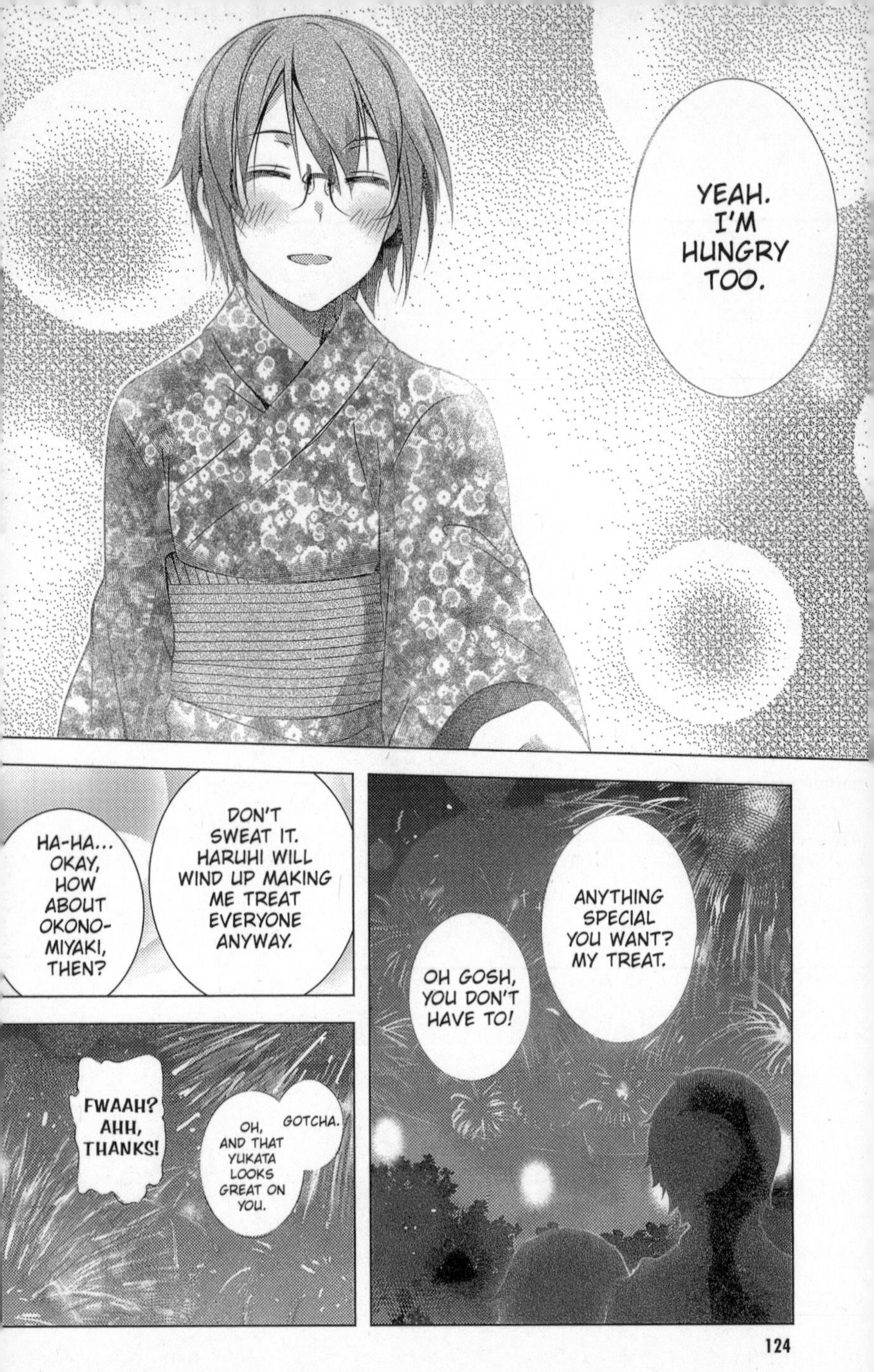
YEAH. I'M HUNGRY TOO.
ANYTHING SPECIAL YOU WANT? MY TREAT.
OH GOSH, YOU DON'T HAVE TO!
DON'T SWEAT IT. HARUHI WILL WIND UP MAKING ME TREAT EVERYONE ANYWAY.
HA-HA... OKAY, HOW ABOUT OKONO-MIYAKI, THEN?
GOTCHA.
OH, AND THAT YUKATA LOOKS GREAT ON YOU.
FWAAH? AHH, THANKS!

8

Epilogue 39>> Summer Vacation: Homework

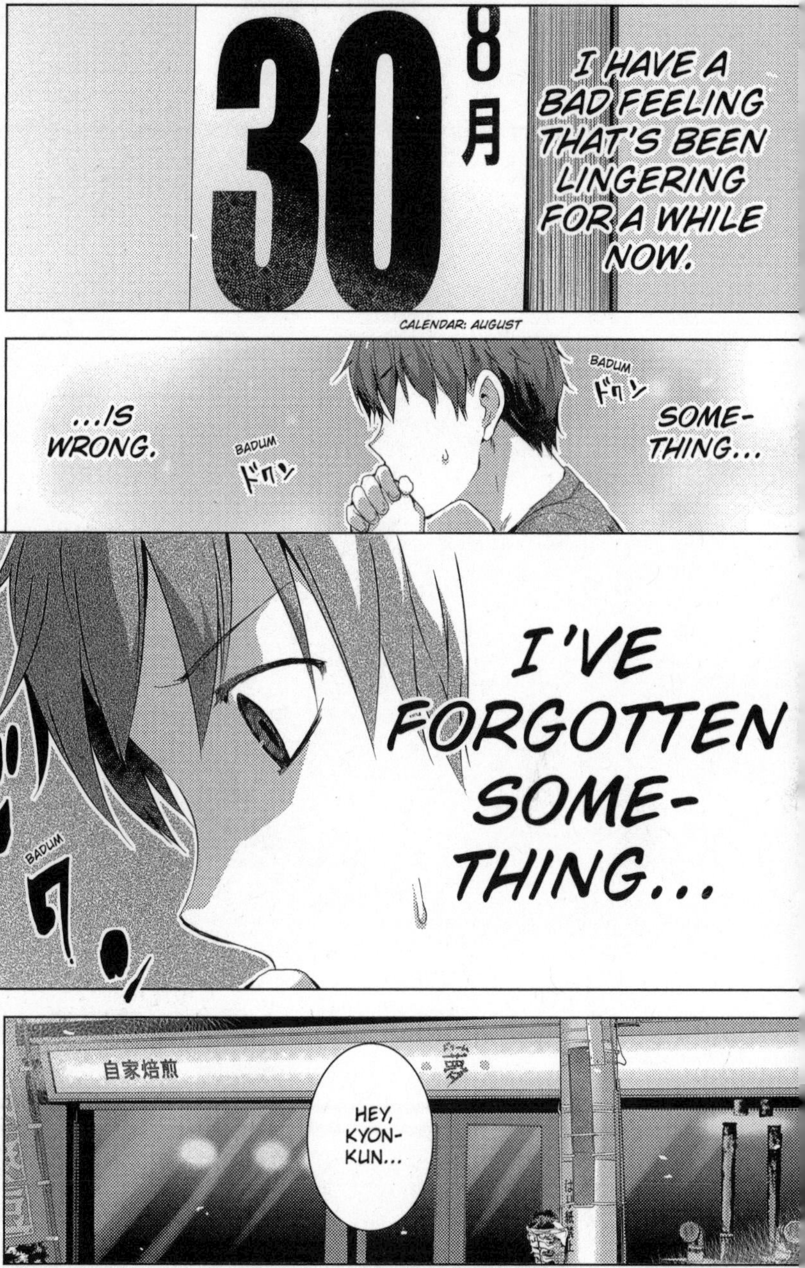
30
8
月
I HAVE A BAD FEELING THAT'S BEEN LINGERING FOR A WHILE NOW.
CALENDAR: AUGUST
SOME-THING...
BADUM
ドクン
BADUM
ドクン
...IS WRONG.
I'VE FORGOTTEN SOME-THING...
BADUM
ドクッ
自家焙煎
夢
HEY, KYON-KUN...

SIGN: HOUSE-ROASTED / DREAM

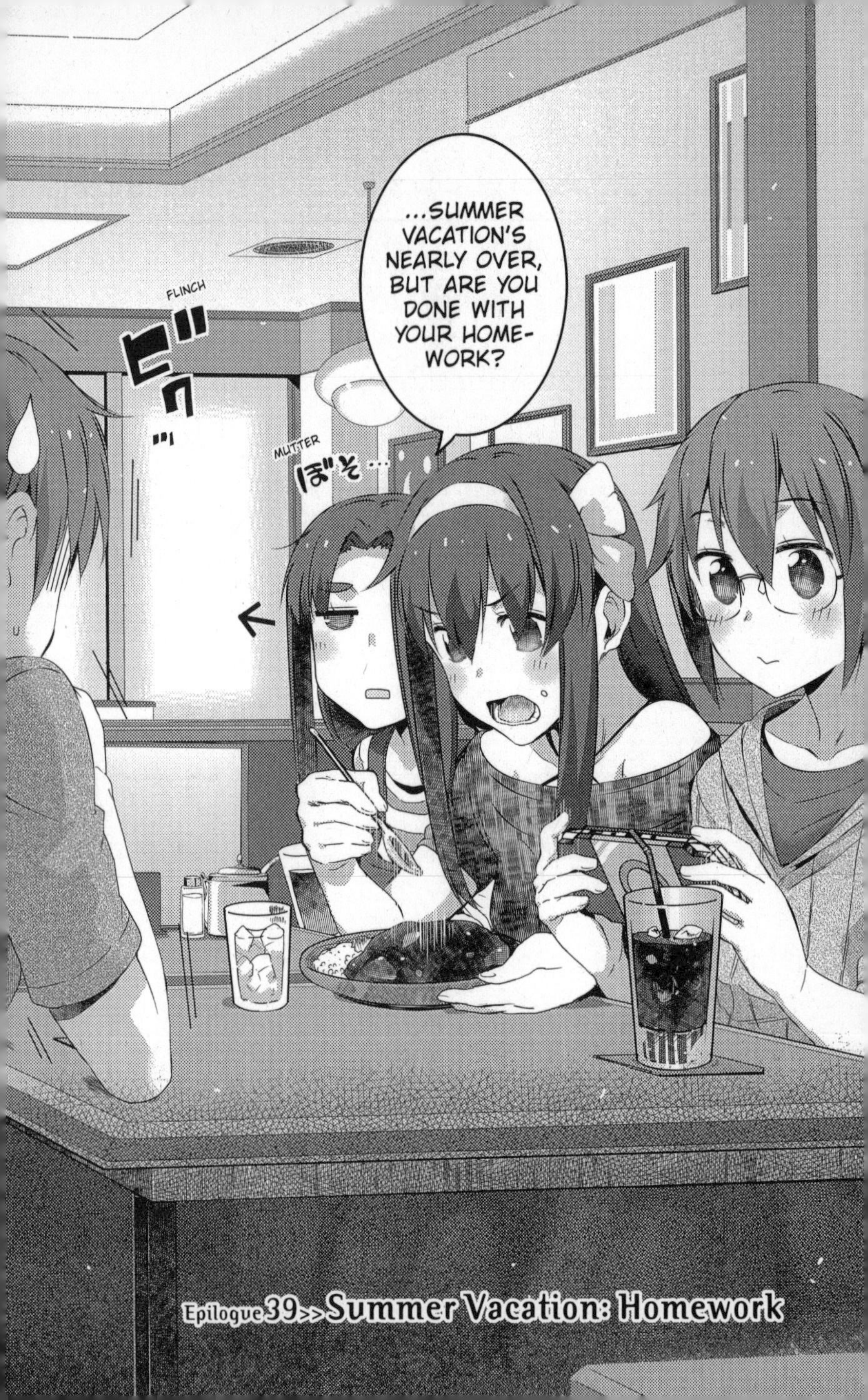
...SUMMER VACATION'S NEARLY OVER, BUT ARE YOU DONE WITH YOUR HOME-WORK?
FLINCH
ビクッ
MUTTER
ぼそ…
Epilogue 39>> Summer Vacation: Homework

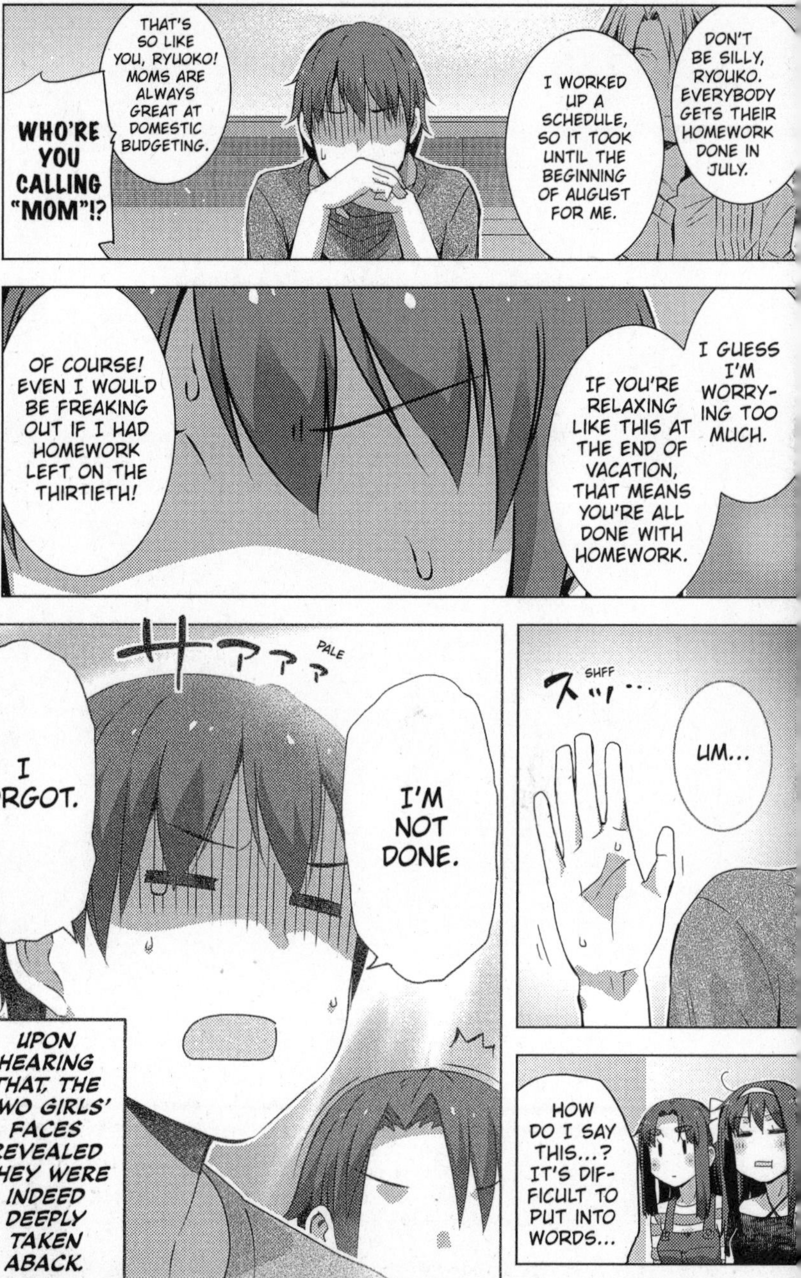
DON'T BE SILLY, RYOUKO. EVERYBODY GETS THEIR HOMEWORK DONE IN JULY.
I WORKED UP A SCHEDULE, SO IT TOOK UNTIL THE BEGINNING OF AUGUST FOR ME.
THAT'S SO LIKE YOU, RYUOKO! MOMS ARE ALWAYS GREAT AT DOMESTIC BUDGETING.
WHO'RE YOU CALLING "MOM"!?
I GUESS I'M WORRY-ING TOO MUCH.
IF YOU'RE RELAXING LIKE THIS AT THE END OF VACATION, THAT MEANS YOU'RE ALL DONE WITH HOMEWORK.
OF COURSE! EVEN I WOULD BE FREAKING OUT IF I HAD HOMEWORK LEFT ON THE THIRTIETH!
スッ…
SHFF
UM...
HOW DO I SAY THIS...? IT'S DIF-FICULT TO PUT INTO WORDS...
サァァァ
PALE
I'M NOT DONE.
I FORGOT.
UPON HEARING THAT, THE TWO GIRLS' FACES REVEALED THEY WERE INDEED DEEPLY TAKEN ABACK.

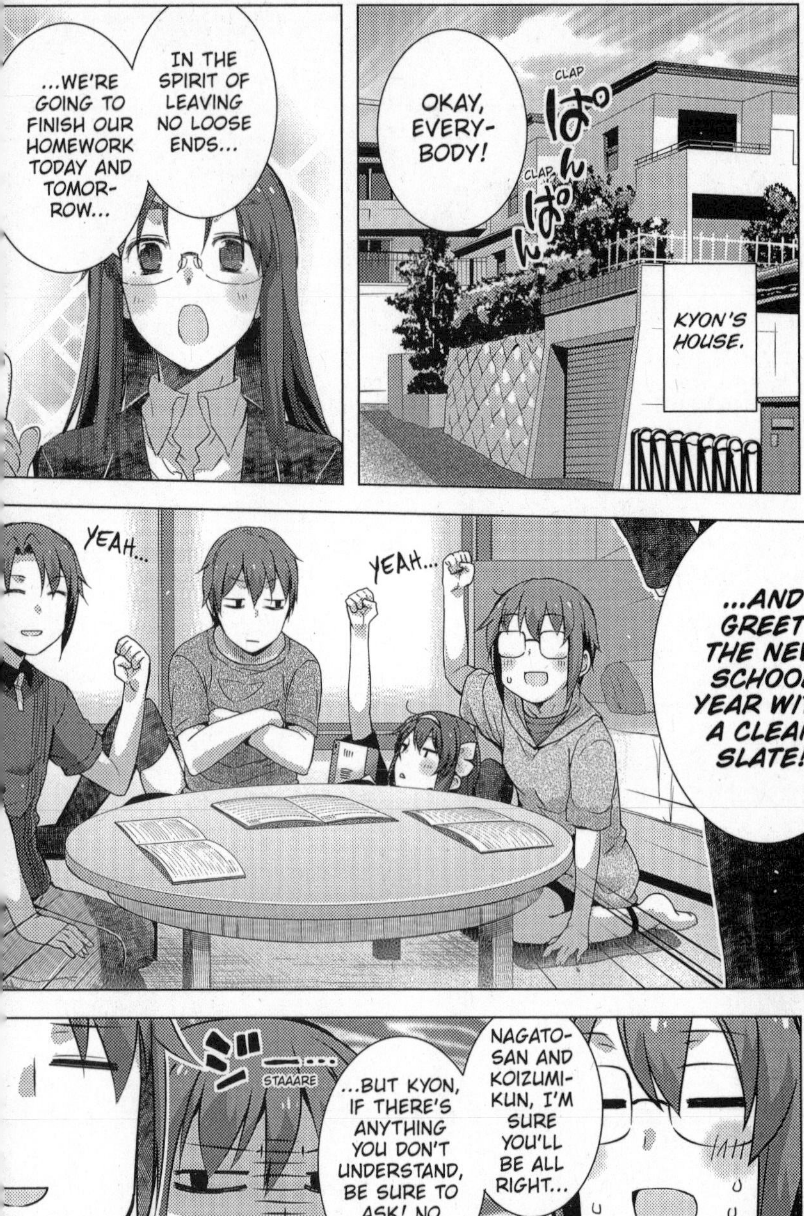
CLAP
ぱん
CLAP
ぱん
OKAY, EVERY-BODY!
KYON'S HOUSE.
IN THE SPIRIT OF LEAVING NO LOOSE ENDS...
...WE'RE GOING TO FINISH OUR HOMEWORK TODAY AND TOMOR-ROW...
...AND GREET THE NEW SCHOOL YEAR WITH A CLEAN SLATE!
YEAH...
YEAH...
NAGATO-SAN AND KOIZUMI-KUN, I'M SURE YOU'LL BE ALL RIGHT...
...BUT KYON, IF THERE'S ANYTHING YOU DON'T UNDERSTAND, BE SURE TO ASK! NO COPYING!
ジー...
STAAARE

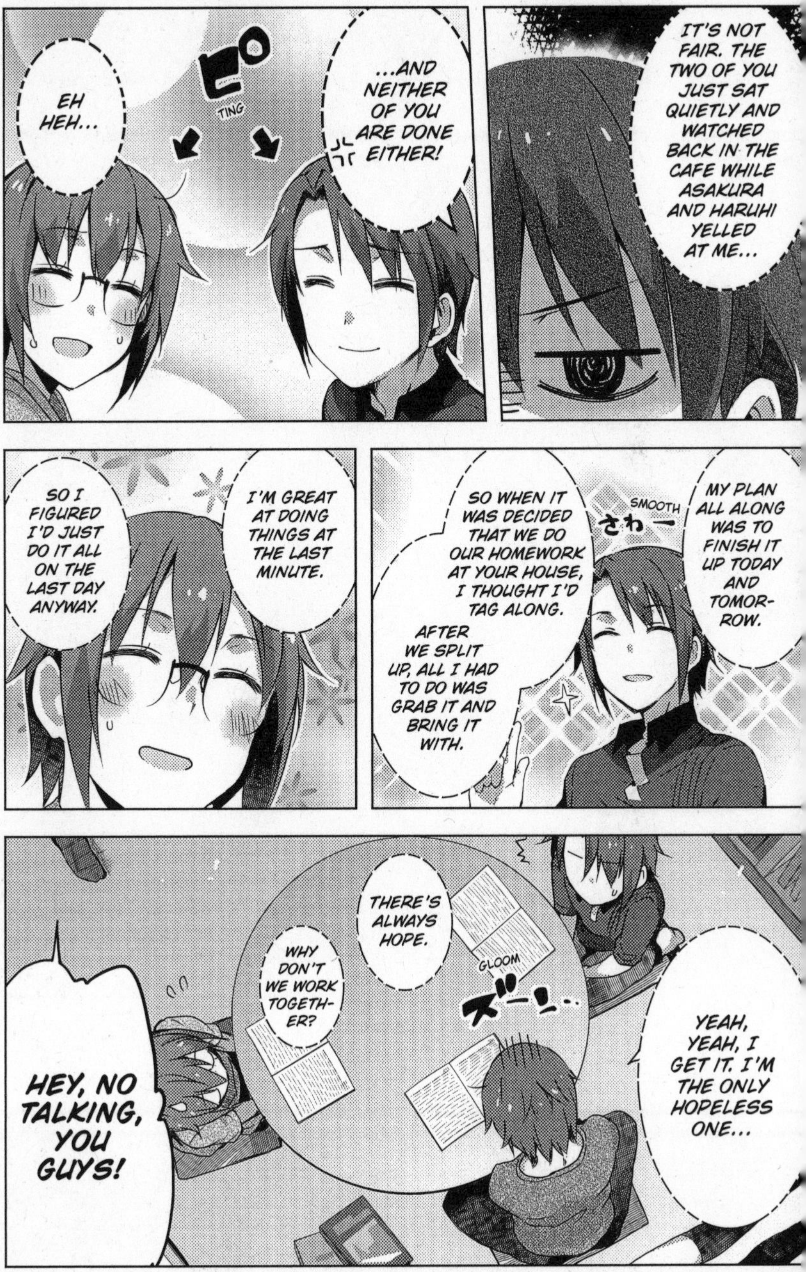
IT'S NOT FAIR. THE TWO OF YOU JUST SAT QUIETLY AND WATCHED BACK IN THE CAFE WHILE ASAKURA AND HARUHI YELLED AT ME...
...AND NEITHER OF YOU ARE DONE EITHER!
TING
EH HEH...
MY PLAN ALL ALONG WAS TO FINISH IT UP TODAY AND TOMORROW.
SMOOTH
さわー
SO WHEN IT WAS DECIDED THAT WE DO OUR HOMEWORK AT YOUR HOUSE, I THOUGHT I'D TAG ALONG.
AFTER WE SPLIT UP, ALL I HAD TO DO WAS GRAB IT AND BRING IT WITH.
I'M GREAT AT DOING THINGS AT THE LAST MINUTE.
SO I FIGURED I'D JUST DO IT ALL ON THE LAST DAY ANYWAY.
YEAH, YEAH, I GET IT. I'M THE ONLY HOPELESS ONE...
GLOOM
THERE'S ALWAYS HOPE.
WHY DON'T WE WORK TOGETHER?
HEY, NO TALKING, YOU GUYS!

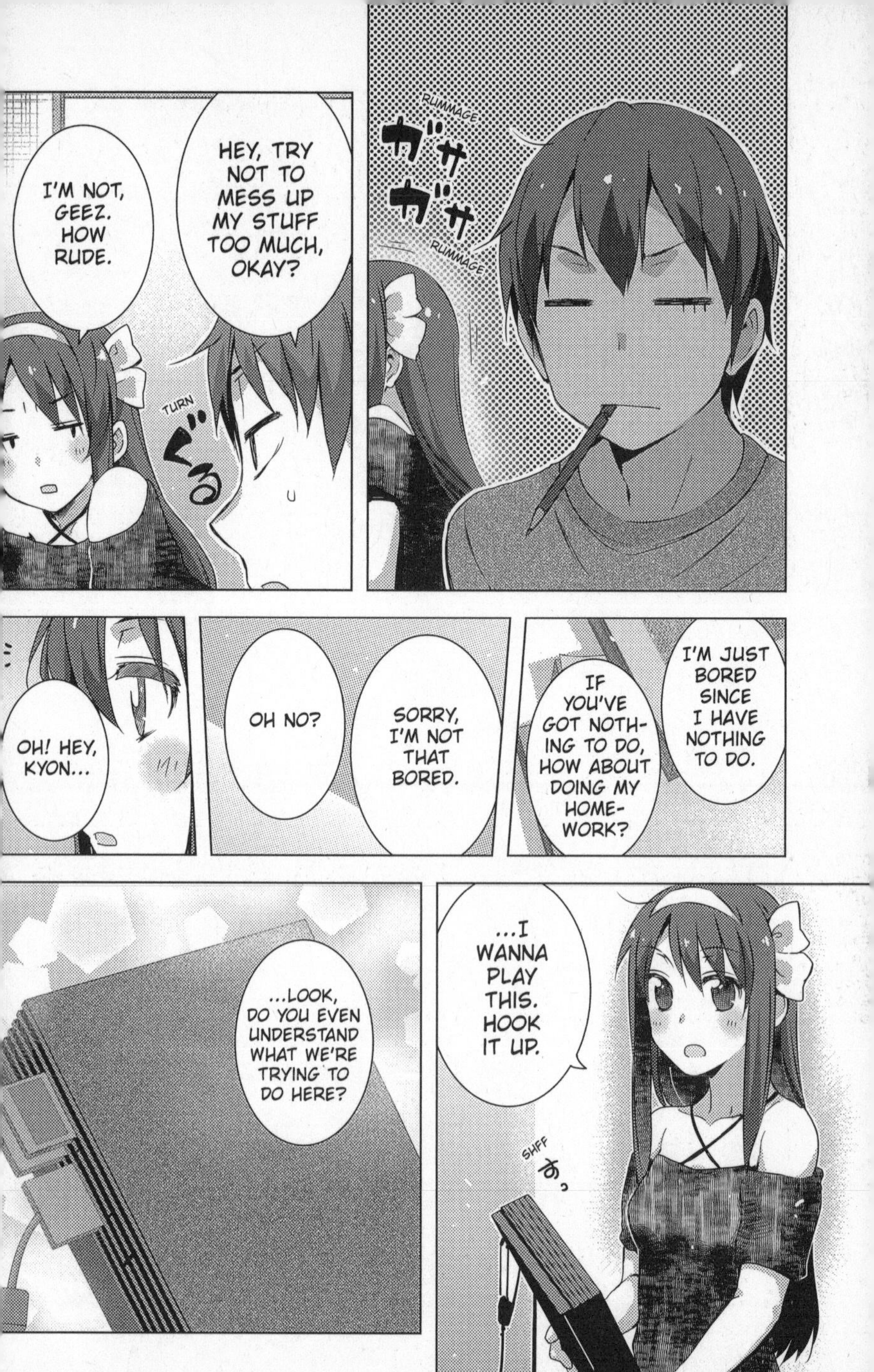
RUMMAGE
RUMMAGE
HEY, TRY NOT TO MESS UP MY STUFF TOO MUCH, OKAY?
TURN
I'M NOT, GEEZ. HOW RUDE.
I'M JUST BORED SINCE I HAVE NOTHING TO DO.
IF YOU'VE GOT NOTHING-ING TO DO, HOW ABOUT DOING MY HOME-WORK?
SORRY, I'M NOT THAT BORED.
OH NO?
OH! HEY, KYON...
...I WANNA PLAY THIS. HOOK IT UP.
SHFF
...LOOK, DO YOU EVEN UNDERSTAND WHAT WE'RE TRYING TO DO HERE?

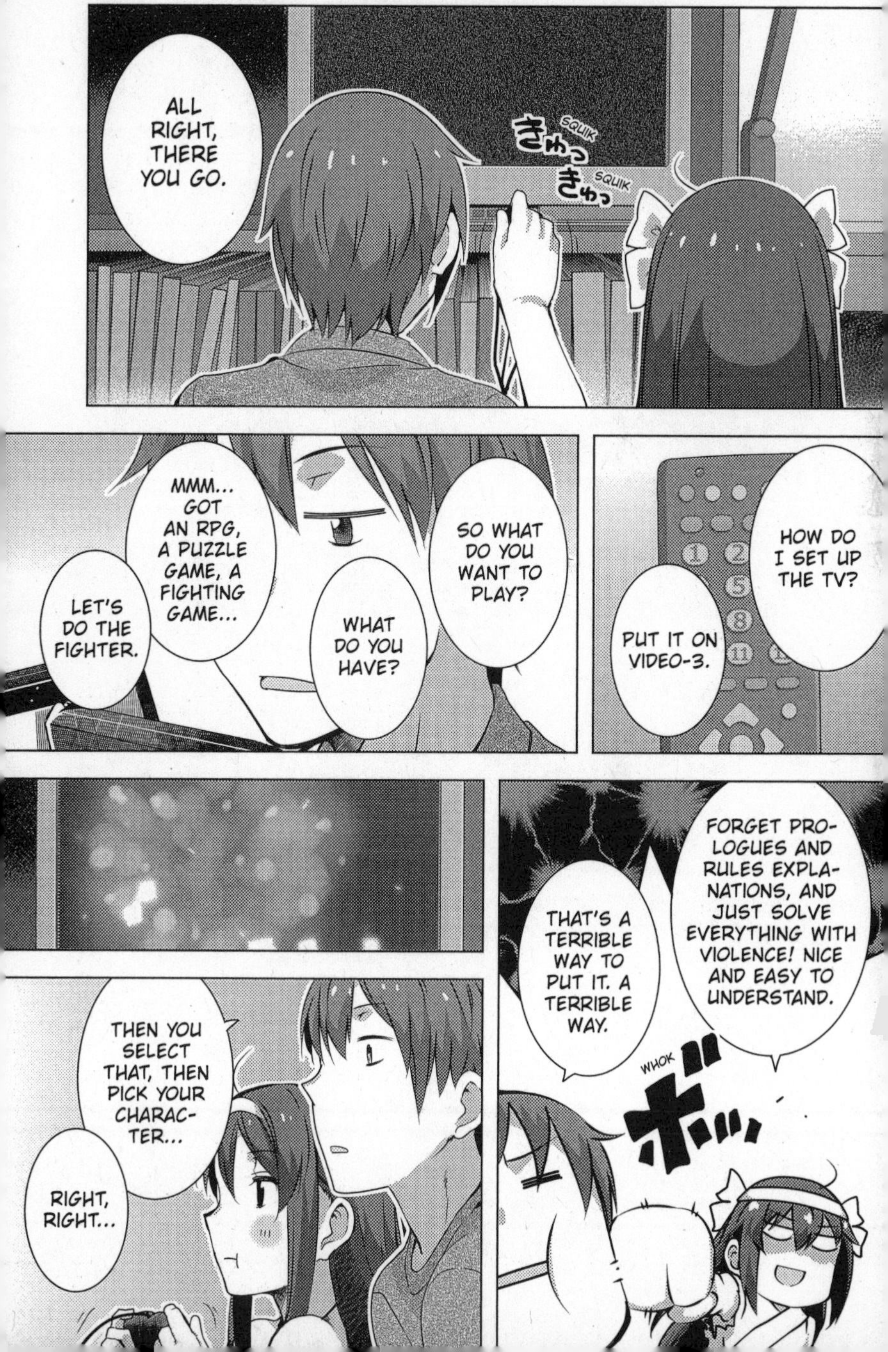
ALL RIGHT, THERE YOU GO.
きゅっ SQUIK
きゅっ SQUIK
HOW DO I SET UP THE TV?
PUT IT ON VIDEO-3.
SO WHAT DO YOU WANT TO PLAY?
WHAT DO YOU HAVE?
MMM... GOT AN RPG, A PUZZLE GAME, A FIGHTING GAME...
LET'S DO THE FIGHTER.
FORGET PRO-LOGUES AND RULES EXPLA-NATIONS, AND JUST SOLVE EVERYTHING WITH VIOLENCE! NICE AND EASY TO UNDERSTAND.
THAT'S A TERRIBLE WAY TO PUT IT. A TERRIBLE WAY.
ボッ WHOK
THEN YOU SELECT THAT, THEN PICK YOUR CHARAC-TER...
RIGHT, RIGHT...

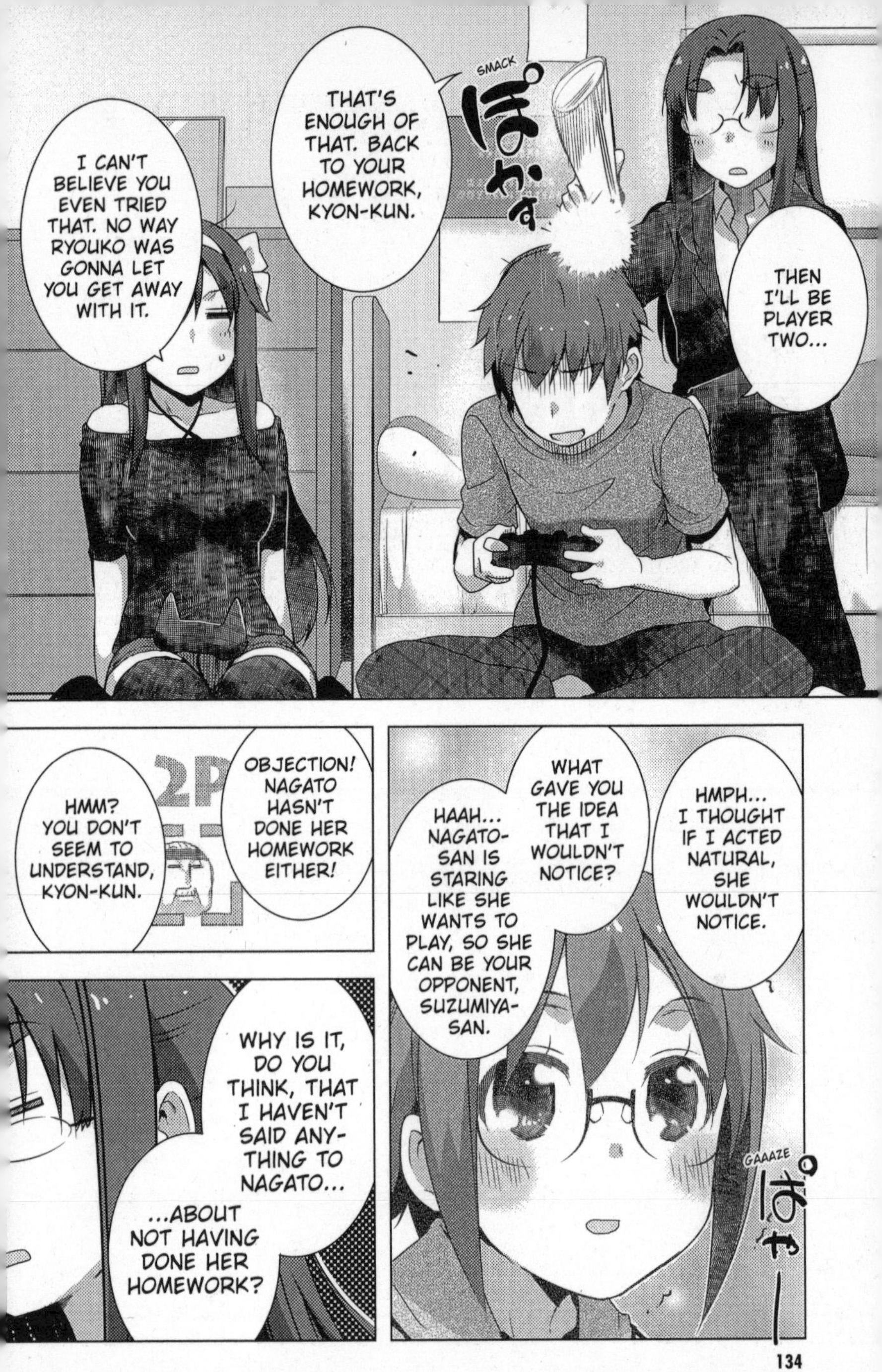
THEN I'LL BE PLAYER TWO...
SMACK
ぽかす
THAT'S ENOUGH OF THAT. BACK TO YOUR HOMEWORK, KYON-KUN.
I CAN'T BELIEVE YOU EVEN TRIED THAT. NO WAY RYOUKO WAS GONNA LET YOU GET AWAY WITH IT.
HMPH... I THOUGHT IF I ACTED NATURAL, SHE WOULDN'T NOTICE.
WHAT GAVE YOU THE IDEA THAT I WOULDN'T NOTICE?
HAAH... NAGATO-SAN IS STARING LIKE SHE WANTS TO PLAY, SO SHE CAN BE YOUR OPPONENT, SUZUMIYA-SAN.
GAAAZE
ぱー
OBJECTION! NAGATO HASN'T DONE HER HOMEWORK EITHER!
2P
HMM? YOU DON'T SEEM TO UNDERSTAND, KYON-KUN.
WHY IS IT, DO YOU THINK, THAT I HAVEN'T SAID ANY-THING TO NAGATO...
...ABOUT NOT HAVING DONE HER HOMEWORK?

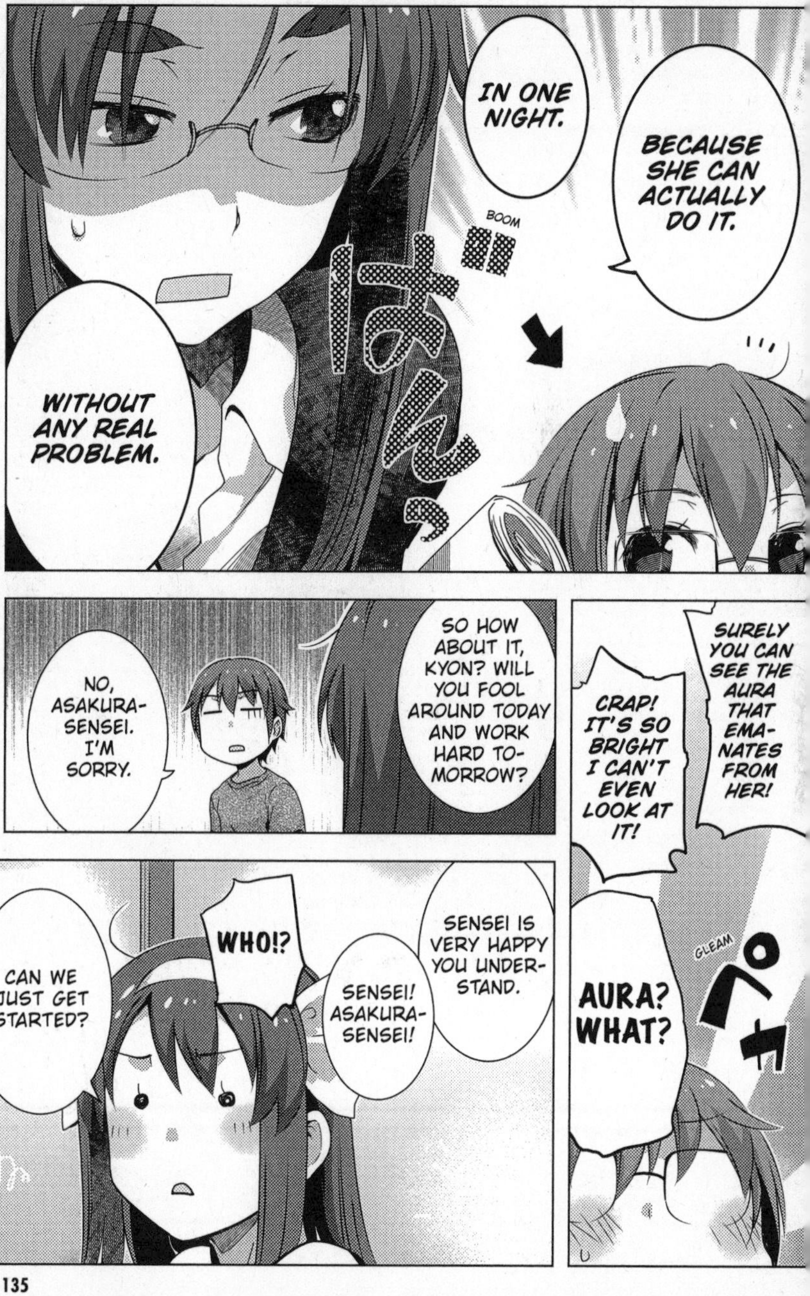
BECAUSE SHE CAN ACTUALLY DO IT.
IN ONE NIGHT.
BOOM
WITHOUT ANY REAL PROBLEM.
SURELY YOU CAN SEE THE AURA THAT EMANATES FROM HER!
CRAP! IT'S SO BRIGHT I CAN'T EVEN LOOK AT IT!
GLEAM
AURA? WHAT?
SO HOW ABOUT IT, KYON? WILL YOU FOOL AROUND TODAY AND WORK HARD TOMORROW?
NO, ASAKURA-SENSEI. I'M SORRY.
SENSEI IS VERY HAPPY YOU UNDERSTAND.
WHO!?
SENSEI! ASAKURA-SENSEI!
CAN WE JUST GET STARTED?

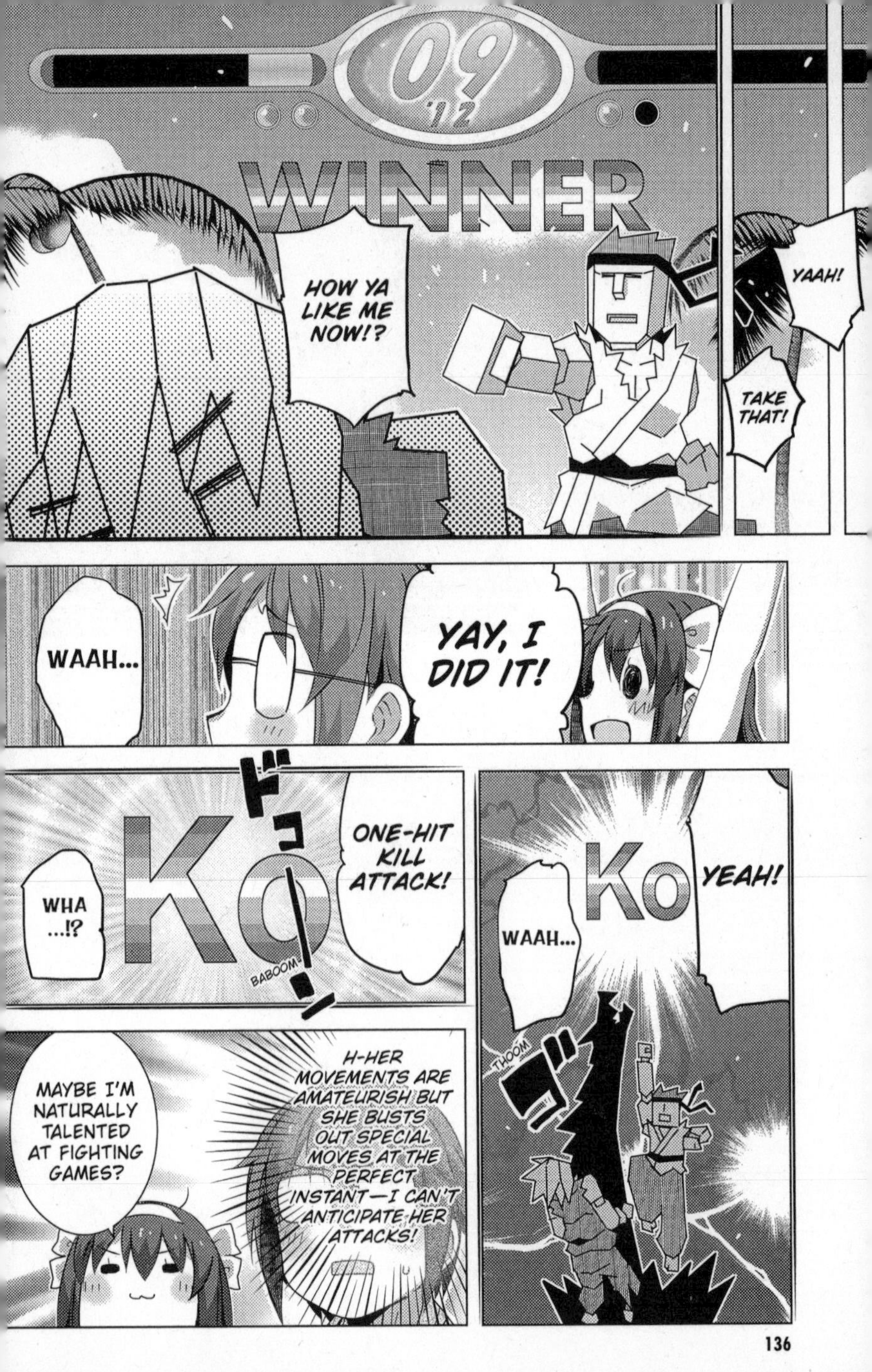
YAAH!
TAKE THAT!
09
'12
WINNER
HOW YA LIKE ME NOW!?
YAY, I DID IT!
WAAH...
YEAH!
KO
WAAH...
THOOM
ONE-HIT KILL ATTACK!
KO
BABOOM
WHA ...!?
H-HER MOVEMENTS ARE AMATEURISH BUT SHE BUSTS OUT SPECIAL MOVES AT THE PERFECT INSTANT—I CAN'T ANTICIPATE HER ATTACKS!
MAYBE I'M NATURALLY TALENTED AT FIGHTING GAMES?

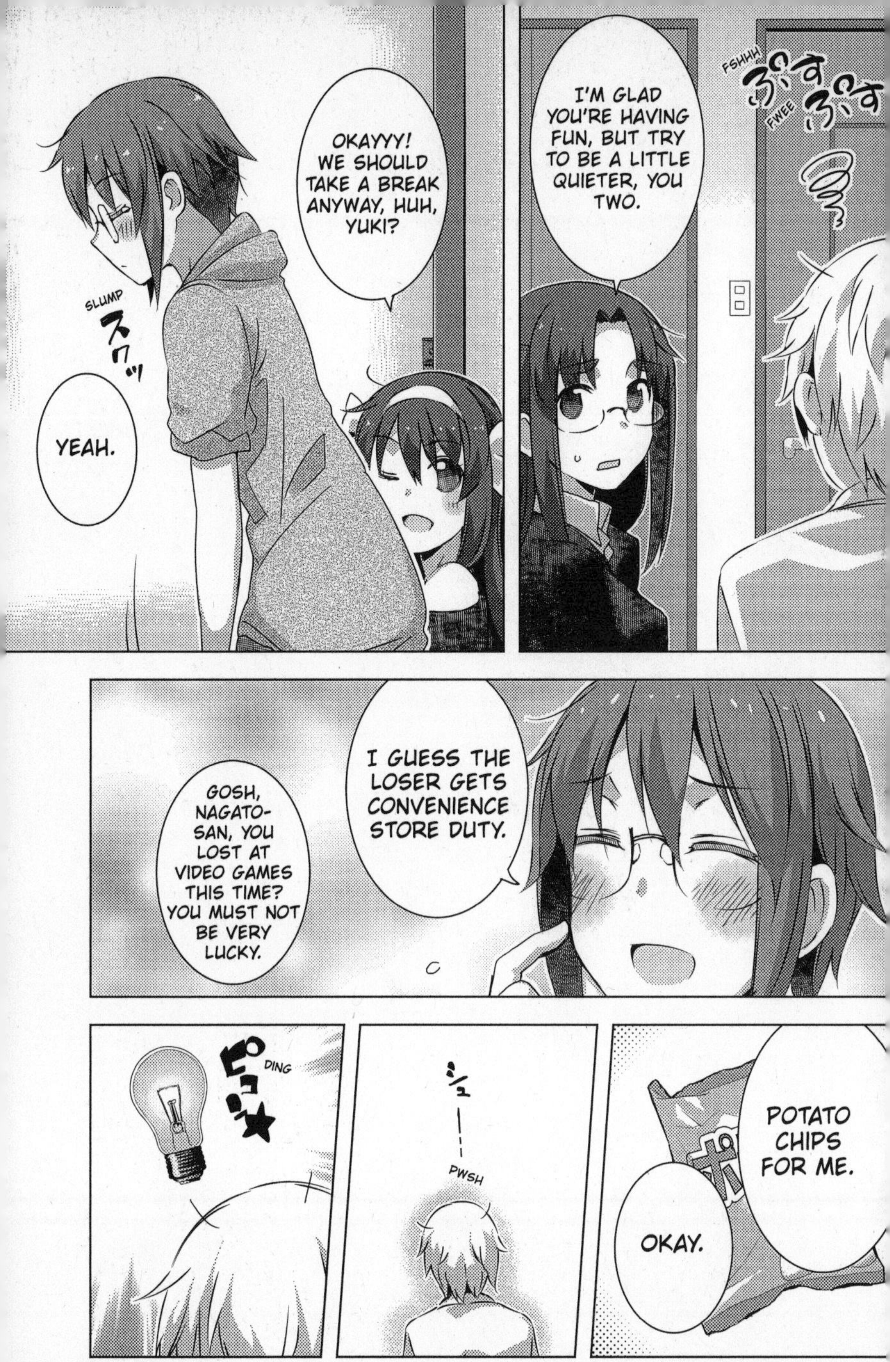
FSHHH
FWEE
I'M GLAD YOU'RE HAVING FUN, BUT TRY TO BE A LITTLE QUIETER, YOU TWO.
OKAYYY! WE SHOULD TAKE A BREAK ANYWAY, HUH, YUKI?
SLUMP
YEAH.
I GUESS THE LOSER GETS CONVENIENCE STORE DUTY.
GOSH, NAGATO-SAN, YOU LOST AT VIDEO GAMES THIS TIME? YOU MUST NOT BE VERY LUCKY.
POTATO CHIPS FOR ME.
OKAY.
PWSH
DING

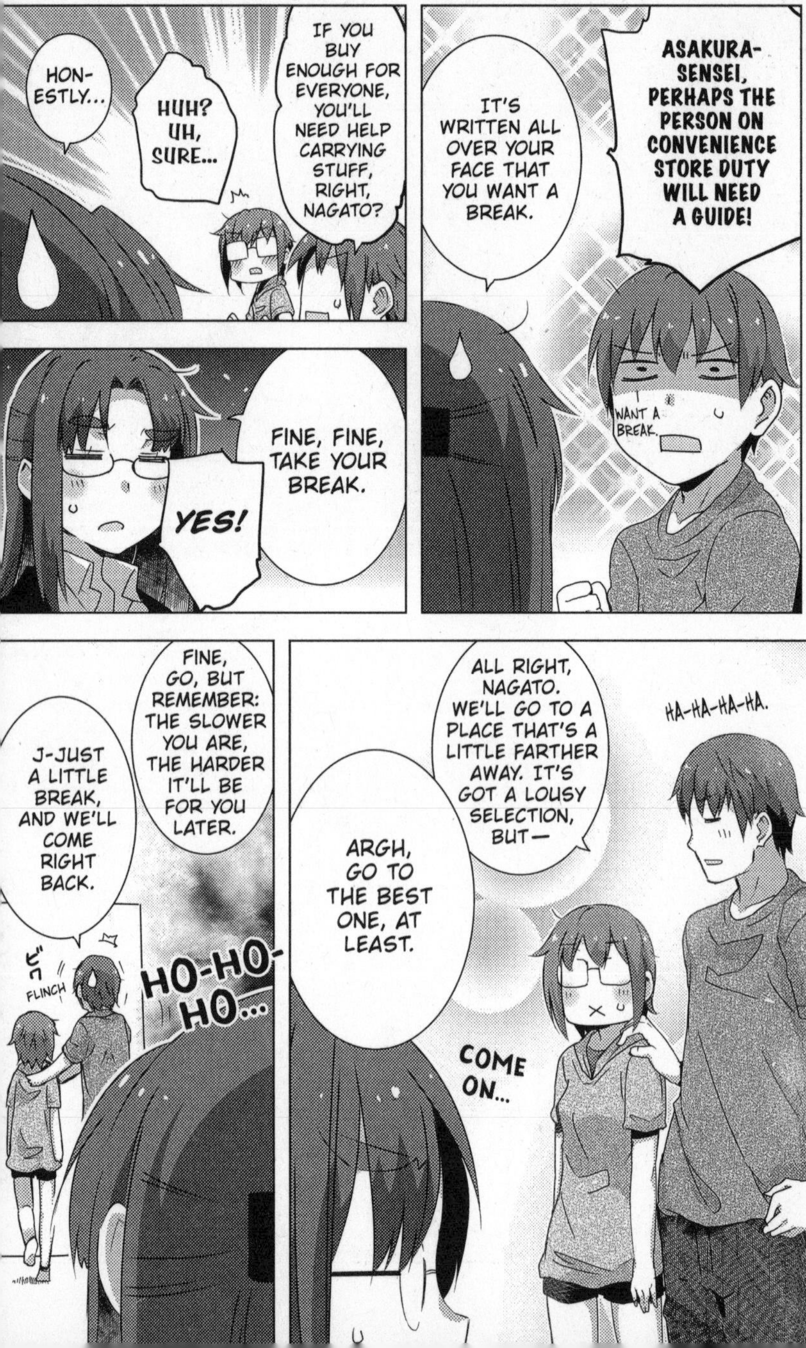
ASAKURA-SENSEI, PERHAPS THE PERSON ON CONVENIENCE STORE DUTY WILL NEED A GUIDE!
IT'S WRITTEN ALL OVER YOUR FACE THAT YOU WANT A BREAK.
WANT A BREAK.
IF YOU BUY ENOUGH FOR EVERYONE, YOU'LL NEED HELP CARRYING STUFF, RIGHT, NAGATO?
HUH? UH, SURE...
HON-ESTLY...
FINE, FINE, TAKE YOUR BREAK.
YES!
HA-HA-HA-HA.
ALL RIGHT, NAGATO. WE'LL GO TO A PLACE THAT'S A LITTLE FARTHER AWAY. IT'S GOT A LOUSY SELECTION, BUT—
ARGH, GO TO THE BEST ONE, AT LEAST.
COME ON...
FINE, GO, BUT REMEMBER: THE SLOWER YOU ARE, THE HARDER IT'LL BE FOR YOU LATER.
J-JUST A LITTLE BREAK, AND WE'LL COME RIGHT BACK.
ビク
FLINCH
HO-HO-HO...

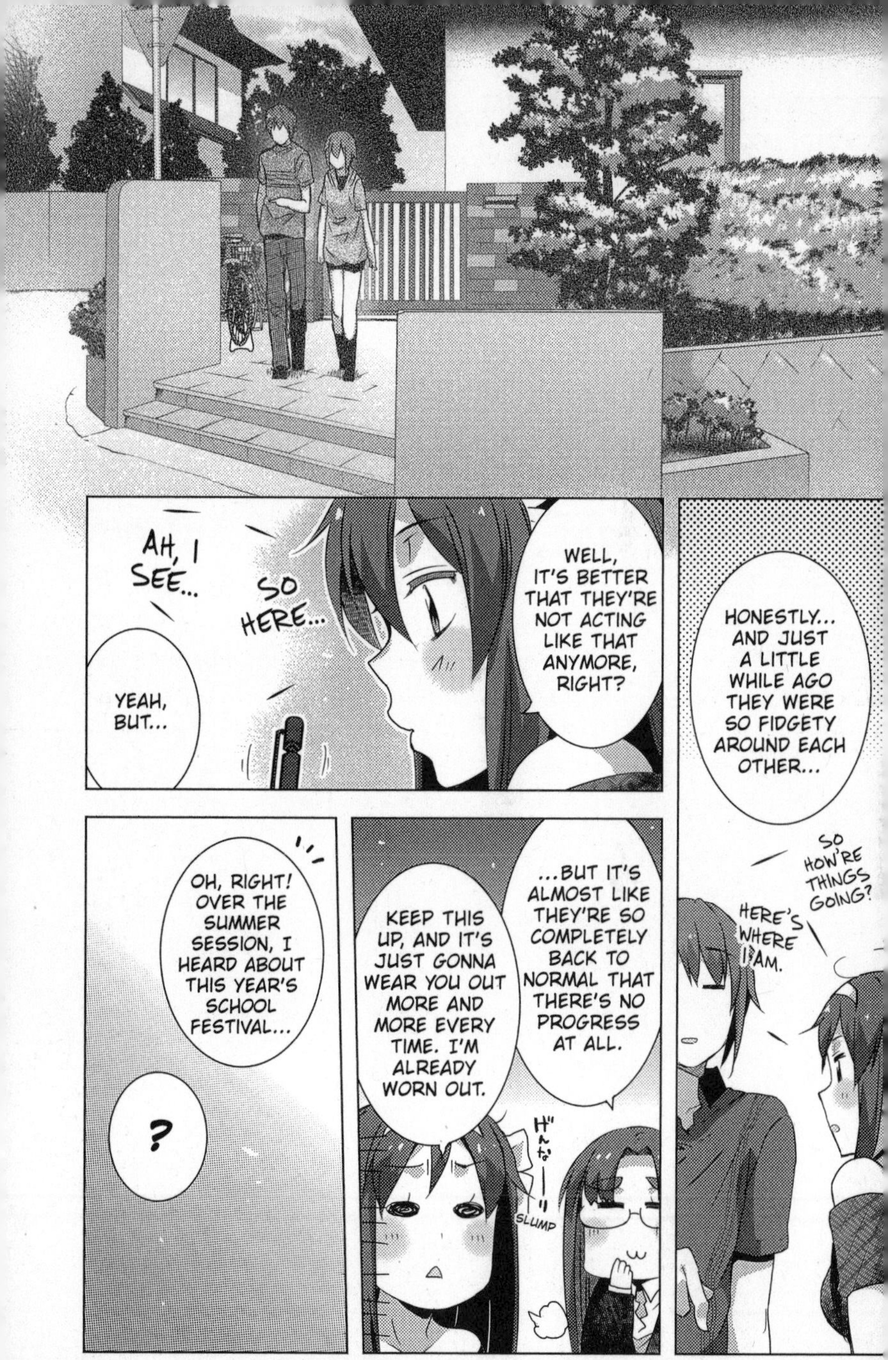
HONESTLY... AND JUST A LITTLE WHILE AGO THEY WERE SO FIDGETY AROUND EACH OTHER...
SO HOW'RE THINGS GOING?
HERE'S WHERE I AM.
WELL, IT'S BETTER THAT THEY'RE NOT ACTING LIKE THAT ANYMORE, RIGHT?
SO HERE...
AH, I SEE...
YEAH, BUT...
...BUT IT'S ALMOST LIKE THEY'RE SO COMPLETELY BACK TO NORMAL THAT THERE'S NO PROGRESS AT ALL.
KEEP THIS UP, AND IT'S JUST GONNA WEAR YOU OUT MORE AND MORE EVERY TIME. I'M ALREADY WORN OUT.
SLUMP
OH, RIGHT! OVER THE SUMMER SESSION, I HEARD ABOUT THIS YEAR'S SCHOOL FESTIVAL...
?

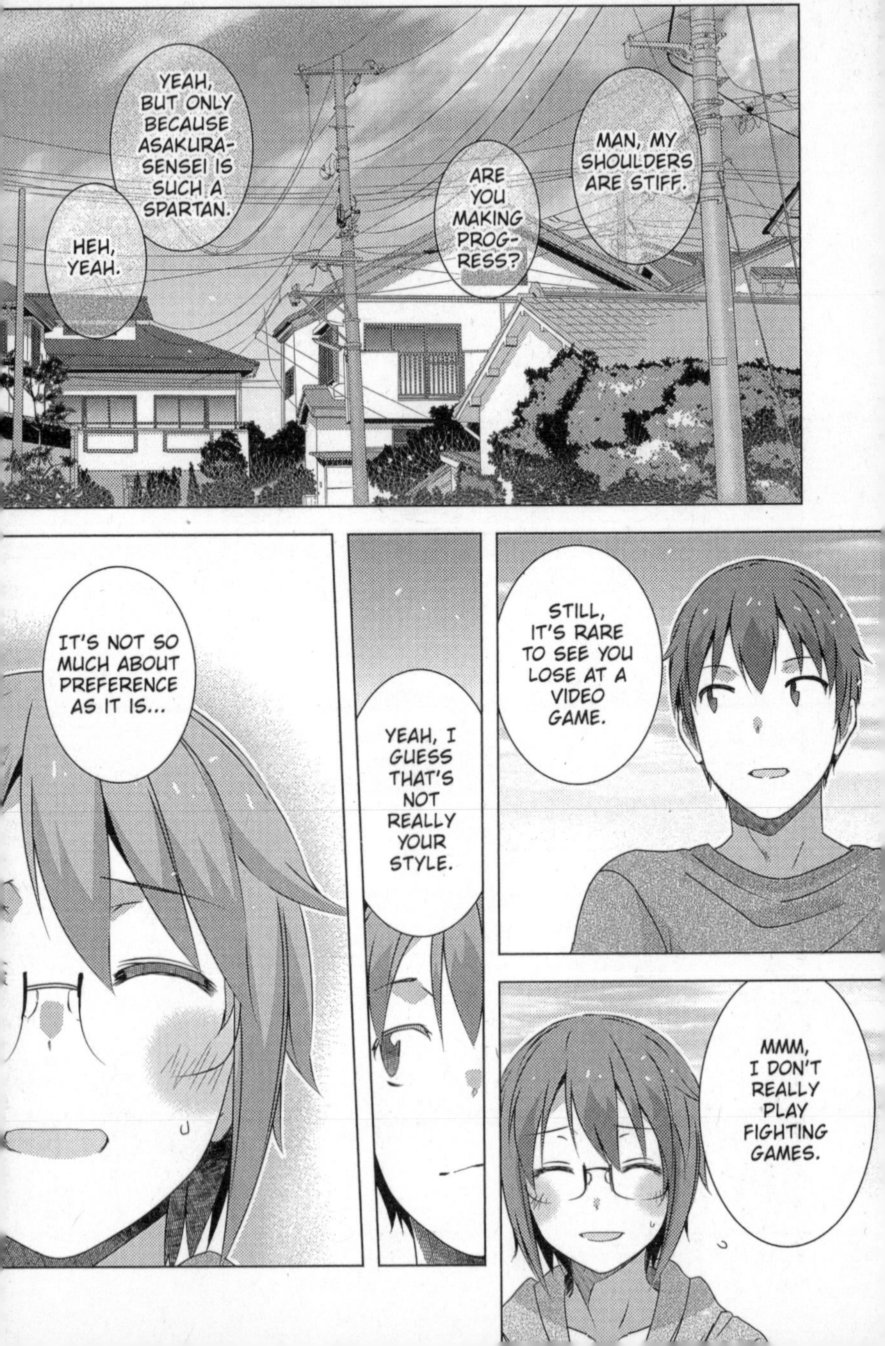
MAN, MY SHOULDERS ARE STIFF.
ARE YOU MAKING PROG-RESS?
YEAH, BUT ONLY BECAUSE ASAKURA-SENSEI IS SUCH A SPARTAN.
HEH, YEAH.
STILL, IT'S RARE TO SEE YOU LOSE AT A VIDEO GAME.
MMM, I DON'T REALLY PLAY FIGHTING GAMES.
YEAH, I GUESS THAT'S NOT REALLY YOUR STYLE.
IT'S NOT SO MUCH ABOUT PREFERENCE AS IT IS...

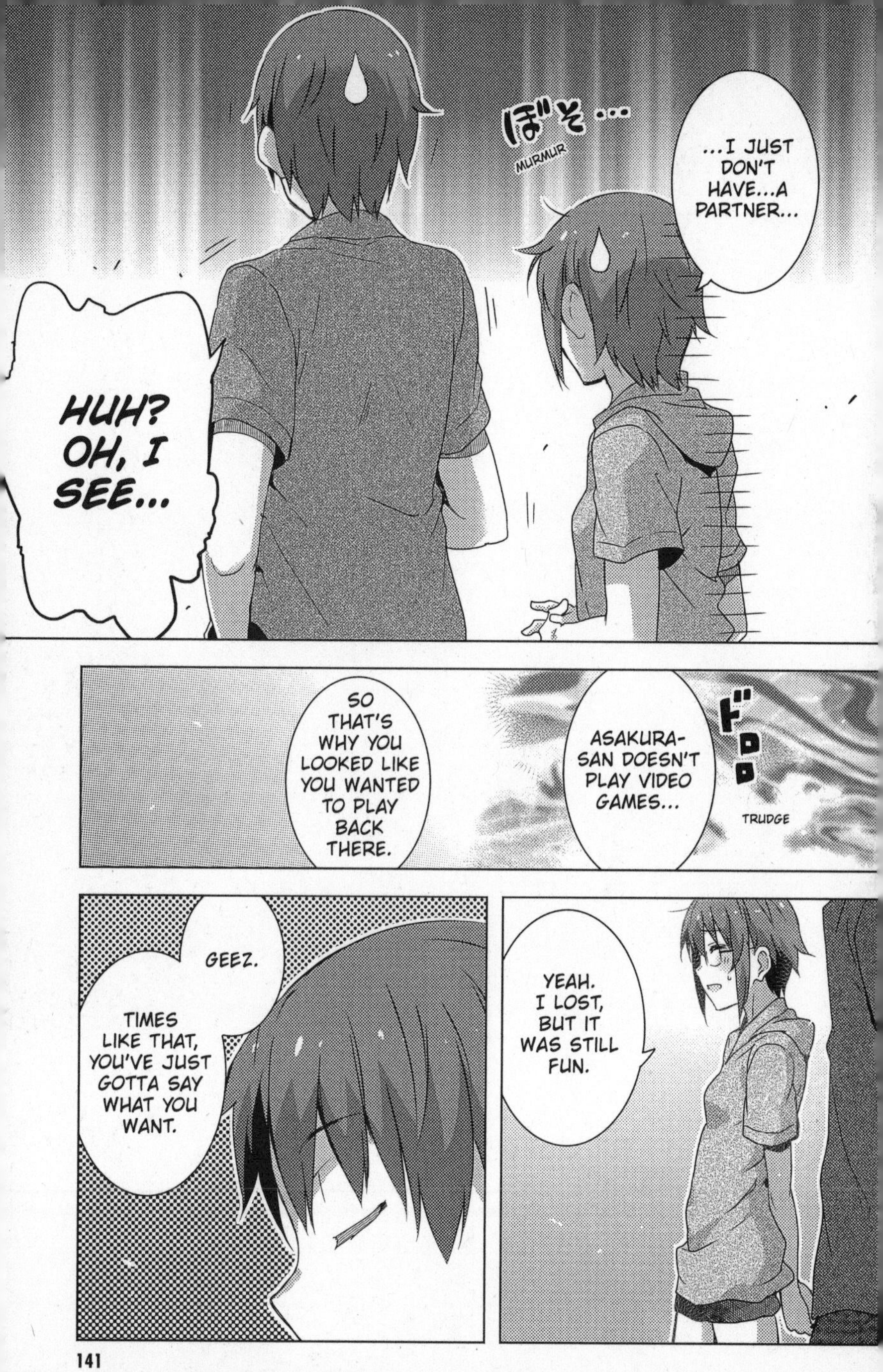
ぼそ...
MURMUR
...I JUST DON'T HAVE...A PARTNER...
HUH? OH, I SEE...
ドロ
TRUDGE
ASAKURA-SAN DOESN'T PLAY VIDEO GAMES...
SO THAT'S WHY YOU LOOKED LIKE YOU WANTED TO PLAY BACK THERE.
YEAH. I LOST, BUT IT WAS STILL FUN.
GEEZ.
TIMES LIKE THAT, YOU'VE JUST GOTTA SAY WHAT YOU WANT.

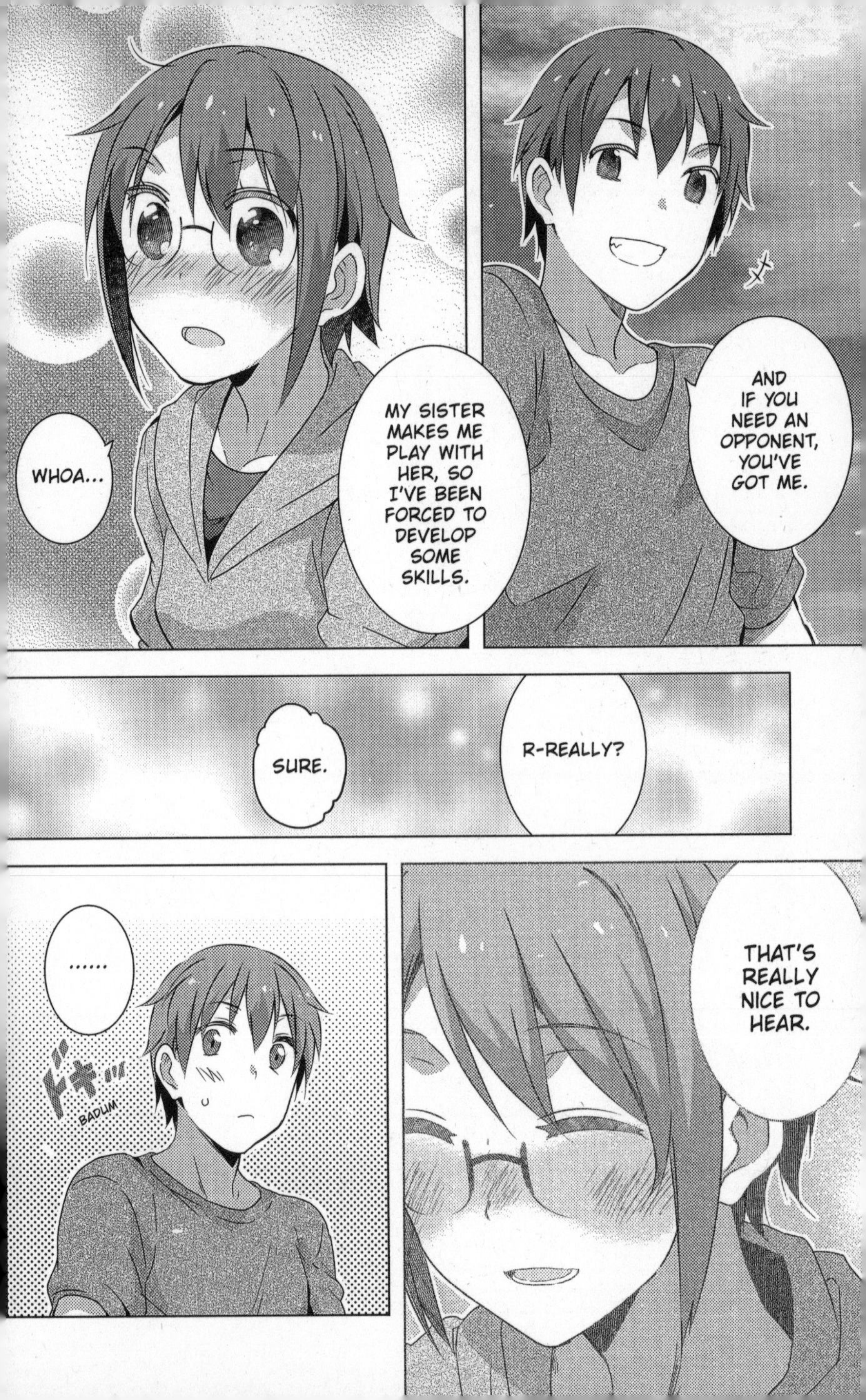
MY SISTER MAKES ME PLAY WITH HER, SO I'VE BEEN FORCED TO DEVELOP SOME SKILLS.
AND IF YOU NEED AN OPPONENT, YOU'VE GOT ME.
WHOA...
R-REALLY?
SURE.
THAT'S REALLY NICE TO HEAR.
......
ドキッ
BADUM

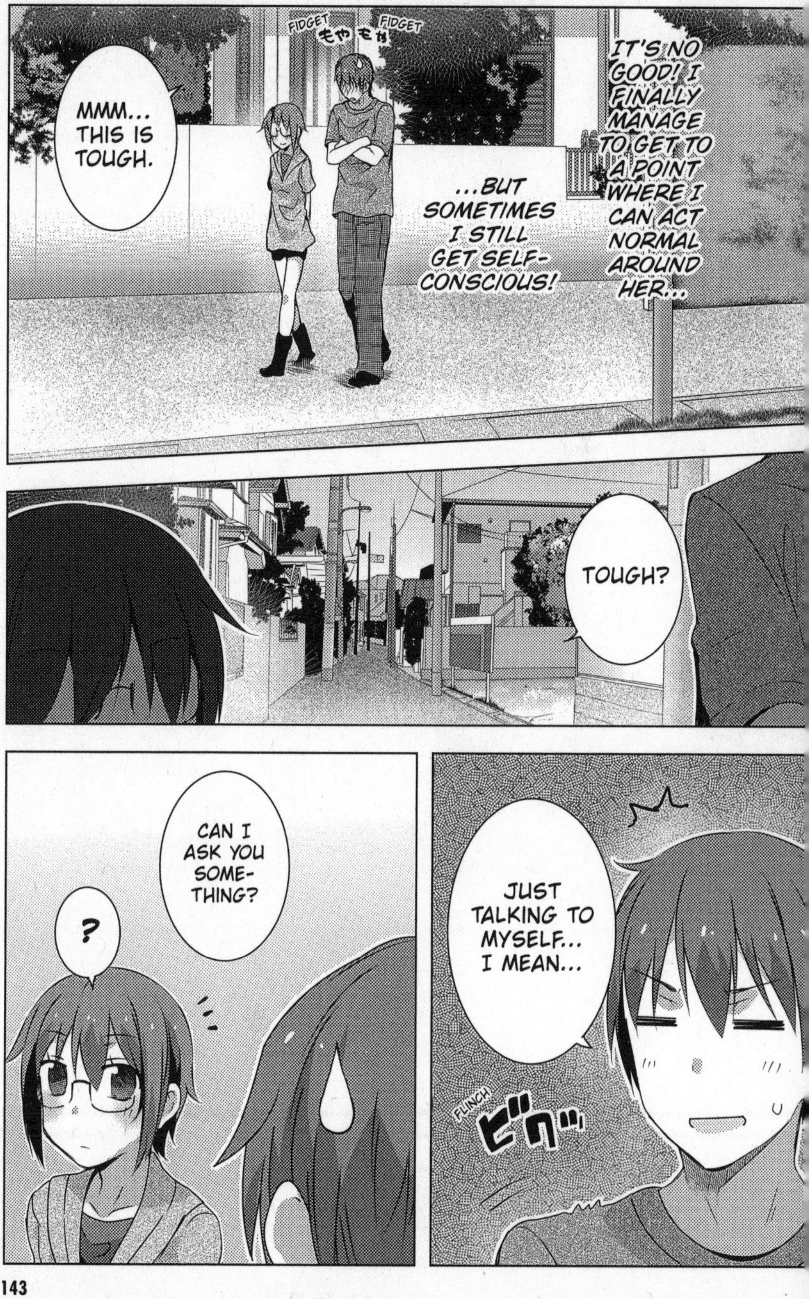
IT'S NO GOOD! I FINALLY MANAGE TO GET TO A POINT WHERE I CAN ACT NORMAL AROUND HER...
FIDGET FIDGET
...BUT SOMETIMES I STILL GET SELF-CONSCIOUS!
MMM... THIS IS TOUGH.
TOUGH?
JUST TALKING TO MYSELF... I MEAN...
FLINCH
CAN I ASK YOU SOMETHING?
?

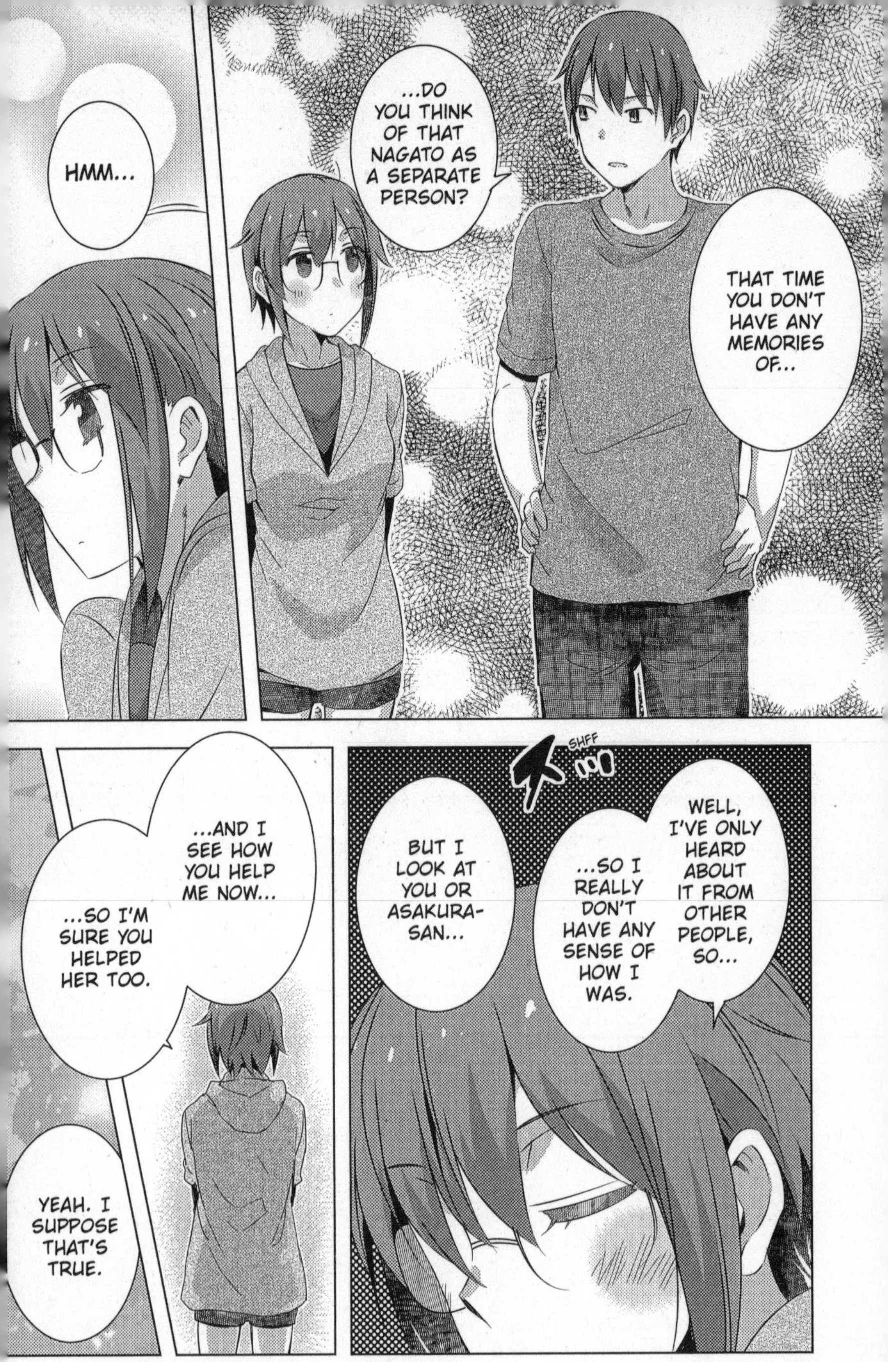
...DO YOU THINK OF THAT NAGATO AS A SEPARATE PERSON?
THAT TIME YOU DON'T HAVE ANY MEMORIES OF...
HMM...
SHFF
WELL, I'VE ONLY HEARD ABOUT IT FROM OTHER PEOPLE, SO...
...SO I REALLY DON'T HAVE ANY SENSE OF HOW I WAS.
BUT I LOOK AT YOU OR ASAKURA-SAN...
...AND I SEE HOW YOU HELP ME NOW...
...SO I'M SURE YOU HELPED HER TOO.
YEAH. I SUPPOSE THAT'S TRUE.

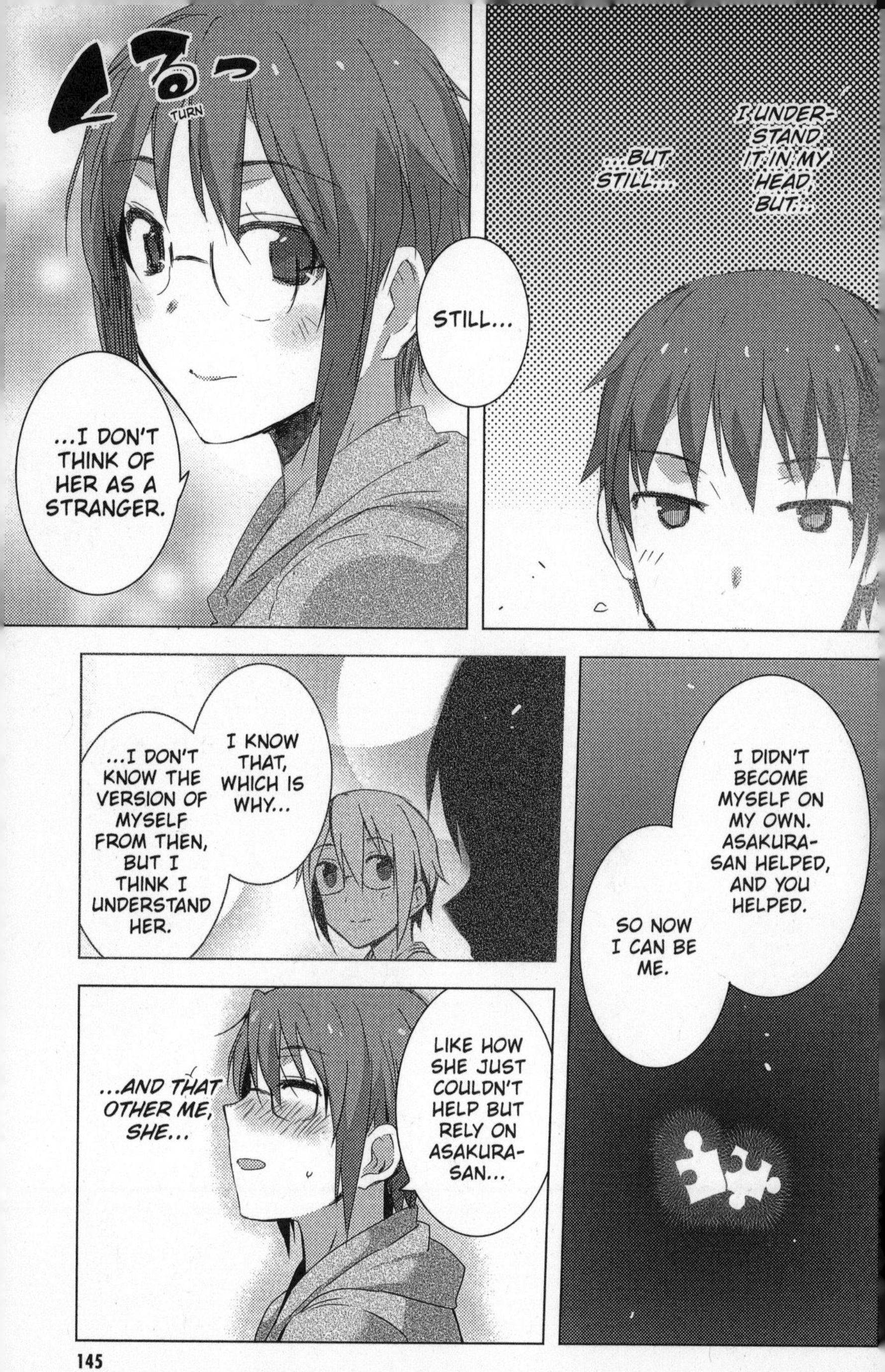
I UNDERSTAND IT IN MY HEAD, BUT...
...BUT STILL...
TURN
STILL...
...I DON'T THINK OF HER AS A STRANGER.
I DIDN'T BECOME MYSELF ON MY OWN. ASAKURA-SAN HELPED, AND YOU HELPED.
SO NOW I CAN BE ME.
I KNOW THAT, WHICH IS WHY...
...I DON'T KNOW THE VERSION OF MYSELF FROM THEN, BUT I THINK I UNDERSTAND HER.
LIKE HOW SHE JUST COULDN'T HELP BUT RELY ON ASAKURA-SAN...
...AND THAT OTHER ME, SHE...

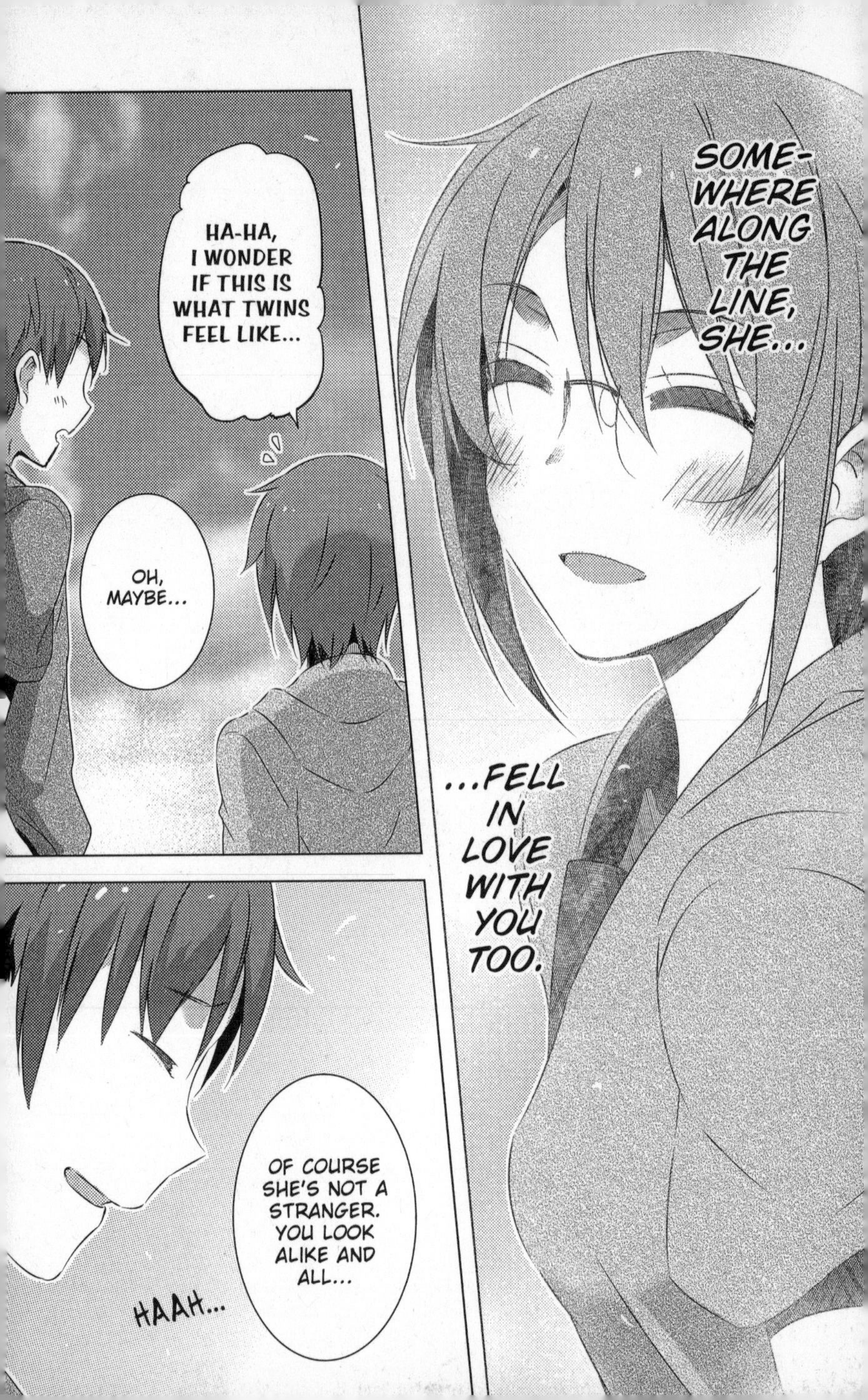
SOME-WHERE ALONG THE LINE, SHE...
...FELL IN LOVE WITH YOU TOO.
HA-HA, I WONDER IF THIS IS WHAT TWINS FEEL LIKE...
OH, MAYBE...
OF COURSE SHE'S NOT A STRANGER. YOU LOOK ALIKE AND ALL...
HAAH...

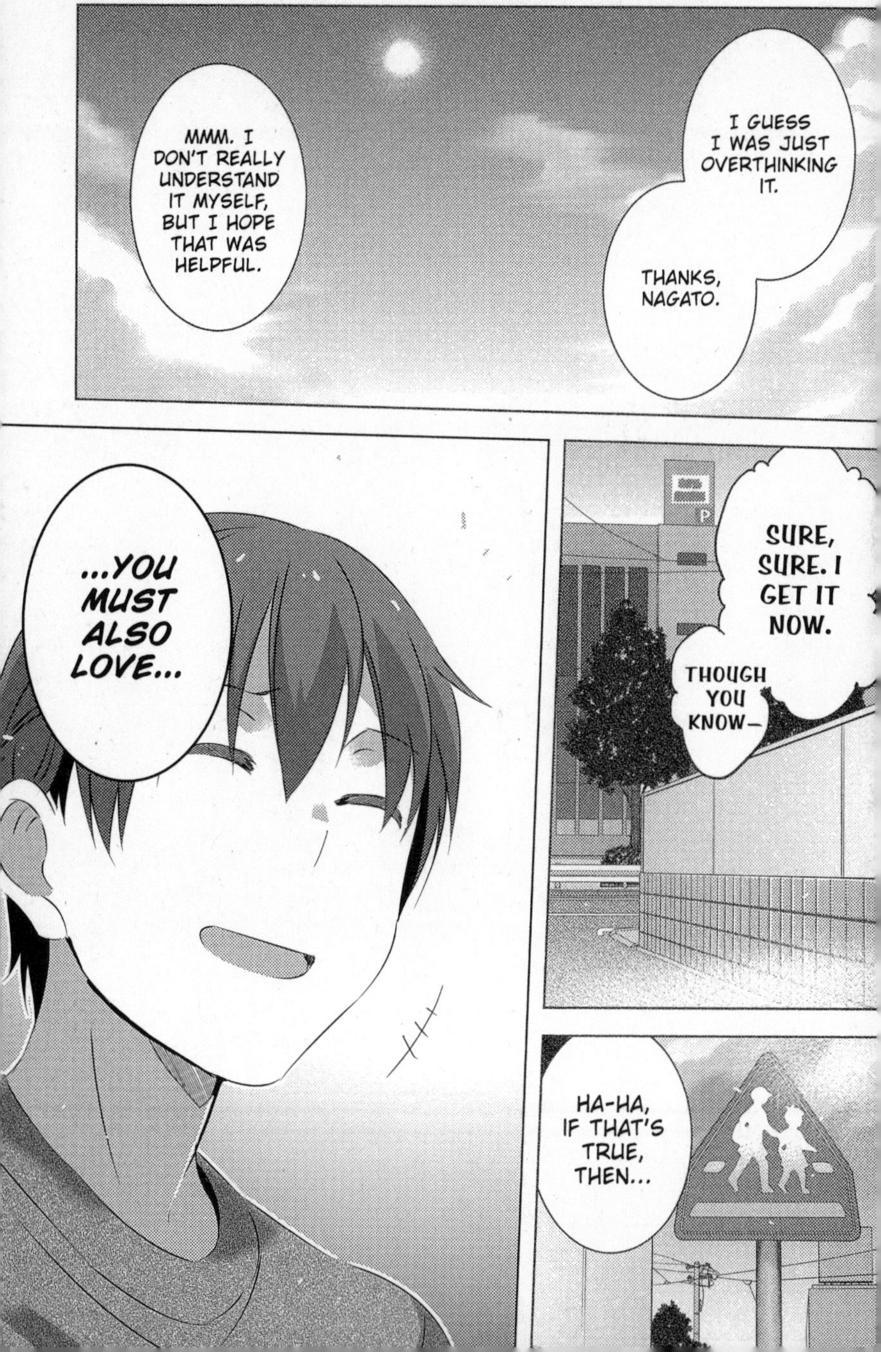
I GUESS I WAS JUST OVERTHINKING IT.
THANKS, NAGATO.
MMM. I DON'T REALLY UNDERSTAND IT MYSELF, BUT I HOPE THAT WAS HELPFUL.
SURE, SURE. I GET IT NOW.
THOUGH YOU KNOW—
HA-HA, IF THAT'S TRUE, THEN...
...YOU MUST ALSO LOVE...

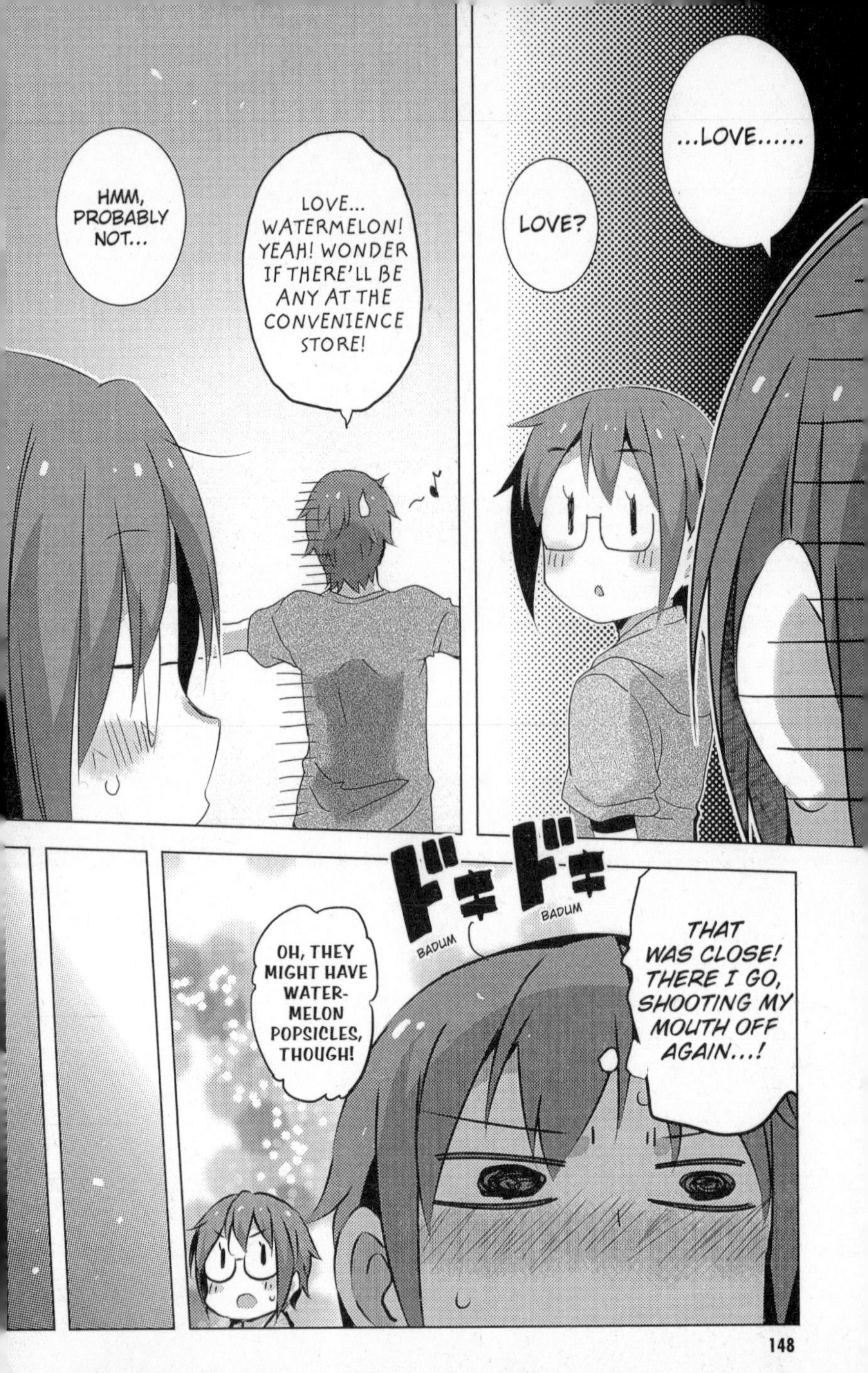
...LOVE......
LOVE?
LOVE... WATERMELON! YEAH! WONDER IF THERE'LL BE ANY AT THE CONVENIENCE STORE!
HMM, PROBABLY NOT...
THAT WAS CLOSE! THERE I GO, SHOOTING MY MOUTH OFF AGAIN...!
ドキドキ
BADUM
BADUM
OH, THEY MIGHT HAVE WATER-MELON POPSICLES, THOUGH!

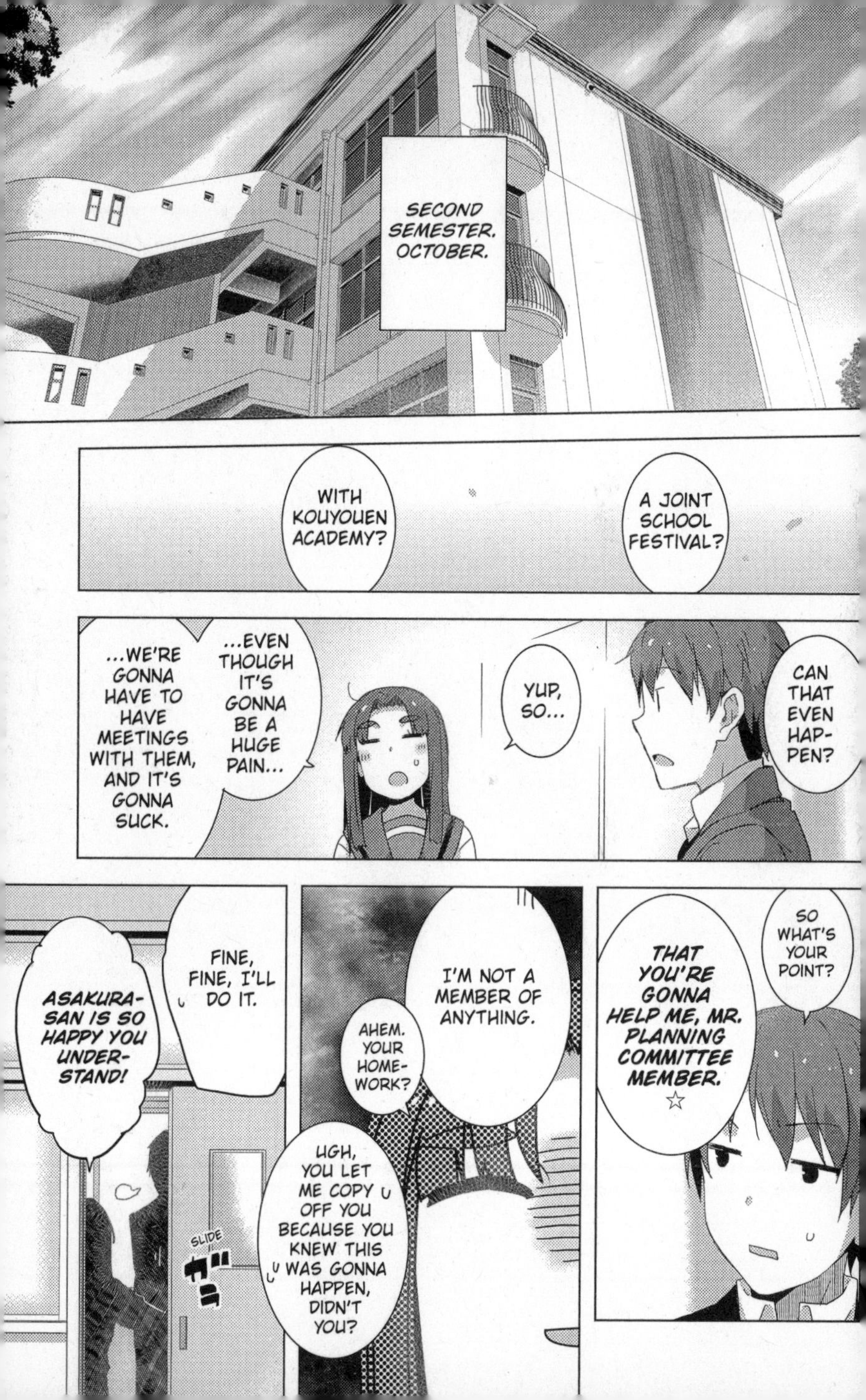
SECOND SEMESTER. OCTOBER.
A JOINT SCHOOL FESTIVAL?
WITH KOUYOUEN ACADEMY?
CAN THAT EVEN HAPPEN?
YUP, SO...
...EVEN THOUGH IT'S GONNA BE A HUGE PAIN...
...WE'RE GONNA HAVE TO HAVE MEETINGS WITH THEM, AND IT'S GONNA SUCK.
SO WHAT'S YOUR POINT?
THAT YOU'RE GONNA HELP ME, MR. PLANNING COMMITTEE MEMBER. ☆
I'M NOT A MEMBER OF ANYTHING.
AHEM. YOUR HOMEWORK?
UGH, YOU LET ME COPY OFF YOU BECAUSE YOU KNEW THIS WAS GONNA HAPPEN, DIDN'T YOU?
FINE, FINE, I'LL DO IT.
ASAKURA-SAN IS SO HAPPY YOU UNDERSTAND!
SLIDE

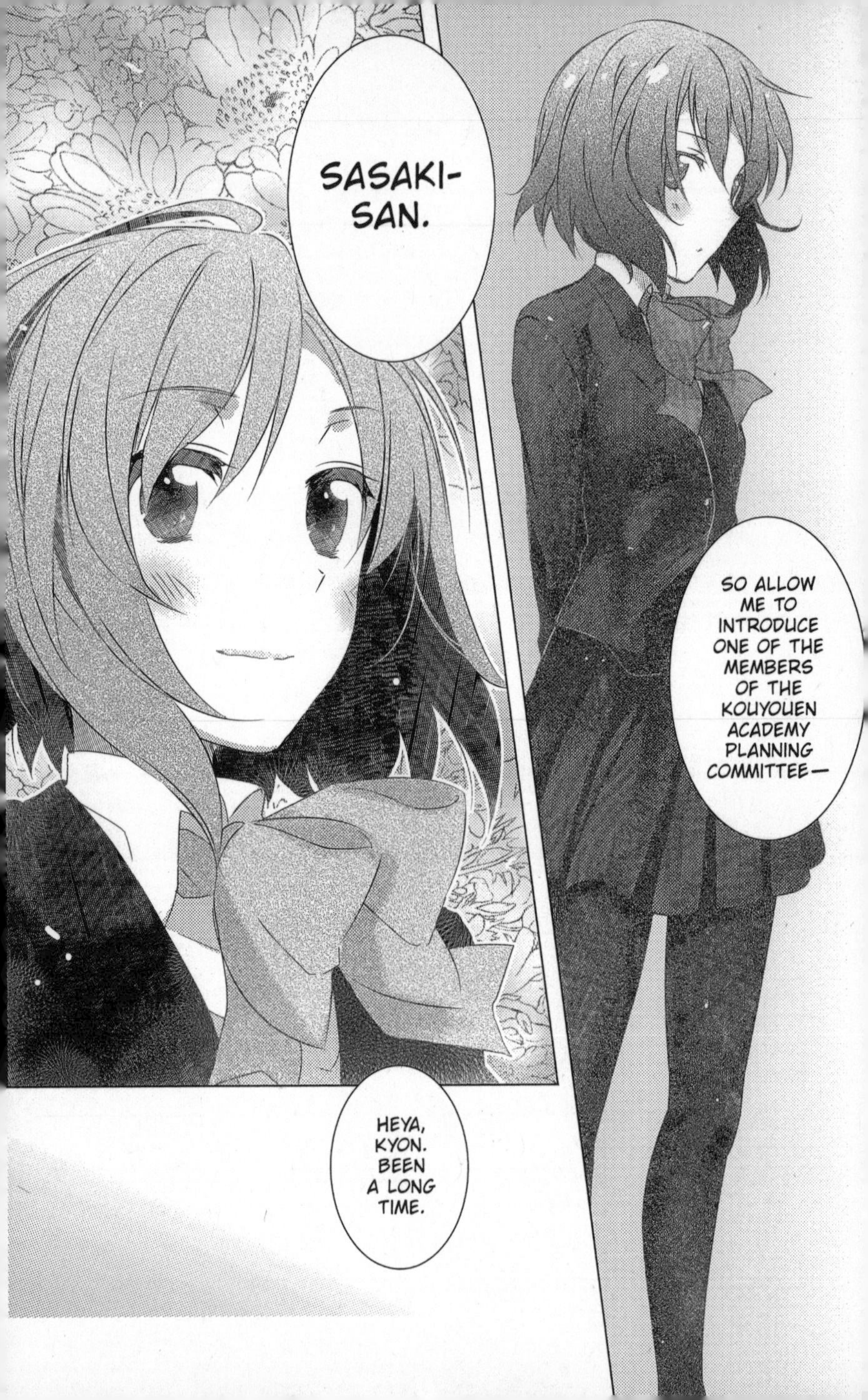
SO ALLOW ME TO INTRODUCE ONE OF THE MEMBERS OF THE KOUYOUEN ACADEMY PLANNING COMMITTEE—
SASAKI-SAN.
HEYA, KYON. BEEN A LONG TIME.

TO BE
CONTINUED
IN THE NEXT
VOLUME!

THESE ARE
BONUS COMICS
THAT RAN IN
NANO ACE.

PUYO

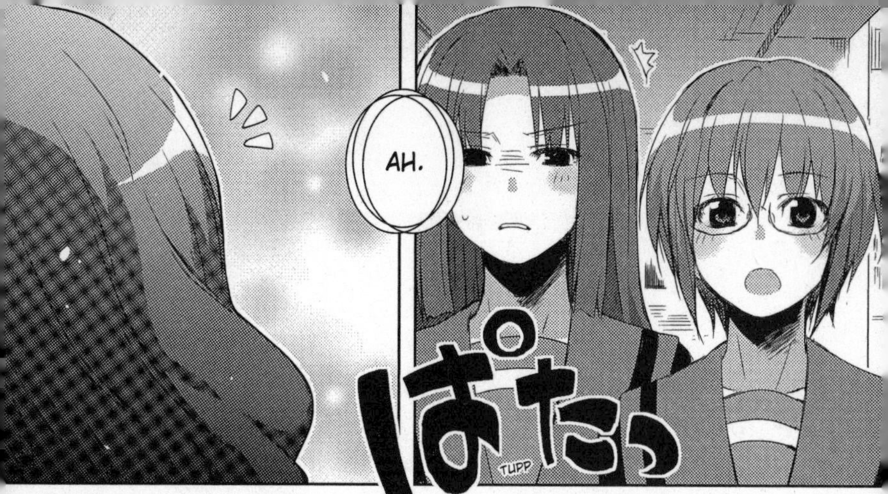
AH.
ぱたっ
TUPP

Bonus Material>> Senpai

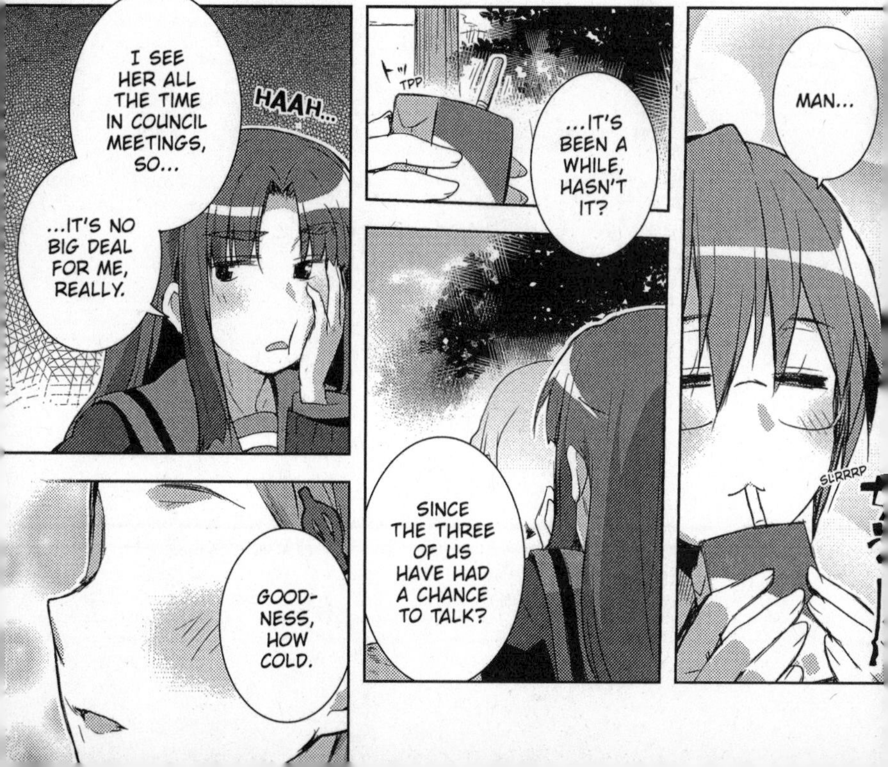
MAN...
SLRRRP
TPP
...IT'S BEEN A WHILE, HASN'T IT?
SINCE THE THREE OF US HAVE HAD A CHANCE TO TALK?
I SEE HER ALL THE TIME IN COUNCIL MEETINGS, SO...
...IT'S NO BIG DEAL FOR ME, REALLY.
HAAH...
GOODNESS, HOW COLD.

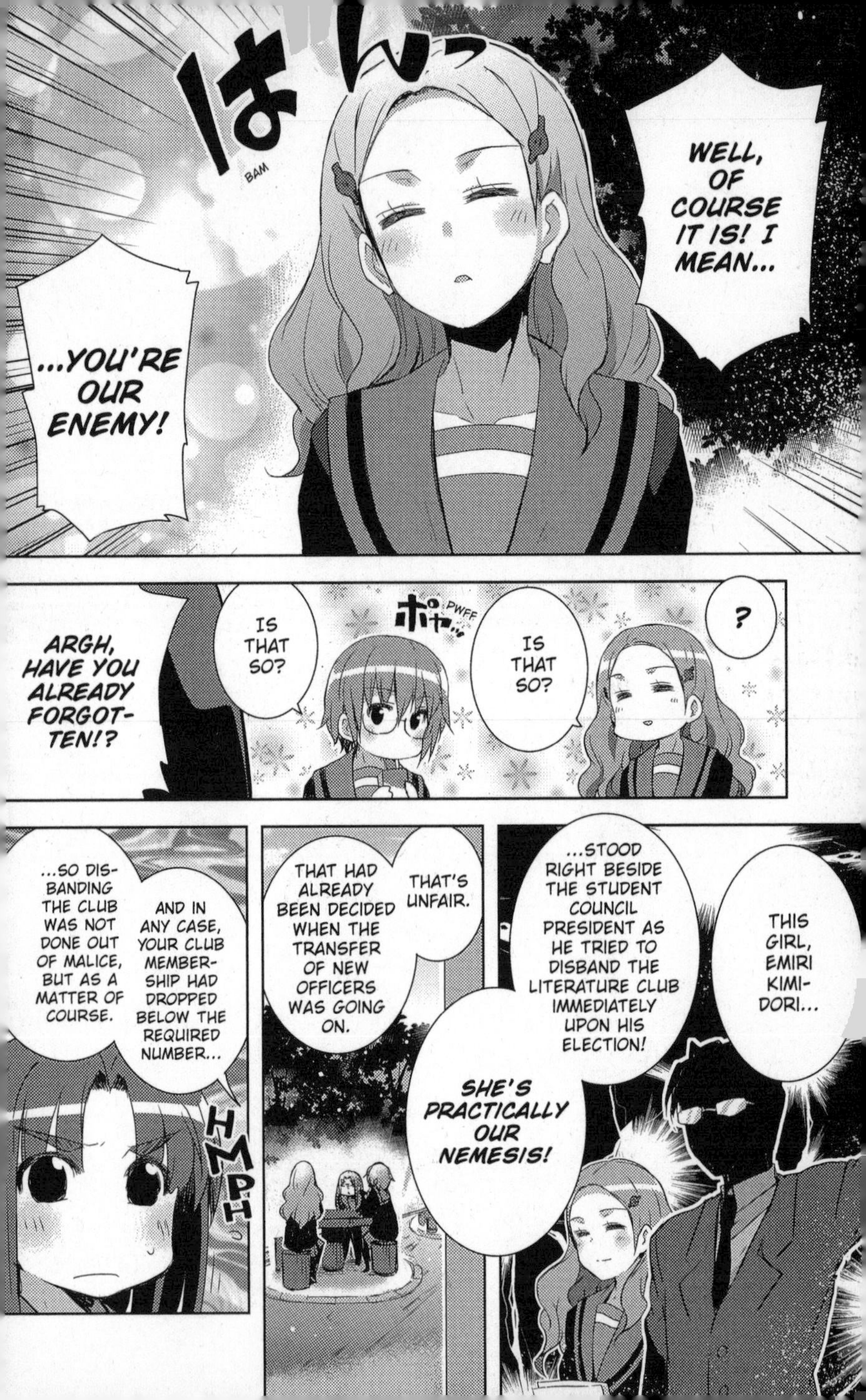
WELL, OF COURSE IT IS! I MEAN...
はんっ
BAM
...YOU'RE OUR ENEMY!
?
IS THAT SO?
ポヤ…
PWFF
IS THAT SO?
ARGH, HAVE YOU ALREADY FORGOT-TEN!?
THIS GIRL, EMIRI KIMI-DORI...
...STOOD RIGHT BESIDE THE STUDENT COUNCIL PRESIDENT AS HE TRIED TO DISBAND THE LITERATURE CLUB IMMEDIATELY UPON HIS ELECTION!
SHE'S PRACTICALLY OUR NEMESIS!
THAT'S UNFAIR.
THAT HAD ALREADY BEEN DECIDED WHEN THE TRANSFER OF NEW OFFICERS WAS GOING ON.
AND IN ANY CASE, YOUR CLUB MEMBER-SHIP HAD DROPPED BELOW THE REQUIRED NUMBER...
...SO DIS-BANDING THE CLUB WAS NOT DONE OUT OF MALICE, BUT AS A MATTER OF COURSE.
HMPH

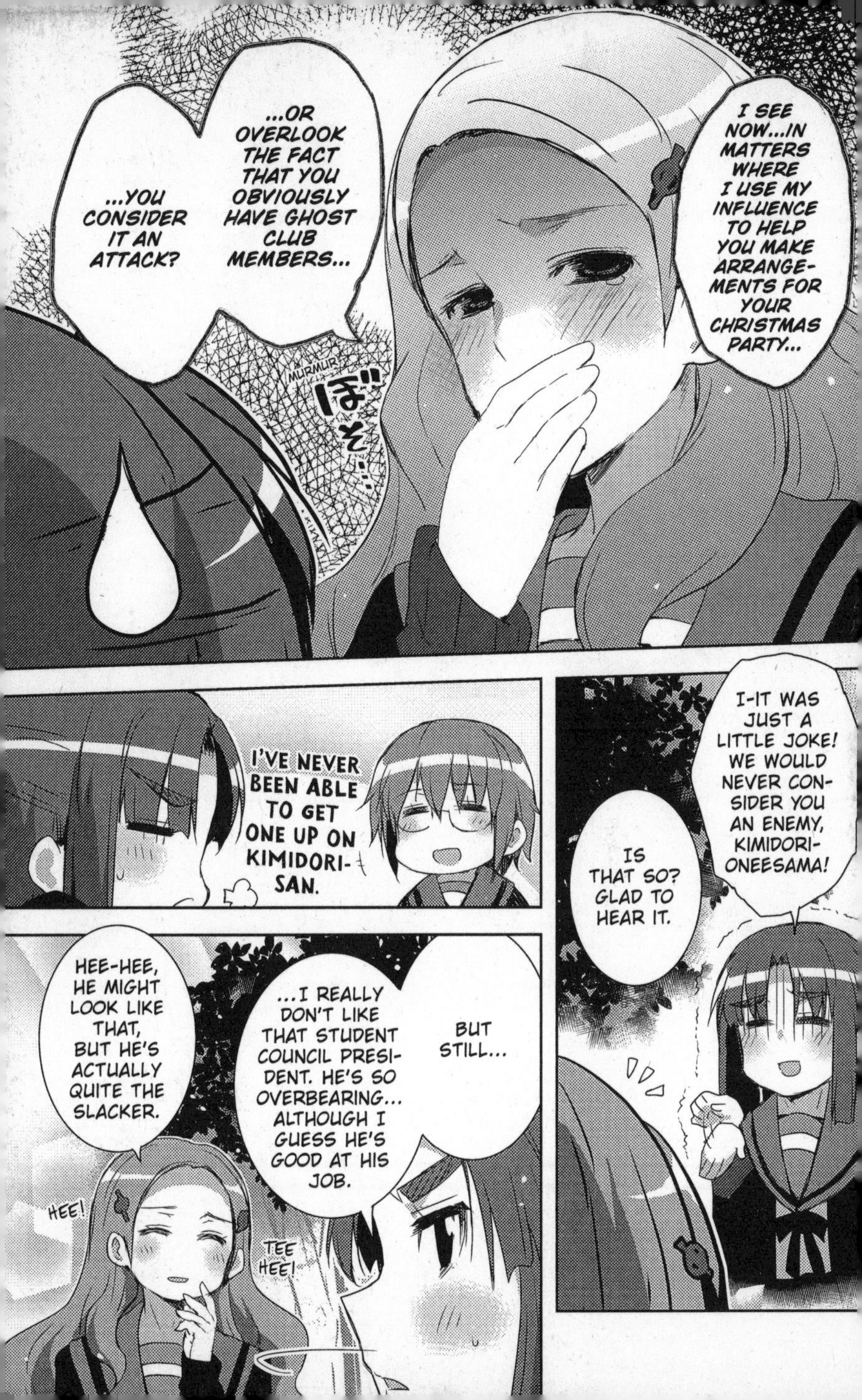
I SEE NOW...IN MATTERS WHERE I USE MY INFLUENCE TO HELP YOU MAKE ARRANGE-MENTS FOR YOUR CHRISTMAS PARTY...
...OR OVERLOOK THE FACT THAT YOU OBVIOUSLY HAVE GHOST CLUB MEMBERS...
...YOU CONSIDER IT AN ATTACK?
MURMUR
ぼそ…
I-IT WAS JUST A LITTLE JOKE! WE WOULD NEVER CON-SIDER YOU AN ENEMY, KIMIDORI-ONEESAMA!
IS THAT SO? GLAD TO HEAR IT.
I'VE NEVER BEEN ABLE TO GET ONE UP ON KIMIDORI-SAN.
BUT STILL...
...I REALLY DON'T LIKE THAT STUDENT COUNCIL PRESI-DENT. HE'S SO OVERBEARING... ALTHOUGH I GUESS HE'S GOOD AT HIS JOB.
HEE-HEE, HE MIGHT LOOK LIKE THAT, BUT HE'S ACTUALLY QUITE THE SLACKER.
HEE!
TEE HEE!

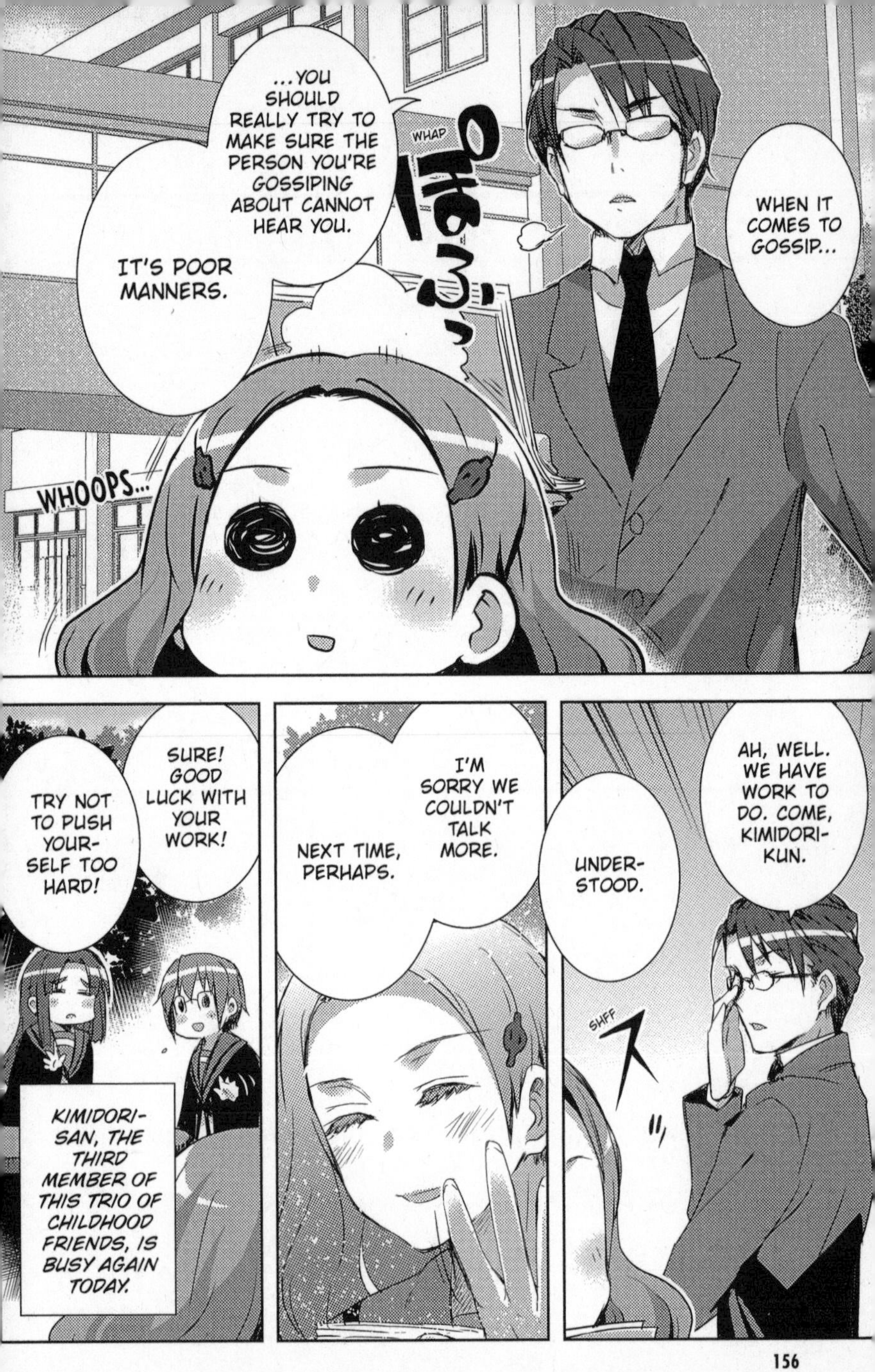
WHEN IT COMES TO GOSSIP...
...YOU SHOULD REALLY TRY TO MAKE SURE THE PERSON YOU'RE GOSSIPING ABOUT CANNOT HEAR YOU.
WHAP
IT'S POOR MANNERS.
WHOOPS...
AH, WELL. WE HAVE WORK TO DO. COME, KIMIDORI-KUN.
UNDER-STOOD.
SHUFF
I'M SORRY WE COULDN'T TALK MORE.
NEXT TIME, PERHAPS.
SURE! GOOD LUCK WITH YOUR WORK!
TRY NOT TO PUSH YOUR-SELF TOO HARD!
KIMIDORI-SAN, THE THIRD MEMBER OF THIS TRIO OF CHILDHOOD FRIENDS, IS BUSY AGAIN TODAY.

WONDER IF
I'LL EVER BE
IN THE REAL
STORY.

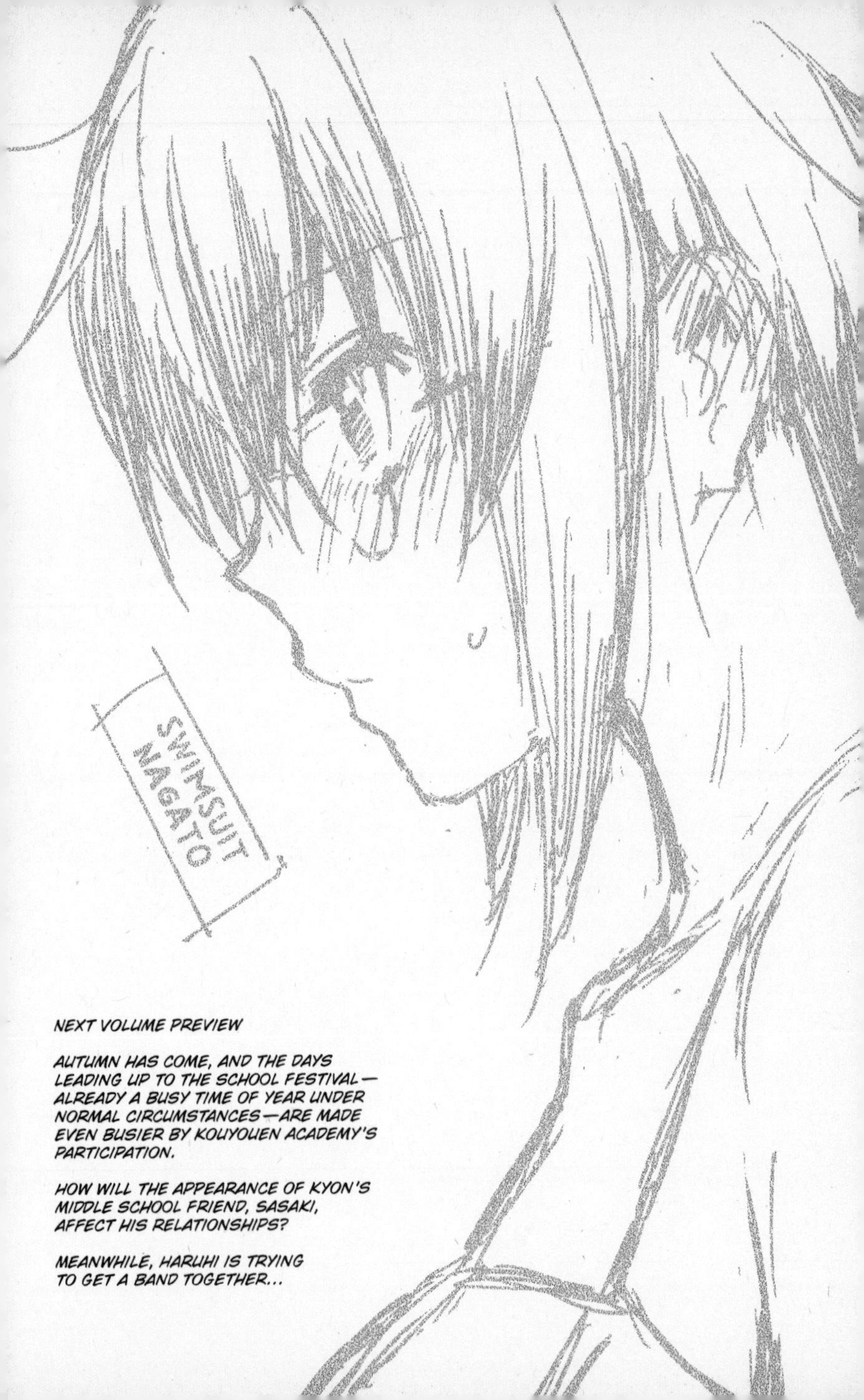
SWIMSUIT NAGATO

NEXT VOLUME PREVIEW

AUTUMN HAS COME, AND THE DAYS LEADING UP TO THE SCHOOL FESTIVAL—ALREADY A BUSY TIME OF YEAR UNDER NORMAL CIRCUMSTANCES—ARE MADE EVEN BUSIER BY KOUYOUEN ACADEMY'S PARTICIPATION.

HOW WILL THE APPEARANCE OF KYON'S MIDDLE SCHOOL FRIEND, SASAKI, AFFECT HIS RELATIONSHIPS?

MEANWHILE, HARUHI IS TRYING TO GET A BAND TOGETHER...

To become the ultimate weapon, one boy must eat the souls of 99 humans...

...and one witch.

Maka is a scythe meister, working to perfect her demon scythe until it is good enough to become Death's Weapon—the weapon used by Shinigami-sama, the spirit of Death himself. And if that isn't strange enough, her scythe also has the power to change form—into a human-looking boy!

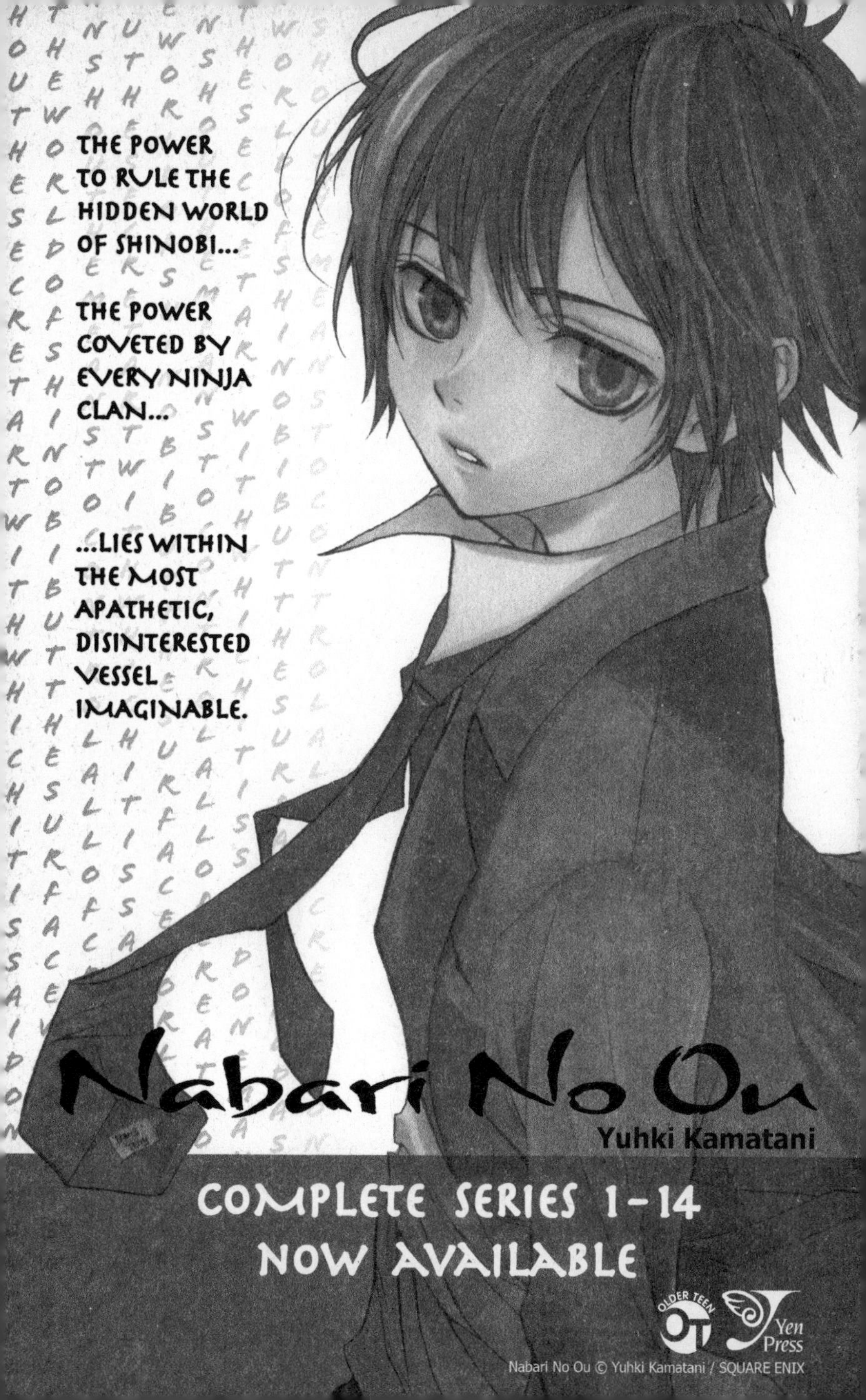

THE POWER TO RULE THE HIDDEN WORLD OF SHINOBI...
THE POWER COVETED BY EVERY NINJA CLAN...
...LIES WITHIN THE MOST APATHETIC, DISINTERESTED VESSEL IMAGINABLE.
Nabari No Ou
Yuhki Kamatani
COMPLETE SERIES 1-14
NOW AVAILABLE
OLDER TEEN OT
Yen Press
Nabari No Ou © Yuhki Kamatani / SQUARE ENIX

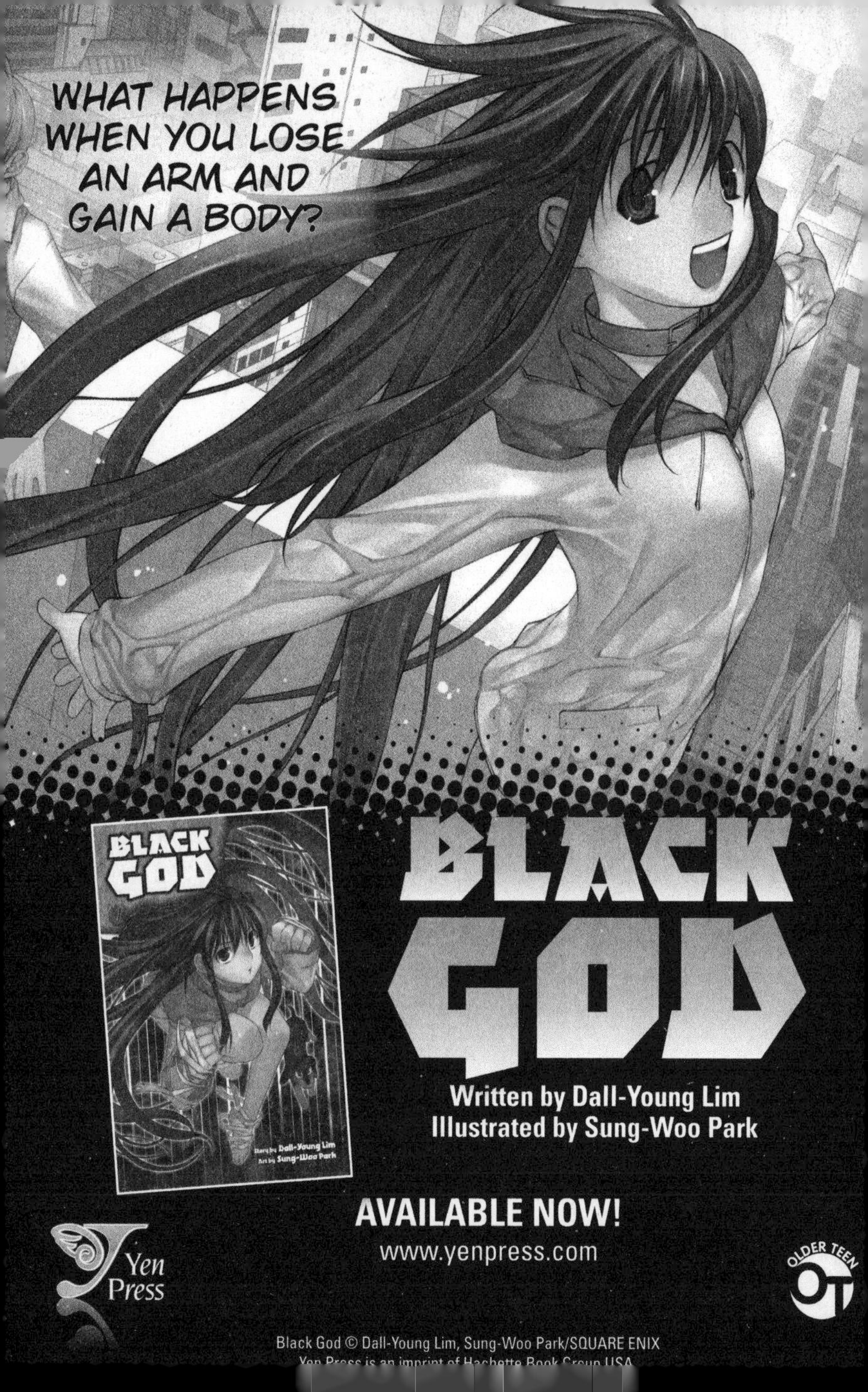
WHAT HAPPENS WHEN YOU LOSE AN ARM AND GAIN A BODY?
BLACK GOD
Written by Dall-Young Lim
Illustrated by Sung-Woo Park
AVAILABLE NOW!
www.yenpress.com
Yen Press
OLDER TEEN
OT
Black God © Dall-Young Lim, Sung-Woo Park/SQUARE ENIX
Yen Press is an imprint of Hachette Book Group USA

THE DISAPPEARANCE OF NAGATO
YUKI-CHAN
❺

Original Story: Nagaru Tanigawa
Manga: PUYO
Character Design: Noizi Ito

Translation: Paul Starr
Lettering: Abigail Blackman

This book is a work of fiction. Names, characters, places, and incidents are the product of the author's imagination or are used fictitiously. Any resemblance to actual events, locales, or persons, living or dead, is coincidental.

NAGATO YUKI CHAN NO SHOSHITSU Volume 5
© Nagaru TANIGAWA • Noizi ITO 2012 © PUYO 2012.
Edited by KADOKAWA SHOTEN
First published in Japan in 2012 by KADOKAWA CORPORATION, Tokyo.
English translation rights arranged with KADOKAWA CORPORATION, Tokyo,
through TUTTLE-MORI AGENCY, INC., Tokyo.

Yen Press
Hachette Book Group
237 Park Avenue, New York, NY 10017

www.HachetteBookGroup.com
www.YenPress.com

Yen Press is an imprint of Hachette Book Group, Inc.
The Yen Press name and logo are trademarks of Hachette Book Group, Inc.

First Yen Press Edition: February 2014

ISBN: 978-0-316-32235-5

10 9 8 7 6 5 4 3 2 1

BVG

Printed in the United States of America